SOCIAL TRANSFORMATION OF INDIAN TRIBES

SOCIAL TRANSFORMATION OF INDIAN TRIBES

Edited by
R. Singh

ANMOL PUBLICATIONS PVT. LTD.
NEW DELHI - 110 002 (INDIA)

ANMOL PUBLICATIONS PVT. LTD.
4374/4B, Ansari Road, Daryaganj
New Delhi - 110 002

Social Transformation of Indian Tribes

First Edition, 1999
ISBN 81-261-0452-X

PRINTED IN INDIA

Published by J.L. Kumar for Anmol Publications Pvt. Ltd., New Delhi - 110 002 and Printed at Tarun Offset Press, Delhi.

Contents

Preface

THE book Social Transformation of Indian Tribes is a critical and comprehensive study of nature and motivation of the social transformation during past few decades. Several books on tribal social structure of India are published but very few have threw proper light of tribal social transformation in modern perspective. The process of social transformation has been discussed in six chapters.

Community, composition and social order has been discussed in the first chapter. Second chapter deals with the basic unit of social structure: family, clan and kinship. The nature and composition are important aspects of family of the tribal community. It plays a very decisive role in all aspects of their collective and co-operative living. Thus any study per training to tribal community cannot afford to leave out of consideration this most nearly universal human group, namely family, clan and kinship.

Whether social transformation is myth or reality? This question has been widely discussed in the third chapter. While, fourth chapter deals with plans, policies and development. Since independence much endeavour has been made to focus on the problem of the Indian tribes. Some practical suggestions have been put forward for the eradication of different problems of the tribal communities. Fifth chapter throws light on the socio-economic status of tribal women in eastern India. Social interaction among the tribes has been described in sixth chapter and the last chapter deals with the concept and composition of tribal caste and nation.

In completing this study, I have taken support from various books and Journals. I am thankful to all those scholars whose works has been cited or substantially included in this work.

I am thankful to Mr. J. L. Kumar, Managing Director, Anmol Publications Pvt. Ltd., New Delhi for acceding to publish this work.

No doubt, social anthropologists, scholars and teachers in the field concerned besides the policy planners and developmental administrators will find this volume of utmost use.

ONE

Community, Composition and Social Order

SINCE early, students of Indian life have been impressed by the social organisation of some of the Scheduled Tribes that, owing to their isolation or insulation, had kept up their tribal state. Capt. Sherwill[1] writing notes on his tour through the Rajmahal Hills in the middle of the last century has described it, if partially, at least in main outlines. He noted that the Santal villages were generally in thick jungles, arranged so as to form one long street with houses on either side. Almost to every house was attached a pig-sty or a dove-cot, while bullock or buffalo-sheds were distributed throughout the village.

In every village according to Sherwill there stood a small thatched roof supported upon one or more wooden posts. Under it there was a small earthen platform raised a foot above the ground. It was called according to Sherwill Manji, but as we know from other literature it must have been called *manjithan,* a spot where *manji* meets the villagers and where perhaps some of the older famous *manjis* were buried.[2] As Biswas has pointed out it is generally in the centre of the village and near the *manji's* or the headman's house. He further states that at the base of the central post a wooden block sometimes shaped as a human head and daubed with vermilion is to be seen. Above it from the roof stands suspended an earthen pot containing water for spirits to drink with a peacock's head by its side. Sometimes *manjithan* stands at the end of the village as observed by Bradley-Birt in the village of Sagarbhanga. According to Sherwill *manjithans* of some of the villages at least would appear to have been named after some important *manji* and known by that name. Thus in the village Jhilmilli, the *manji* spot is known as *Bora manji*. The headman of the village and it would appear his helpmates of the village meet and talk over the village affairs here. According to Risley[3] the headman was entitled to certain perquisites at marriages and such other occasions from the family in which that event took place, over and above the rent-free land that he held.

The *manji* is both a civil and moral authority. In his civil functions he is assisted by his sub-headman whom the Santals call *paranik;* but as pointed out by O'Malley and others it is the Sanskrit term *paramanik* which is thus contracted. According to Dalton[4] the specific business of the *paranik* was to attend to the farming arrangements of the village, and it was his duty to see that the land was fairly and justly distributed for cultivation among the villagers. His was the duty also to provide for guests, levying contributions for the purpose.

In the discharge of the moral functions of the *Manji* he is assisted by an official *jog-manji. Jog,* as is very clear, is the same as Sanskrit *yoga* meaning control (*sic* moral control). He is not only the master of ceremonies at birth and marriage but is responsible for the morals of the youth of the village. His authority, according to Mukharji[5] who wrote in 1938 has dwindled and he is also more prone to corruption. There appears to be an opposite number to *jog-manji,* who is known as *jog-paranik* but is merely his assistant.[6]

Both the *manji* and the *paranik* are helped by the village official called *gorait* who acts as messenger.

After the civil and moral aspects of life have been entrusted and provided for, the religious or sacred aspect is not expected to be left out. In every village there is a priest called, according to Dalton, *naia,* but according to Risley, Mukharji, Biswas and Datta-Majumdar,[7] *naeke.* Both Biswas and Datta-Majumdar give the additional information that the *naeke* is really called *ato naeke* and his assistant is distinguished as *kudam naeke,* this latter being so distinguished by Mukharji too.

Thus there are altogether seven officials in a Santal village. These officials, generally hereditary, and some elders of the village form the panchayat. Over the village panchayat is the panchayat of a group of villages which may vary from five to ten or twelve.[8] This panchayat has a headman who is called *pargana* or *parganait* and consists of all the headmen of the component villages. The *pargana* has also an assistant who is called *desh-manji.*[9]

We may call this part of social organization socio-administrative and compare and contrast similar sections of the organization of some other Scheduled Tribes. Let us begin with the Mundas who are believed to have kept their tribal organisation almost intact. We may note that though the Santal word for village, whatever it may be, is not much in evidence, the cognate tribes of the Mundas and the Hos call it *hatu.*[10]

The Munda village was primarily centred round the members of a single exogamous sept. In actual practice, however, an exogamous sept and the village were not coterminous, more than one exogamous sept being found in a number of villages and one and the same sept having its members distributed in more than one village. Whether owing to the remembrance of the actual descent of exogamous septs or as a result of administrative considerations, in actual practice, villages have been grouped together into a larger unit called *parha* by the Mundas, or *patti* by ruling folks. It must be noted that *patti* is a regular north Indian term of village organization, indicating a particular type of land division or land holding.[11]

The Mundas call the headman of their village *Munda* and not *manji.* If the *munda* is the civil officer, *pahan* is his religious counterpart though originally he too had civil functions.[12] Roy[13] informs us that a *patti* or *parha* generally included twelve villages. The most influential headman was elected as the chief of the *patti* and was called *manki.* The *parha* or *patti* panchayat was thus under the guidance of the most influential of the headmen of the twelve villages. Both the *munda* and the *pahan* were hereditary officials.

There are other small officials but they seem to be either unimportant or receive specifically a Mundri name.

The social organization of the Hos, on the socio-administrative side, is better structured in certain matters. Lieut. Tickell[14] informs us that the Hos of Kolhan were divided into twenty-four *pirs* or *parganas* which, as Roy has pointed out, is linguistically the same thing as the *parha.* They also call their village *hatu* and the headman of their village, *munda.*[15]

Hunter[16] writing about 1875 states that the *parha* or the federal union of a group of villages under a divisional headman called *manki* was an original feature of Munda-speaking peoples and had almost died out in Chotanagpur proper. In Kolhan, according to him, this system in which a cluster of five to twenty villages formed a unit was still surviving, though from his own account, forty years before his statement the arrangement sanctioned by government envisaged a group of five to fifteen villages.

In the account of the social organization prevalent in Kolhan given in the District Gazetteer of Singhbhum by O'Malley[17] in 1910, it is stated that the total number of *pirs* in the Kolhan was twentysix and that for the purposes of administration the government had recognized seventythree local divisions, the name for which, if any, is not given. It is this local division that comprised a group of five to twenty villages. D. N. Majumdar,[18] writing about the Hos forty years after O'Malley, while describing the country of the Hos mentions only twentysix *pirs* in Kolhan and he equates a *pir* with the division stating *inter alia* that some of the larger *pirs* are divided into a number of sub-divisions. It is this sub-division, according to him, of which the headman is a *mankis* managing them. They are thirtysix. Whether the total number of *mankis* is seventythree, as we are led to expect from O'Malley's account given in the *District Gazetteer* of *Singhbhum,* or some other number, which cannot be less than fiftyeight in view of Majumdar's statement, we do not know. But we know from Majumdar that whereas the total number of villages in Kolham was 622 in 1837, about 1950 they numbered 917.

In 1868 according to a Survey the number of villages was 847. A report of 1866 mentions the number of *mundas* in the Kolhan to be 710 and the number of *mankis* as sixtyeight.[19]

Whatever is the exact number of manki-led divisions among the Hos in Kolhan, it is interesting that the federated unit which is known among the Mundas as *parha,* and among the Santals as *pargana* is called by the Hos *pir* which according to Hunter is the same as *Pirhi.* It will interest the readers to know that *para* at least is a term used in Gujarat and some parts of northern India to denote the section of a town and in Marathi *pada* is a regular term for a hamlet. As it will be seen later, among the Oriya Khonds a street of a village is also known as *para* which Lieut. Frye[20] writing a century ago translates as side or quarter. That *pirhi* is a bio-social term common to a number of Indo-Aryan languages becoming in Marathi *pidhi,* meaning a generation, may also be noted.[21] O'Malley however derives *pir* from *piri* meaning upland. Need we conclude that the use of the word among the Hos reflects a clear indication of the communal memory about the genetic connection between the villages of a *pir*?

Among the Hos of Dalbhum, Kharsawan, Parahat and in Saraikala the headman of a village is known as *pradhan;* and he is generally helped by a *paramanik* as his deputy, in some parts *kotwal* taking his place.

As Dalton noted 95 years ago, the social organization of the Oraons is almost the same as that of the Mundas with this addition that sometimes there is a third additional officer called *mahato* among them who seems to be almost either a replica or a deputy of the *munda.* All these three officials including the hereditary priest *pahan* have hereditary pieces of land which are called *khunts. Khunt* it should be remembered, is a word which occurs as far south as the southern confines of Maharashtra and means a post, sic fixed post. Oraon's saying speaks of only the *pahan* and the *mahato* but not the *munda.* They say, a *pahan* makes the affairs of a village, the *mahato* administers them.[22] Besides these the other village officials in an Oraon village are the *ahir,* the *lohar,* the *gorait* and the *kumbar.* The *pahan* has an understudy in the *pujar* or *pani bora* or *tahalu* having a *khunt* of his own; but both the *pahan* and the *pujar* are elective offices and not hereditary.[23]

The *parha* or the federal organization of villages of the Oraons as Roy informs us is based on local contiguity. In former times a *parha* comprised of either seven, nine, twelve, twenty-one or twenty-two villages. When Roy studied the *Oraons* he met with parhas having only five, four or even three villages each. The description of the *parha* panchayat leaves no doubt that the *parha* organization was largely influenced by the rajahs of Chotanagpur.[24] The *parha* panchayat meets only one a year and deals with matters of interest to whole villages and the community, such as the dates of festivals and disputes about village flags which are distinctive emblems.

As Colonel Dalton[25] observed eightyfive years ago the social organization and the government of the Khonds closely resemble the tribal polity of the Mundas. The headman of each Khond village is called *obbaye.* Number of adjacent villages have in the words of Dalton, "a district *abbaye,*" both the offices, the village *abbaye* and the district *abbaye* being hereditary. O'Malley,[26] however, has called headman of the village, *malika* and that of the *mutha, mutha malika* and has added the further information that for administrative purpose there is generally over the *mutha malika* an official called *sardar.* Lieut, Frye[27] writing about Oriya Khonds in 1858 informs us that they, like the other Oriyas, named their village after its founder, only differing from the latter in that instead of their *gam* the Khonds used the word *millaka.* Thus Diggo Millaka was a village founded by Diggo. Even one street in a village was named after its original inhabitants; only the suffix or the ending added was either *para* or *khando.* Large divisions in the hill country are called *maliahs, malos,* or *mals* from the last of which the region of the Khonds is known as the Khondmals. Each federal unit of villages is called *mutha.* Over and above the village headman who is called the *malik* there is also a tribal *malik* or *abbaye.* And over all the *mals* there is a tribal chief known as *mahamalik.* In the Oriya area of the Khonds, where they have been more in contact with the other plains folk, in each *mutha* and sometimes in each large village there is an Oriya officer called *bisoi.* In some parts of the country the *mutha* is otherwise known by the usual term *pargana,* as for example in Chinna Kimedy, where also *maji* was used as a concurrent term for a Khond village headman. As Dalton observes this is no doubt the same as the Mundari and Ho *manji.*[28]

Carmichael[29] reporting on the organization of the Khonds of the district of Vizagapatam wrote that in the Godairy taluka where the villages were rented, the renter, quite often almost hereditary, was himself considered the *maji* (headman) of the village and was also known by the usual plains term *patro.* The *mutha,* at least in this part of the Khond region, consisted of six to thirty three villages Each.[30]

A Khond village of Vizagapatam district as described by Carmichael has generally two streets each with a double row of huts, one occupied by the Khonds themselves and the other by people, termed *pariahs* by him but called by the Khonds, *paich, Dombo or Pano*. These latter wove the coarse cloth which is required by the Khonds and also made tinsel ornaments for them and officiated as musicians at their festivals.[31]

It is to be specially noted that the Khonds have tended to hold their village lands jointly, in theory individual possession being permitted for the sake of convenience.[32]

The Gond village as pointed out by Rudman[33] is more often than not a collection of scattered hamlets varying from two to twelve, each one being called *tola* or even *khera* (this is the standard world for village in most Indo-Aryan languages). The headman is generally known as the *mandal* or *bhoi*. Other castes, either as village servants or not, to be generally found in Gond villages are the *ahir,* the *barai,* the *lohar,* a 'baiga' priest and some *pankas*. In Chanda, and it would appear in some other localities, however, even the Gond village is a single group unit, with the house of the village headman in the centre. It is called *gurri;* but instead of the *mandal,* the malguzar *or* the *patel* of the village resides in it: and then it is the house of this dignitary, which is called the *bara* and not *guree,* that takes its place.[34]

In Gond villages there is evidence of social stratification in the form of *Raj* Gonds or the aristocracy, the *Dhur* Gonds literally dust Gonds or the common peasantry and the tenantry generally formed by some Gonds or Gond-like people called Pardhans and Ojhas, the former being the musicians and bards and the latter priests and soothsayers.[35]

T. H. Hendley[36] describing the Mewar Bhils more than eighty years ago stated a fact about them which further a field and further down history has been true. And that is that generally they live in scattered hamlets each one consisting of a few huts which are not unusually even half a mile apart. According to S.C. Roy[37] such a hamlet was called by them a *phala.* To us it appears that this word *phala* is the same as the Gujarati word *phalio* which means a section or a quarter of a township. Thus Nagarphalio would mean the quarter of a township where the people of Nagar caste live in that town. According to Hendley these scattered hamlets are grouped together and the unit-group of such hamlets is called *pal.* Roy has made it clear that a *pal* is a group of *phalas* or hamlets and has pointed out that it is generally a group of between ten to twelve *phalas*. The Bhils who have this organisation are known as Palia Bhils as against others more backward than they who are known as Kalia or black Bhils. It should be pointed out that the Bhil word *pal* for a group of hamlets cannot be utterly different from the Sanskrit word *palli* which is one of the words in that language for a village.

According to Hendley[38] The headman of a village, evidently of a *pal,* is called a *gammaiti.* He speaks of the panchayat without any further statement about its constitution. Luard[39] writing about the Bhils of Central India Agency in 1901 mentions that the presiding officer of the panchayat is known either as *patel* or a *tarvi.* He too does not give any constitution and we must take it that the panchayat was of the ordinary type, comprising of some five respected Bhils of the locality. The headman, the *tarvi,* according to Luard was hereditary.

Luard further gives the interesting information that at least three other castes are associated with the Bhils in their village organisation. Of these it is very interesting to note that the Balais and the Chamars are required, in the naive observation of the Bhils themselves, to do this Bhils' village work, and the Gachhas or sweepers evidently to clean it. It is further interesting to note that they look upon the Gachhas as not only untouchables but as unapproachables because if a Gachha were to approach too near any food that is being cooked by the Bhils it is considered to be defiled. Needless to say that the Gachhas are, or rather were, not allowed to draw water from the village wells of the Bhils. The Balais and the Chamars on the other hand can or could do so.[40]

The *gammaiti* of the Palia Bhils is substituted by the *gaddo* among the Kalia Bhils.

An account of Panchmahal Bhils written within a few years of Hendley's account given in the Gazetteer[41] states that the head of a village clan of Bhils was distinct from the government patel and was called *tadvadi* and that each clan had its panchayat consisting of five Bhils. T. B. Naik[42] writing about the Rajpipla Bhils, that is to say Gujarat Bhils, about 1950 states that the Bhils call their village *gam,* like any other Gujarat caste. And it consists generally of between three to forty families, the houses lying scattered. When a cluster of houses is located in one street it is called *foli*. May it not be that this *foli* is the same thing as *phala* of Roy or the *phalio* of the other Gujaratis? The village headman, according to Naik, is called *vasawo*. And *pardhan* is the second official in the village; but he, like the patel of the other areas, is an official appointed by government. In the Bhil villages of this area too there is untouchability observed by the Bhils about one caste, namely Gori whose huts stand at one end of the village.

The headman of a Kol village, in consonance with regional usage, is called the *mahato,* and he presides over the panchayat. All Kols, who in their own words, are 'possessors of piety and property' (*dharam aur dhan*) are members of it. There is a further federal integration of villages. Each such federal unit consists from twenty to thirty separate villages. It seems that the panchayat of a village as a whole acts also to represent it in this federal organisation.[43]

Having studied in general outline the socio-administrative parts of the social organisation, we may pass on to the next important item, namely the socio-aesthetic and the socio-marital parts. To begin with the socio-aesthetic the *akhara* claims our first attention. *Akhara,* is unmistakably the same word which in Marathi appears as *akhada.* It means the place where one performs athletics; and in one form or another it occurs in North India even in ascetic organisations.[44] For the scheduled tribes this *akhara* is an open space generally beneath some spreading tree cleared and levelled and is a scene of many a dance whether festive or ordinary.

Among the Santals the *akhara* is generally in front of the *jog-manji's* house.[45]

Associated with the *akhara* generally, among the scheduled tribes as we shall have occasion to pint out, there is another item of the social organisation and that is the dormitory for the bachelors and sometimes also a separate one for the spinsters of the tribe. But as Dalton[46] pointed out years ago there is no separate dormitory in a Santal village, the boys and girls sleeping with their parents in their own houses.

There is among many of these tribes a fourth institutional unit which is almost wholly connected with the disposal of the dead and the religious customs and beliefs associated with it. We shall speak of it in another chapter.

The north-western neighbours of the Santals, the Malers are almost equally fond of dancing and though the dancing place or the arena has not been specifically named by either Bradley-Birt or other students of the Malers, Atkinson, an administrator of the Rajmahal Hills of those times is quoted by Hunter[47] to the effect that there was a dancing place in every Maler village where dances took place on occasions when drinking was indulged in. Both Dalton[48] and Hunter have invoked the authority of a missionary at Bhagalpur to assert that the Malers had the dormitory like the Oraons, the bachelors having a separate one from those of the maidens.

The Munda institution of the *akhara* or the dancing arena is usually located almost in the centre of a Munda village. It fulfils among others, the additional function of being the meeting place, the panchayat hall so to say, or the *Manjithan* of the Santals. Underneath the spreading tree there are large stone slabs on which the villagers sit for their meetings. The Mundas are rather reticent about the place where their bachelors and maidens sleep, particularly the latter; but Roy[49] asserts that after some acquaintance they reveal the whereabouts of the sleeping place (*gitiora* in Mundari) which generally is provided in the hut of an elderly male Munda for the bachelors and that of a widow for the maidens. It should be noted that the portion of any house where the members sleep is called *giti-ora* as against the *mandi-ora,* that portion of the house where people eat; and the cattle may have a separate shed called *unri-ora,* but may also be accommodated in the *giti-ora* portion of the house itself.

Among the Hos the *akhara* or the dancing arena generally stands in the centre of the village and their *giti-ora* or the dormitory stands in front of it and opens out into it. The arena itself is open but is surrounded by large spreading trees. Dr. Majumdar who makes this assertion on page 45 of his book[50] amplifies and modified his statement of facts by stating that, according to the tribal customs still current, the Hos have to "send the children as soon as they attain a certain age to the village dormitory, the boys to the bachelors' hut, and the girls to the hut for unmarried girls," and in the villages which do not have a hut for girls they are distributed for purposes of sleeping among the window of the village who can spare accommodation.[51] He also adds categorically that wherever a hut for girls exists it is under the charge of an elderly female. With all this, however, he unwittingly though emphatically contradicts himself when he makes the statement: "Most of the villages do not possess the dormitory house . . . ."[52]

Among the Oraons too there is the village *akhara* or the dancing arena and the bachelors' dormitory which adjoins it. *Dhumkuria* is a Hindi word for bachelors' dormitory for which the Oraon word is *jonk-erpa.* The institution of the dormitory was fast disappearing when S. C. Roy[53] more than nearly fortyfive years ago studied the people. His reaction to that institution was far from happy. The Oraons who tended to be reticent about this place were naturally still more so about the dormitory for the maidens called in their language *pel-erpa.*

According to Dalton[54] each Khond village has two dormitories one for bachelors and the other for maidens, the latter according to some being under the charge of an elderly matron. They are described as having been fond of dancing like the Oraons, dancing even for burial service round a flag fixed at the place of the funeral pyre for ten days.

Carmichael[55] described Bissemcuttack in Vizagapatam district as a town and the capital of a feudatory head Jeypore Raja. It contained 500 houses and in the centre of it stood what Carmichael describes as "a good sized gymnasium where these fellows [the Oriya followers] wrestle and box and perform feats *Khusruth* generally." And in the description of other places which are purely Khond ones no such gymnasium is mentioned. We may treat this as a support of our observation about *akhara,* being a term of general use in Indo-Aryan languages for a gymnasium, and may further suggest that the institution itself may not necessarily be of non-indo-Aryan origin.

A proper Gond village has a village dormitory called the *gotul* which as Inrajit Singh[56] observes is "the pivot of social activities." Among the Maria Gonds it seems to fulfil some wider functions. In the *gotul* it is clear that both boys and girls are accommodated. Among the section of the Gonds of Chanda district there are three separate dormitories in a village—one for bachelors, another for unmarried women and a third for married couples. Among some Gonds there are two dormitories, one for bachelors and the other for maidens. As Indrajit Singh has pointed out the distribution of the *gotul* institution among the Gonds is rather peculiar. Such districts of Gond concentration as Mandla, Chhindwara, Balaghat and Betul do not have it. In direct contradiction of Russell and Hiralal's statement that it existed among the Chhatisgarh Gonds, Indrajit Singh has stated very clearly that his investigations in the three districts of Chhatisgarh namely, Bilaspur, Durg, and Raipur did not reveal its existence. His conclusion therefore makes it clear that only among the Gonds of Bastar and Chanda districts the *gotul* institution flourishes. It would appear that there is generally a big *agana* [*angana*-courtyard?] or courtyard in front of the gotul and within its fence. This spacious compound is used as a playground and must be considered to be the equivalent of the *akhara* of the other scheduled tribes.

Neither the Bhils nor the Kols have the institutions described above, though the Bhils at least have been described as fond of dance at the Holi and at all other feasts, their women joining them but not mixing with them in carrying out the dance. One dance however called *ghanna* in which coloured staves are used to strike together is solely performed by women.

REFERENCES

1. *J.A.S.B.,* Vol. XX (1851), p. 551.
2. P. C. Biswas, *Santals of the Santal Parganas* (1926), pp. 14, 15; also *Bihar District Gazetteers, Santal Parganas,* 2nd ed., p. 141; and F. B. Bradley-Birt, *op. cit.*, pp. 247-248.
3. *Census of India,* 1901, Vol. I, *Ethnographic Appendices,* p. 148.
4. E. T. Dalton, *op. cit.*, p. 213.
5. *Bihar District Gazetteers, Santal Parganas,* 2nd ed, (1938), p. 135.
6. Datta-Majumdar, *The Santals* (1956), p. 46.
7. P. C. Biswas, *op. cit.*, p. 108; and Datta-Majumdar, *op. cit.*, p. 46.
8. Mukharji, *op. cit.*, p. 136; and Datta-Majumdar, *op. cit.*, p. 46
9. Mukharji, *op. cit.*, p. 131.
10. S. C. Roy, *Mundas and their Country,* pp. 115-117; 413-418; *Bihar and Orissa District Gazetteers, Ranchi* (1917), pp. 20-25.

11. B. H. Baden-Powell, *The Indian Village Community,* (1896), pp. 328, 329 f.n., 340-341.
12. *Bihar and Orissa District Gazetteers, Ranchi* (1917), p. 65.
13. *Mundas and their Country,* p. 120.
14. *Op. cit.*, p. 698.
15. W. W. Hunter, *Statistical Account of Bengal,* Vol. XVII, pp. 74, 114; also see *Bihar District Gazetteers, Singhbhum,* etc., p. 95; and D. N. Majumdar, *The Affairs of a Tribe,* pp. 16-17.
16. *Statistical Account of Bengal*, Vol. XVII, pp. 74.
17. *Bihar District Gazetteers, Singhbhum, Saraikella,* etc., pp. 49, 163-166.
18. *Op. cit.*, p. 7.
19. W. W. Hunter, *op. cit.*, p. 76.
20. *J.R.A.S.,* Vol. XVII, p. 7
21. *Op. cit.*, p. 49.
22. E. T. Dalton, *op. cit.*, p. 247; also S. C. Roy, *Oraons of Chotanagpur,* pp. 111-112.
23. S. C. Roy, *Oraons of Chotanagpur,* pp. 69-72, 116-117.
24. *Ibid.*, pp. 49-53; also *Bihar and Orissa District Gazetteers, Ranchi* p. 76.
25. *Op. cit.*, pp. 293, 294.
26. *Bengal District Gazetteers, Angul* (1908), p. 35.
27. *J.R.A.S.,* XVII, p. 7.
28. *Bengal District Gazetteers, Angul* (1908), pp. 291, 299.
29. Carmichael, *op. cit.*, p. 9.
30. *Ibid.*, pp. 9-11.
31. *Ibid.*, p. 90.
32. *Bengal District Gazetteers, Angul* (1908), p. 52.
33. *Central Provinces District Gazetteers, Mandla,* pp. 92, 93, 94.
34. Indrajit Singh, *op. cit.*, pp. 51-54.
35. *Ibid.*, pp. 55, 56.
36. *J.B.A.S.,* XLIV (1875), pp. 356-359.

37. *J.B.O.R.S.*, Vol. XX, p. 102.

38. *Op. cit.*, p. 359.

39. *Op. cit.*, p. 57.

40. *Ibid.*

41. *Gazetteer of the Bombay Presidency,* Vol, III (1879), p. 221.

42. *The Bhils: A Study* (1957), pp. 45-52.

43. W. G. Griffiths, *op. cit.*, pp. 47-50.

44. G. S. Ghurye, *Indian Sadhus* (1953), pp. 116, 209, 210.

45. F. B. Bradley-Birt, *op. cit.* p. 252; and Biswas, *op. cit.*, p. 47.

46. *Op. cit.*, p. 214.

47. *Statistical Account of Bengal,* Vol. XIV, p. 296.

48. *Op. cit.*, p. 272.

49. *Mundas and their Country,* pp. 383, 385, 387.

50. *The Affairs of a Tribe.*

51. *Ibid.*, pp. 45, 101, 102.

52. *Ibid.*, p. 112.

53. *Oraons of Chotanagpur,* pp. 172, 211, 212-214, 260-261.

54. *Op. cit.*, pp. 295, 300, 301.

55. *Op. cit.*, p. 11.

56. *Op. cit.*, pp. VII-VIII, 51, 59, 60, 62.

TWO

Composition and Social Order

Socio-Anthropologic Composition

TRIBES in India generally represent those populations groups, who are the decedents of the races, who entered Indian soils during prehistoric ages to the later vedic period of history. Their entry was mostly through the land routes. As the inflow continued for a long time and ever new entrant race was an invader for the former settlers, the already settled races receded to the interior parts and hid in the densely forested zones and the rims of the mountains. H. H. Risley found the identifiable population groups of Dravidians, Indo-Aryans, Mongoloid, Arya-Dravidians, Mongoloid-Dravidians, Sytho-Dravidians, Turko-Iranian etc. in Indian Population in 1901. Risley however, has skipped various groups which are still found. He was based his guess on the language groups. The Negrito mixture in Indian population has not been separated in Risley's analysis. Later historians have tried to identify *Pulaya, Yurali, Kanikkar* population groups in present Cochin as decendents from Negrito immigrants. Giuffrida has formed four groups of the tribes in India e.g. Negrito, Australoids, Dravidians, and Dolicho-Cephalic. He has claimed that Negrito are *Vaiddah* of Srilanka and forest tribes of South India. *Santhal, Oran, Munda, Hans,* etc. groups of tribals in India are said to be belonging to Australoid group. The population groups who belong to Tamil and Telegu language today are from the Dravidian group of settlers in India. The *Toda* and *Kadar* tribes of Nilgiri and Cochin respectively are from tall Dolicho-Cephalic groups.

Haddon classifies the population of India in mainly three groups; Indo Aryans like kenites of Himachai in Kulu valley, Punjab, Rajasthan and the Kashmir valley. But to the Himalayan parts these are intermixed with the Tibetan stock. With these there are the Mongoloid indo-Aryans who belong to the areas of Nepal, Bhutan, Gurrang, Gorkha, Lepcha, and Newar and are more close to the Mongols, Kenites in Lahaul Spiti are quite distinctly identifiable. The groups in the Kashmir, Rajasthan, Punjab and the *Jats, Gujjars, Rajput,* etc. who are distinct from others in long head, tall stature, wider forehead straight nose, and white wheatish colour. Some what closer to them are the people living in the Sivaliks of Himachal and extended parts intruding in U.P. Himalaya. Towards South India there are the Dravidian populations consisting broadly four sub-groups (i) Pre-Dravidians covering the *Santhals, Panyans, Kadars, Mundas, Kanikkars, Erula, Kurumba, Kolari, Bhil, Gond,* and *Konds;* (ii) Dravidians consisting *Nayyar, Baraga, Tiyans, Kanari, Ijuvans,* and Brahmins in Tamil group. The language groups like Kannada, Malayalam, Tamil and Telgu are from this stock; (iii) The southern Brachy Cephals are separable human kind spreading between northern Arcat to Tirunalvalli district. These are fishermen of *Paniyan* and *Parva* groups, and (iv) There are the western Brachy-Cephals who generally settle in the western parts spreading from Gujarat to Kerala in the western coast. *Nagar, Prabhu, Marathas,* etc. are in these groups. B.S. Guha has tried to separate the Tibeto-Mongloid groups from rest of the Indians in the main land. People in Laddakh, Eastern Kashmir, north eastern Himachal, northern Uttar Pradesh, Nepal, Bhutan, Sikkim, and north eastern tribes are from the Mongoloid groups of population of India. Present scheduled castes of India are generally the Proto Australoids spreading in the wider plains of India while those in the Hilly tracts are intermixed with Mongoloids in their physical feature composition. Some of them have Negrito features mingled with the other groups. The tribal groups are called a submerged humanity because their identity is fast withering away and they have joined the main stream of Indian national life to day. Indian culture bears a stamp of their distinct contribution in various ways.

Grass-roots of Growth Differentials

Spatial disparities in levels of living are quite notable in some areas which have long kept lagging for historical, economic, and sociological reasons. These areas are the hilly and tribal concentrations which are the focus of our attention in our development Plans, policy, and programmes. The growth potentials of these areas are being assessed under special schemes so as to raise the levels of living and to ensure social justice and participation of these areas in national growth. Much is still left undone in this direction specially in terms of gathering adequate information on the nature, identification, patterns of composition, and the diagnosis of the social order and working of the interlocked system of socio-economic stratification. These communities are known for peculiar characteristics requiring very appropriate instruments of social engineering for amelioration in economic conditions of these communities.

Some of the developmental problems arise due to the basic limitations imposed by the physio-geographic constraints. Thin and very unproductive resources and those too distributed in a very uneven pattern cause the fundamental weakness for the highlanders while joining the race of economic and technological growth with other communities of the country. The low density of population itself constitutes a bottleneck in growth because the cost of building an infrastructure for growth becomes very prohibitive. The maintenance of roads in isolated areas of mountains terrain cost so high and the return is so low that the budget priorities can never favour such investments. Due to the utter neglect of these areas by the ruling Governments, the resource endowments of these regions were never scaled in the past and the force of the ballot is always poor in low population density areas. The experience regarding development of difficult terrain yeas is also lacking with the government and officials do not want to work in difficult areas and the schemes for them are not attended seriously. The National Commission on Agriculture (1976) remarked very aptly, ". . . . The problem of development of tribal areas is primarily linked with the general backwardness of these areas, poverty of the tribals, exploitation by the non-tribals and the absence of social and cultural integration of the tribes with the rest of the population". (N.C.A., p. 50-52). The hill areas in Laddakh, Kashmir, Himachal, Uttar Pradesh, East Indian states, Madhya Pradesh, Andhra, Orissa, Karnataka, Kerala, Maharashtra, Gujarat etc. or the climatically inaccessible areas have populations organized in typical social systems and they follow typical traditions of life uncommon in other areas. Therefore, it is a prerequisite for successful planning for growth to deeply investigate and understand their social systems. Any attempt at this needs precise definitions of the terms which we use and the classification adopted for the study.

Connotation of 'Tribe'

Tribe, caste, sect and class are the various categories of social stratification found in India. A tribe is a collection of families or groups of families, bearing a common name, members of which occupy the same territory, speaks the same language and observe certain taboos regarding marriage, profession or occupation and have developed a well assessed system of reciprocity and mutuality of obligations. A tribe is ordinarily an endogamous unit, the members of which confine their marriage within the tribe. Several clans constitute a tribe, each of which claims kinship between the members belonging to it, based either on totemistic division, territorial contiguity or common residence. A tribe is a political unit in the sense that the tribal society owns a political organization, either recognizes hereditary tribal chiefs or the several sections of it are welded into a territorial group rule over by class chiefs of hereditary kings.

'Tribe', 'caste', 'sect' and 'class' are used synonymously and therefore, many castes are described as tribe and many tribes have been described as 'caste'. It is a difficult job to separate social groups as 'castes' and 'tribe'.

Some sociologists and anthropologists define tribes as a social groups speaking a common dilect. W. J. Perry observes, . . . "tribe is a group speaking a common dilect and inhabiting a common territory".

Imperial Gazetteer defines tribe as, 'a collection of families bearing a common name, speaking a common dialect, occupying or professing to occupy a common territory and it not usually endogamous, though originally it might have so'. All tribe-members, within the Tribe, quote their common origin and workship common Dieties (Pande, 1975).

Notified Tribal Population in India

India is a country of many castes and tribes. There are more than a hundred different tribes in India and are found mostly in hill regions of India. India's tribal population which stood at approximately 22.5 million in 1961 can now be roughly estimated to have exceeded the thirty two million mark. Of this the number of tribal people pursuing the traditional way of life and not considerably affected by the surrounding Hindu or some other cultural tradition is very small indeed. Again a number of such tribes retain a tribal name and are, hence, included in the figures of tribal population but they have otherwise become a part of Hindu society and have merged into the national stream of cultural life.

According to 1961 Census the total population of India was 43.8 crores in which roughly 3 crores were scheduled tribes. The tribal population of India according to 1971 Census was around 4 crore which is 6.94 per cent of total population. The scheduled tribe population is normally living in forests and in Hill areas from a very long time and because of their typical living conditions and lack of proper transport they could not join in the main stream of our national life. State-wise Indian tribal population in 1971 Census, is shown in the following table.

TABLE 2.1

Tribal Population in Indian States and Union Territories

Sl. No.	*Name of State/Union territories*	*Total Population*	*Tribal Population*
1.	Andhra Pradesh	4,35,02,708	16,57,657
2.	Assam	1,49,57,542	19,19,947
3.	Gujarat	2,66,97,475	37,34,422
4.	Bihar	5,63,53,369	49,32,767
5.	Haryana	1,00,36,808	–
6.	Himachal Pradesh	34,60,434	1,41,610
7.	Jammu & Kashmir	46,16,632	–
8.	Kerala	2,13,47,375	269356
9.	Madhya Pradesh	4,16,54,119	8387403
10.	Maharashtra	5,04,12,235	29,54,247

Sl. No.	Name of State/Union territories	Total Population	Tribal Population
11.	Karnataka	2,92,99,014	2,31,268
12.	Nagaland	5,16,449	4,57,602
13.	Orissa	2,19,44,615	50,71,937
14.	Punjab	1,35,51,660	–
15.	Rajasthan	2,57,65,806	31,25,506
16.	Tamil Nadu	4,11,99,168	3,11,515
17.	Uttar Pradesh	8,83,41,144	1,98,565
18.	West Bengal	4,43,12,011	22,32,969
19.	Manipur	10,72,753	3,34,466
20.	Meghalaya	10,11,699	8,14,230
21.	Tripua	15,56,342	4,50,544
Union Territories			
1.	Andaman & Nicobar	1,15,133	18,102
2.	Chandigarh	2,57,251	–
3.	Dadar and Nagar Haveli	74,170	64,445
4.	Delhi	40,65,698	–
5.	Goa, Daman and Deu	8,57,771	7,654
6.	Lakshadweep	31,810	29,540
7.	Arunachal Pradesh	4,67,511	3,69,408
8.	Pondichery	47,707	–

Source: Bulletin of Harijan and Social Welfare in U.P. (Hindi) Director Harijan and Samaj Kalyan, Lucknow, 1974-75, pp 66.

State Tribal Population

In U.P. the schedule tribes are living from a very early period but they were not recognised as Tribes from administrative side up to 1967. In 1967 President of India proclaimed an ordinance and recognized five social groups as scheduled tribe. These are *Tharu, Boksas, Bhotia, Raji and Jaunsaris.* These tribes are mainly inhabited in hill areas and Tarai area of Kumaon and Garhwal regions. On the north, hill are inhabited by Bhotia, Raji and Jaunsari tribes and the foothills and Terai parts are mainly inhabited by Tharu and Boksas tribes. Some other social groups are also like a "tribe" but they are not recognised by the Government as a "tribe". These are Gujars, Agariyas, Bagi, Bheel, Chero, Kol and Gonds, etc.

According to 1971 Census the tribal population of Uttar Pradesh was 1,98,565 which is 0.22 per cent of total population of the State.

TABLE 2.2

District-wise Tribal Population in U.P.

Sl. No.	*Name of District*	*Tribal Population* *Total*	*Rural*	*Urban*
1.	Dehradun	61,672	61,107	565
2.	Naini Tal	52,660	52,297	263
3.	Almora	1,874	1,665	209
4.	Pauri Garhwal	409	372	37
5.	Tehri Garhwal	435	432	3
6.	Chamoli	8,155	6,629	1,526
7.	Uttarkasi	282	274	8
8.	Pithoragarh	15,247	15,118	229
	Total of Hill Districts	1,40,734	1,36,894	2,840
9.	Jhansi	70	1	69
10.	Jalaun	2	–	2
11.	Hamirpur	–	–	–
12.	Banda	233	209	14
13.	Kanpur	627	96	531
14.	Fatehpur	148	116	32
15.	Lucknow	142	–	142
16.	Unnao	317	317	–
17.	Rai Bareilly	42	42	–
18.	Sitapur	213	132	82
19.	Hardoi	539	490	49
20.	Kheri	18,254	18,224	30
21.	Barabanki	4	–	4
22.	Deoria	320	240	80
23.	Azamgarh	1,592	1,592	–

Sl. No.	Name of District	Tribal Population		
		Total	Rural	Urban
24.	Jaunpur	10	10	–
25.	Gazipur	582	572	10
26.	Balia	181	173	8
27.	Basti	332	331	1
28.	Behraich	1,680	1,668	12
29.	Allahabad	676	435	241
30.	Faizabad	21	3	18
31.	Gorakhpur	1,715	1,673	42
32.	Gonda	7,752	7,743	9
33.	Mirzapur	1,840	1,308	532
34.	Pratapgarh	16	16	–
35.	Sultanpur	2	2	–
36.	Varanasi	276	130	146
37.	Saharanpur	2,053	1,861	192
38.	Muzaffarnagar	1,445	1,012	533
39.	Meerut	2,235	693	1,442
40.	Bulandsahar	986	44	842
41.	Aligarh	420	281	139
42.	Mathura	800	2	798
43.	Agra	2,183	2	2,181
44.	Mainpuri	1	1	–
45.	Etah	216	216	–
46.	Bareilly	451	186	265
47.	Bijnor	3,173	754	419
48.	Badaun	365	168	197
49.	Moradabad	2,302	394	1,908
50.	Rampur	917	112	805
51.	Sahjahanpur	1,455	761	694
52.	Pilibhit	467	224	243
53.	Farukhabad	285	274	11
54.	Etawa	401	366	35
	Total of Plain Districts	57,831	45,874	12,867
	Total of Hill and Plain District (U.P)	1,98,565	1,82,768	15,707

Source: The data are for 1971. Director of Harijan & Social Welfare U.P. *Harijan & Samaj Kalyan in U.P., Lucknow,* 1974-75, pp 69-70.

Aboriginals of U.P. Himalayas

Kumaon revenue division is situated on the northern part of Uttar Pradesh. In Kumaon, there are only four recognized tribes. These are Tharu, Boksa, Bhotia and Raji. Geographically most part of the division is hilly. In the hills Bhotias and Rajis are found while in Terai areas main tribes are Tharus and Boksas. From the point of view of tribal population, Naini Tal district has the biggest number of tribals and Pithoragarh district stands second in accommodating tribal population.

It is said that these tribes were found in vedic period and are frequently mentioned even afterwards. Different Gazetteers and historical writing establish this truth. History tells that in the period of British rule in India the administrator assigned little importance to tribal development. Due to this fact in 1885 there was a full-fledged revolt by some tribes in Bihar against the ruler of the time. After this incidence the Britishers formulated some laws and lent their attention to tribal development. About the origin of the tribes of Kumaon there is no authentic information available. Some writings and Gazetteers have compiled a little information basing on the legends and historical documents. We have used these sources towards introduction to Tribes.

Tharwat in U.P. Himalaya

Areas in habited by exclusively Tharu tribe is "Tharwat". The tribe is found in the Terai belt at the foot hills of the Himalayas. It is said that they are also found in Nepal near Indian border. In Naini Tal district the mostly inhabited places by Tharus are the villages around Banbasa, Khatima, Sitaranj and Nanakmatta. The origin of Tharus has formed the subject of much controversy. Some claim that they are originally Mongols. Pande, (1958) says that they are like Nepali. There is no doubt that they are similar to Mongols in some of their features. William Crooke observes. ". . . A tribe which has its headquarters in the Himalayan Terai and colonies in the Gorakhpur division and northern Oudh" (Crooke, 1974) Tharu tribe is spread over a long Terai belt stretching from east Kumaon to Gorakhpur. According to D. N. Majumdar, the Tharus resemble the artisan caste in body characters, the Bhantu and the Habura in facial characters and some of the higher castes in nasal character . . . the Mongoloid features are definite among them, and even the skin colour is yellow brown and oblique eyes are numerous". Majumdar, 1961). He establishes that Tharus are Mongols.

Some authors believe that the word Tharu is derived from the Hindi work "*Thahrey*" because they are said to have halted, after the fight with Gurkhas, in the forests. Some claims that the word "Tharu" is a Hindi word and used in English as wet in allusion of the swampy tracts in which they live. Others attribute the origin of the word Tharu to "Daru" (wine) because they are habitual of drinking wine. Other say that Tharu means the resident of Terai. Tharus say that they are Rajputs. Their ancestors came from Chittor, when the great war of Hastinapur was fought. Their ancestors fled away from the battle and came to the Terai and became the residents of Terai.

It is also commonly held that Tharu males were not Rajputs but their females were Rajputs. Tharu males were the servants of Rajputs, working with them at the time of Hastinapur battle. At the battle they saved the life of Rajput females and fled away to these forests, along with the Rajput ladies. For long, they continued in the relationship of devoted servants. It is proved by the fact that Tharus females have higher status even today and are more powerful in all decisions than their males in these families. Tharu males can not even go to their household kitchen and dine with ladies. The males, thus, still have a lower status. Tharu people deny any validity of this saying. They say that they are Rajput and write their sir name as "Rana" but their features indicates their Mongolian origin rather than a birth from Rajputs of Chittor.

Tharus, now called scheduled tribe, are not treated at par with Brahmans and Rajput in Kumaonee society Brahmans and Rajputs say that they are inferior in caste. They do not participate in common Kitchen and dine with Tharus. Now some Tharus are economically better and the Hindu society seems accepting them in common social participations.

It is observed from the Tharu study that Tharus according to their physical features are of Mongolian origin. The body structure does not differ much from other Hindu people, but there are some differences still seen in very obvious distinguishing them from rest of the inhabitants of Terai. We can make-out a Tharu easily.

The male are mostly short statured. They have a flat face, dark complexion and scanty growth of beard. In females dark complexion is also found but they are healthy and flat nose and have round faces. Males wear dothi, kurta and coat and usually cover heads with a cap. Females wear lahenga and waist. But now the new generation is adopting the new fashions. Tharu females are very fond of jewellery. The jewellery often used by the women are made from silver, while gold ornaments are rarely found among Tharus. This is a dissimilar feature from Rajput ladies of Chittor.

Buxas or Boksas of Himalyan Terai

In Nainital district of Kumaon division the second tribe, which is numerous is Boksa. This tribe is found in western part of Terai. Boksas are very near to Tharus in physical features. It is said that this tribe is living in Kumaon from a very long period because their description is found in Kumaon geography and history.[1] Dr. Stewart describes Boksas of Bijnor as follows "The members of the tribe are of short stature and sparse in habitat. In both respects they are somewhat different from the ordinary Hindu peasant of the district. They do not however, differ much in general built-in or in complexion. The eyes are small, the opening of the eye lids being narrow, linear and horizontal (the inner angle not ending downward so far as observed); the face is very broad across the cheek bones, and the nose is depressed, thus, increasing the general flatness of the face, the jaw is prognathous and the lower lip is thick and the moustache and beard are very scanty. . . ." The features of Boksas of Kumaon are also exactly the same.

Boksas claim that they are connected with Panwar dynasty of Rajputs and assert that their chief Udaijeet, was driven by Jagat Deo from their home in a quarrel, which arose between brothers Udaijeet and Jagat Deo. The Raja of Dharnagar, Udaijeet, came to dwell with a few followers at Banbasa on the bank of Sarada River. Udaijeet had not been there long when his aid was solicited by the Raja of Kumaon, whose territories required defence against some of the neighbouring powers. Success attended the efforts of Udaijeet Panwar, and the gratitude of the Raja of Kumaon induced him to offer an asylum to his defenders in his territory. They having been given western Terai areas left Banbasa and took up their residence in their present abodes called "Buksad".

Elliot described that there are no features of Rajputs in Boksas of Kumaon and claims that these are non-Aryan people. These are not similar to those people who are immigrated from outside to Kumaun. Those are near to Tharu in physique. Buksad, the area on which this tribe is living, is described in *Aain-i-Akbari*. The province was densely populated at that time and some Sikh population was also found. May be these so called Sikhs were Boksa and due to Nanakmatta Gurudwara, they changed their religion. This is of course, only a speculation that Boksas looked like 'Sikhs' or were converts due to the influence of Nanakmatta, literally the followers of Nanak. There is not sufficient evidence to prove this. The links between 'Sikh' and Bhoksa are not rooted in history. In present form, Boksas have not similarity with Sikhs. Boksas are the aborigins of western Terai areas and have somewhat closer similarity with Tharus.

High-landers of Bhotauchal

'Bhotia' is a hill tribe. In Kumaon Division Bhotia tribe is generally found in district Pithoragarh and Almora. Pithoragarh district has the highest population of Bhotia community. In district Almora they are found in a very small number. In Pithoragarh district, tehsil Dharchula and tehsil Munsiyari are mostly inhabited by this tribe and in Almora they are found in Bagheswer tehsil. The area where Bhotia tribe is found is called Bhotia Mahalas. Atkinson writes, "Bhotia mahal or fiscal sub division of the tract called "Bhot" comprises the inter Alpine valley of the snowy range bordering on Tibet-Byans, Chaundas and Darma on the east, Johar in the middle and Painkhanda on the west."

Bhotia settlements, as described by S.D. Pant, read as ". . . If we draw a straight line across the district from Kapkot to Askote, the area to the north-east of this line constitutes the region locally known as the Bhot or Bhotia tract, which is entirely distinct from the remaining, south western portion of the district"

Bhot is the name of the area inhabited by "Bhotia" tribe. The word refers to the people living between India and Tibet. 'Bhot' or more correctly 'Bad' is really the same word as Tibet". They are claimed to have come from Tibet, in remote past and had marital links with Tibet and were trading with India.

Some authors claim that Bhotias are of Hindu origin. They have not immigrated to Bhot, from any other place. They are Hindu Rajput as Sanskritayana says, while some anthropologists confuse them with Tibetans of mongoloid origin on the basis of certain similarities in language, customs and physical appearance, they are originally Hindu and most probably of Rajput origin "Bhotias also subscribe this view."

Sherring observes that Bhotias are originally from Tibet. He says "the Bhotias are of Tibetan origin though they themselves have still current among them they belief that they were originally Hindus" 'Bhot' is used by outsiders for Tibet as Haimendorf says "the average Nepalis of the Kathmandu valley and the middle ranges refer to all these populations of Tibetan culture and language in discriminately as, 'Bhotias' or 'Bhotis', generic term derived from 'Bhot', the Nepali name for Tibet".

Grierson speculates that "a Tibetan is Bod-pa, and this word has been changed to Bhulla, Bhotia, etc. by the Hindus. The name Bhotia is now applied by them for the Tibetans living on the borders between India and Tibet, while the people of Tibet-proper are called Huniyas, and the country is called Hundesh. Usually 'Hunias' of Tibet are more sturdy than average Bhotia". Hunias of Tibet call Bhotias as Monpa and Qunam for Kumaon area.

Sherring in his book *Western Tibet and British Borderland* at one place writes the Rajput colonies were in Tibet in past as a Chinese historian has observed but it is yet not clear whether they were Hindu or not. "It is true that Tibetan and Chinese historians write about Rajput colonies but there is no doubt that they are Mongolians".

Some people hold the opinion that Bhotias came from Bhutan, but Pangtey in his study found that "the Bhotias of Kumaon, however, should not be confused with people of Bhutan who are really of Tibetan stock. He establishes finally that Bhotias are Hindu. Bhotias and Bhutanis do not seen to be very different and carry some similarities.

H.G. Walton expressed the view that the Bhotias are not by any means identical with the present Tibetans, though their features are of an undoubtedly a like cast and structure.

From the above expression we come on this conclusion that about the origin of Bhotias, Sociologists, Anthropologists and Historians are not clear as Majumdar accepts, "our information about the race element in the population of the Himalayan region is extremely meagre". But most of the scholars are of this opinion that Bhotias are of Mongoloid blood and came from Tibet while we can not refute their origin from Bhutanis. Bhotia traders prospered in the past but have lost their ground in later fifties.[2]

Exiled Princes of Deedihaat

There is a Raji tribe, numerically small but having a royal vanity, inhabiting in Pithoragarh district. The word 'Raji' is drawn from "Rajas" or the 'royal people'. "This is a tribe apparently of non-Aryan affinities, found in Askote, in Kumaon and in small numbers along the lower Himalayan ranges" says Crooke. Today, Rajis are few in number. Rajis are found in a small number near Askote, Jauljeewi and Chalthi in Pithoragarh district. It is said that they are living in this region from a very long period. Now their population is not more than 1000. Rajis are called the royal people because they lived in forests and have the claim that they belong to the family rulers of Askote. They are an aboriginal tribe. They do not much care for their clothings and other necessities of material life as they have no social compaisons in a forest life.

They have been identified with the "Raja Kirates" who in early Sanskrit literature, are joined with the Sakas and Saraves as "Dasyus" and are placed by the Varah Samhita between Amarvana and China or between Jageswer and Tibet, and it will mean little either the "princely Kiratas" or the "kiratas of Rajya".

Captain H. Strachey's writes in his Journal of Garjjia Ghat that, "Rajdhai Karinda (agent) caught two of the Banmanus, the wild man of chipula for my inspection. I saw nothing very remarkable about them except an expression of alarm and stupidity in their faces and they are, perhaps, darker and otherwise more like low land Hindustanis than the average Kumaon paharie". In the context of this field study, author contacted the Raji households and had long sittings with them for data collection and group discussions. While it was difficult to understand their dialect, they could communicate well in Kumaonee and also few could speak good manageable Hindi. They were courteous and humble.

The tribe is the descendant of royal prince exiled in dense forests of Kumaun. About their origin, Rajis, tell typical stories, Atkinson writes in *Himalayan Gazetteer,* "... The Rajis' themselves, say that they are of Hindu origin. That when the world began there were two Rajput brothers, of whom the elder was a hunter and lived in the Jungles, whilst the younger cultivated the ground and had a fixed abode. The younger brother received the government of the world and said to his elder brother that there can not be two Rajas in one country, and accordingly the elder brother retired to the forest and his descendants are now called Raji, who neither cultivate the ground nor live in permanent dwellings".

A large number of stories are narrated by the old about Raji tribe. Dr. Preetchand conjectured that the Rajis, usually found along the Himalayan border, are all possessing the physical characters of the Bhotias in general and very unlike the Doms.

During the visit to these areas the author inquired from them about their origin and was told that, they are a princely tribe. Their caste, in rank, is the highest in the world. On enquiring about their relations with other castes, they replied that, they are Rawat Rajput. "Rawat" is derived from the world Raji and Raji from Raja. They are the children of Raja. So they can not establish any marital relationship of equal rank with other groups of society, on whom they are supposed to rule. They claim to be kings in exile. Their patterns of life seem to be the same as of poor Paharies.

The physical features of Rajis are the same as Bhotias but their facial colour is dark. They wear simple woollen cloths in winter and cotton in summer. Males wear *Kurta, pajama* and females wear *Ghagra, Lakya* and *Zarkins*, *Mirzain* etc. By habits and behaviourial character, Rajis are simpler, scared, guileless and avoid dealing with other inhabitants of these areas. Their requirements of life are few and aspirations still less. Their norms of "honesty" and loyalty to God are worth appreciation not evidenced so clearly among others. Now Raji are quite demanding and grudging people but have a poor ballot force.

Introduction to Tharu Habitat

Here we will introduce ourselves with the amenity structure of the inhabited villages of Tharus covered by our sample. The names, location of villages, description about houses, food habits, etc. will be explained regarding each village. The following table presents the village-wise introductory data.

TABLE 2.3

Location and Participation of *Tharu* Village

Habitations of Tharu Tribe	*Distance from Block (HQ)*	*Total tribal population*	*Total land of the village (Hectare)*	*Net cropped land (Hectare)*	*Persons in Govt. & other service of State*	*Animals*	
						Milch	*Drought*
Umraokhurd	2	796	476	414	16	159	179
Naugaon Thagu	6	1302	741	720	6	389	254
Chanda	8	338	364	308	4	85	158
Jhankat	12	746	586	493	3	246	466
Sundrikala	24	423	324	316	8	87	240
Kishanpur	20	186	154	145	3	19	136
Zhankat	27	213	138	126	3	16	78

Umraokhurd

Village Umraokhurd is situated at a distance of 2 km. in the north of the Block headquarters of Khatima. Khatima is the main centre of the village for purchase and sale of village produce. Total area of the village is 476 hectares in which 411 hectares area is use for cultivation and other purposes. Cart road metalled by bricks is constructed for reaching this village from Khatima. Most of the persons are engaged in a agricultural activities. Sixteen persons from this village are in Govt. and other services outside in 1982. Only one person was graduate in the village upto 1976. Main products of the village are paddy, wheat, gram, mustard and maize. Main export of the village is paddy. Number of draught animals was 179 used for transport and ploughing while milch cattle were 159. There seems to have occurred only little change since 1980 yet the contribution of N.R.E.P. projects has been enormous.

Naugaon Thagu

There were 1302 people in the village in 1982 perhaps, Naugaon Thagu is the biggest village from the stand point of population and area in Tharu villages. It is nearly 6 Km. far from the Block headquarter and situated in the south-west of Khatima town. Only 6 persons are in services and rest are employed in agriculture. Paddy, wheat etc. are the main produce of village and paddy is the principal export. Most of the houses are tetched and Kachha. There is a school for children and a bricked path in the village.

Chanda

Chanda is situated in the south of Khatima and 8 km. far from the town. Cart road is available for village. Main market and centre of activities is Khatima. From stand point of population this is a small village, quite neat and clean. Only four persons are employed in Govt. and other services. Primary School is situated very close to the village. Hospital, High School and other facilities are in Khatima, at a distance of eight kilometres. Draught animals are more than milch animals. Houses are mostly Kachha, constructed by wood, grass and mud. Three houses have transistors and one has a black and white television which does not work for a major defect.

Jhankat

Jhankat is situated at both sides of Khatima-Sitarganj main road. This is 12 km. far from Khatima and the direction is to the west of Khatima town. Junior High School, Post Office, and Primary Health Centre facilities are available in the village. No person was graduate in the village but most of the males were well informed. Some houses are constructed with Bricks and Cement but most of the houses are Kachha. Number of the milch and draught animals was the highest among the seven sample villages inhabited by Tharus. Irrigation facilities are very meagre. Few peasants have pumping sets. Main products are Wheat and Paddy. Main export of the village is paddy. Sarson, and 'soya' are also socon by same Tharu peasants. The village has 746 person and 493 hectare total cropped areas.

Sundrikala

Sundrikala is 24 km. far from the Block headquarters Khatima. This is in the north-west of Khatima. A metalled road is constructed for village by Ganna Samiti. Grinding mill is also situated in the village. Wine shop is in the village. Primary school and Post Office are also in the village Nanakmatta is only 2 km. far from the village and this is the main village market. Most of the houses in village are Kachha. Irrigation facilities are negligible. Five persons of the village are in services. Number of drought animals is more than milch animals. A tea stall is also in the centre of the village Intermediate Collage is in Nanakmata. Though village has all of these facilities yet its look and pattern is very traditional some houses are better built. Three farmers had sown sugarcane in their farm. Sugarcane is getting popular in recent years. One of the farmers produced oilseeds in one acre in 1981-82 and the returns were good.

Kishanpur

Five kilometres away from the main bazar Kishanpur is a poor Tharu village. The soils are wet and poor in yields.

The Kishanpur village is situated near Nanak Sagar in the northwest of Khatima and at a distance of 20 km. This is a medium size village. Nanakmatta is the nearest market of this village. Post Office, Primary School, Grinding Mill are at a distance of two kilometres from the village. These are in closer village Sundrikala. Nanakmatta is 5 km. far from the village. All the houses in the village were Kachha. Draught animals are more in number. Per acre production is less than that in other villages due to seepage of Nanak Sagar. The drainage in the village is poor so the land is getting unproductive. Only two persons are in service outside the village. The general condition of village is poor. It has a population of 186 persons and nearly 154 hectares of total land. Most of the land is used for crops. Nearly, 10 hectares land is a waste due to waterlogging.

Zhankat

Zhankat is situated in the west of Khatima and north-west of Nanakmatta. This is at a distance of 27 km. from Khatima and nearly 4 km. from Nanakmatta. Three persons of the village were in Govt. service. The number of draught animals was more than milch animals. Some pucca houses have been constructed with the aid of Government but most of the houses in village are thatched and constructed with mud and kachha bricks. 213 persons have cropped area of 126 hectares. The villagers are poor and uneducated. Children go to school but the children avoid going to school for the harsh behaviour of teachers.

Tharus are cultivators. The land of Terai is fertile and most of the Tharu families have their own possession on most of their land except the patches mortgaged to others. Due to their backwardness and illiteracy they have not utilized their land wisely. Other communities of the area have used it prudently. They do not have means of irrigation at their ownership and the irrigation facilities provided by government are only negligible. In the past, Tharus were a migrating tribe. Due to their migrating character in the past, it was very difficult for them to retain their land in possession. They were very fond of breaking up new soil as Navil has observed, "the Tharu is an excellent cultivator, and will till about four times as much land as men of plains in the same neighbourhood, but his migratory habit and his love for breaking up new soil make it difficult to prevent him from bolting". But now Tharus are very sincere to their occupation. They live in villages permanently. Most of the Tharu families constructed their houses working with own family labour. Houses are built of grass, wood and mud. The housebuilding material is available free of cost, so the cost of construction is only meagre. Some families which are, economically, in better position have designed houses made of bricks and cement. In the Tharu houses usually two rooms and verandah at the front and separate Kitchen are constricted. All houses have a similar style.

Tharus are very fond of fish. They often go for fishing in rivers. In rainy season they collect good quality of small fish and dry them for future use. Basket or net or ordinary cloth sheets are used for fishing. Navil wrote in *Naini Tal Gazetteer* "that the Tharu and Boksas of Terai are great fish eaters". Tharu use rice as their principal food item, chapatis are used very rarely though they produce wheat.

Tharus are at times dead-drinkers. Drinking habits of Tharus increases their indebtedness. Tharu males are known for simplicity and goodness. They are very simple and God fearing people. Money lenders take a exorbitantly higher percentage as interest from Tharus. About Tharus drinking and other habits Navil wrote "Tharus are ... honest, brave, great hunters and good cultivators . . . , their favourite crop being rice. As everywhere the Tharus are superstitious and much under the influence of their priests, their dispute are settled by the tribal council, and at their panchayat gathering and at every possible occasions, they consume large quantity of liquor, distilled from rice. Their hospitality and honesty are worth appreciation. They are fatalists and have strong faith on worship of deities and sacrifices are made in their worship.

Introduction to Boksa Habitat

Here we will introduce the amenity structure of the inhabited villages of Boksa covered by our sample. The following table presents the villages of Boksa covered by our sample. The following table presents the village-wise introductory data about Boksa sample villages.

TABLE 2.4

Location and Particulars of Boksa villages Under Sample

Habitations of Tharu Tribe	*Distance from Block (HQ)*	*Total tribal population*	*Total land of the village (Hectare)*	*Net cropped land (Hectare)*	*Persons in Govt. & other service of State*	*Animals*	
						Milch	*Drought*
Bannakhera	10	245	1443	1420	2	15	100
Khamari	15	454	836	800	7	10	250

Bannakhera

Bannakhera is situated at a distance of 10 km. from Bazpur Block headquarter and is placed in the north-west direction of Bazpur. Bazpur is a big *mandi.* Small household goods are available at even Bannakhera shops. Primary School, Post Office, Grinding Mill, Primary Health Centre are available in the village itself. The climate is very hot in summer. No person in the village is in Govt. service. Houses are most Kachha, made of wood, grass and soil. Milch animals are very rare but the number of draught animals is quite big. Main products of the village are paddy, wheat, Sugarcane, etc. Paddy and sugarcane are the main exports from village. No family has got a tractor in the village. But among the other castes, in which Sikhs are main, have got tractors. Irrigation facilities are available in village. Govt. has constructed a Canal for the village. Pucca road is also constructed by the government. Bannakhera is a rich village. It has fertile land. Farmers grow Fodder and have buffaloes for milk. Draught cattle are more numerous. Cash-crops are also grown.

Khamari

It is a big populous village but land is only little. Buffaloes are of better breed. The people are very good. Village Khamari is very densely populated. This is situated 15 km. far from Bajpur and 3 km. from Bannakhera in the north of Bazpur town. Village post office is in Bannakhera itself. Only 7 persons are in Government and other services. The main products of the village are paddy, wheat and sugarcane. Mostly houses found in village are Kachha but some families have now constructed pucca houses with the aid of Government. Number of draught animals is more than the milch animals. Milk production is only meagre. The people are quite simple and do not believe in raising income by subsidiary occupation. They want the new generation to be educated and want to children to become Government Officials.

Boksas are very simple, honest and God-fearing people. Their disputes are settled by their *tribe council.* They consume a large quantity of wine and are used to smoking. Old ladies are also used to smoking. Most of the Boksa are non-vegetarians. Fish and rice is their delicious food and *chapatis* are seldom used in food. The females are held with respect and they have command over the household.

Boksas are cultivators like Tharus. Per yield is more than Tharu farmers. Irrigation facilities are available in these areas. The main sources of irrigation are canal, constructed by Government. Pumping sets are found only rarely. Boksas are more prosperous than Tharus. Seven Boksa have got tractors and many are found using modern agricultural instruments. They have learnt this from Punjabi immigrants. The main cause of prosperity of Boksas as compared to Tharus is the irrigation facility and roads. Roads are constructed by the public works department with the help of sugar factory of Bazpur. Boksas dress themselves in simple clothes following their traditional patterns. They like coloured cloths and like to be recognised and civilized and cultured.

Like *Tharus* Boksa take keen interest in fairs. Males and females both visit fairs enthusiastically. The Main Markets used by Boksas are Bazpur and Gadarpur. Small shops are also available near villages. Wine shop is more frequently seen as compared to those catering to other needs. Terai climate is very hot. Malaria is a very common disease in this area. Medical facilities are very rare and the quacks fleece the poor exorbitantly. The tribe needs in intensive medical care. The Primary Health Centre Doctors also charge high rates for medicines and the tribals avoid going to P.H.C. of Block due to bad treatment with them by the staff and due to communication barrier (Tripathi, 1980).

The Boksa male wears Dhoti, Pajama, Paints, Kurta, Coat, Cap etc. Old ladies wear *Ghagra* and *Zarki* and young women wear *Sarees, Lahanga* and *Blouse.* Bangles and ornaments are loved by young and old equally. Ornaments used by Boksa woman are made of silver and gold. Gold ornaments are not very frequently seem now. Some old males also wears, ornaments and ear-rings which is called *Kundal.* ". . . . It is held that Boksa ladies are abnormally skilled in magic spell and can grip-over the males of their choice and keep them enslaved. But author in course of his survey 1982 checked the validity of this saying and found no logical ground to believe this.

Introduction to Bhotia Habitat

The following table presents the village-wide introduction data of Bhotia sample villages namely Sirkha, Roonga, Daranti, Tejam and Palli Pharsali.

TABLE 2.5

Location and Particulars of Bhotia Villages

Village	*Distance from Block*	*Total tribal population*	*Total land of the village*	*Net cropped land (Hectare)*	*Persons in Govt. & other service*	*Animals*	
						Milch	*Drought*
Sirkha	48.1	247	744	87	28	25	78
Roonga	49.2	136	290	78	16	15	110
Daranthi	6.5	109	258	115	14	16	112
Tejam	38.0	172	569	236	13	33	126
Palli Pharsali	8.6	96	602	201	16	75	156

Sirkha

A village of enthusiastic youth at the top elevations is Sirkha. Sirkha village is in Dharchula Block. It is situated at a height of 8000 feet above sea level and at a distance of 45 km. in the north-east of Dharchula. The climate of the village is very cold. Out of 297.6 hectare of land only 34 hectare is fit for cultivation. The people of the village are permanent residents of the village and they do not migrate in winter. Post Office, Primary School and Janmilan Kendra are in the village itself. Drinking water is supplied by a pipeline. Educated youth of the village offer free tuition to the boys. The boys have play ground where they organize games and sports for their young friends. There is good unity and integration. There are no road facilities. One link is formed recent by rural employment project. Metalled road is upto Tawaghat and beyond this there is no way other than to go on foot. Slopes in these hills are very steep and the rocks are extremely weak. There is a P.W.D. Rest House near the village. Twenty-five persons of the village are in Government service. All the houses in the village are pucca and built by stones and slate roof. Houses are double storeyed. Lower or ground floor of the house is used for animal shed and upper part for residential purpose. Most of the time is consumed in preparing woollen goods. The female labour is very hard working in, both, agriculture and cottage level crafts. The old, and young children also devote to cottage industry and utilize every bit of spare time.

Roong

The village is on the lofty Himalayan range having extremely cold climate. Village 'Roong' is situated 48 km. far from Dharchula in the north-east direction. The altitude of the village above sea level is nearly 7500 feet. The entire tract is hilly. Primary School is in village itself. Post Office is 2 km. far from the village. Ayurvedic Dispensary is in this village. Seventeen persons were in Government service during 1976, 4 persons were taking higher education and there were two Graduates. Net cultivatable area is only 30 hectares because of steep slope and shallow land in these hills. Draught animals are more in number than milch. Drought cattle are also used for transport. Main products of the village are Potato, Wheat, Uwa and Barley. One fair price shop is also in the village. All houses are constructed by stones and all the houses are double storeyed. The young generation including girls are keen to get education specially science education. Migraton for services it felt necessary and the males have a longing for going to armed forces and if they can't find an entry in army, they want to go for business.

Daranthi

Daranthi is 5 km. far from the Block headquarters Munsiyari. This is in the south from the Munsiyari. The altitude of the village is nearly 7000 feet above sea level. Post Office and Primary School are very near to village. Most of the facilities are available at Munsiyari. Eighteen persons are in Government services. Fourteen are permanent and 4 in daily wages. Seven persons are Graduates. One person is Divisional Forest Officer. One is selected in engineering course. Number of draught animals is higher. Land, due to steep slopes and cold climate is not much in use. Main agricultural products of the village are Wheat, *Jhungra,* Barley etc. Woollen goods are produced in the village. Main exports are woollen goods such as Thulmas, Blankets, Dan, Mufflers, Shawls, Sweaters, etc. Per household value of such disposed goods is Rs. 250 to 300 annually.

Tejam

Tejam is situated in the south-west of Block headquarter Munsiyari at a distance of 35 km. on Munsiyari - Pithorgarh road. The altitude of the village is nearly 4000 feet. The climate is not so much cold. Primary School, Post Office, Primary Health Centre are in village itself. Some shops are also in the village in which all the household items are of course in very prices. Water is available at a distance of 200 yards down. Ram Ganga river is in close proximity to this village. Twelve persons are in government services, in which 6 are Medical Doctors. Nine are taking advanced Medical Education in Medical Colleges and one is in Engineering College, Gorakhpur. Draught animals number high. Bhotias have small holdings. So their principal occupation is weaving and knitting of woollen goods. The main exports from the village are woollen goods. Six persons of the village were shop-keepers. The houses are pucca and double storeyed. The general look and expression of inhabitants indicates higher cultural traditions. There were two student leaders and social workers in the village. The Khadi Commission organizer serves raw-wool to the spinners.

Palli Pharsali

The village is a mini-industrial centre for woollen fabrics. Palli Pharsali is in Kapkot Block of District Almora. This is 8 km. far from Kapkot in the north-east direction. The village is one km. far from Bharari-Sama motor road. The village market is Bharari which is also the bus station. Post Office, Primary School are very near to the village. There is carpet training centre, where mostly ladies are the trainees. Water is available for drinking and to some extent irrigation is also available. The Bhotiyas of this village are not mainly cultivators because their holdings are very small and which are not sufficient for the livelihood of the family. So the main occupation of this village of Bhotia is production of woollen goods. They bring raw wool from the carpet training centre and prepare yarn from that. Carpet centre gives them wage according the length and quality of yarn. The agricultural products of the village are Wheat, Jhungra, Paddy, Pulses, etc. Potato is grown in small terraces quite successfully.

The houses in all the villages of Bhotias in the block are pucca. No village in the area is having purely Bhotia population. From Bharari to Loharkhet the road construction work is going on. This is the way for Pindari Glacier and other Bhotia villages of the area. There are four English speaking boys working devotedly to crafts and serving as teachers.

The *Bhot* is a hilly region. The best suitable parts of this region for cultivation and living are the narrow valleys lying between the great peaks of Himalaya. The whole Bhotia region is divided among five parganas in which four are in Pithoragarh district and one in Almora district. Dharchula, Byans, Chaundas and Darma three parganas are mostly inhabited by the Bhotias. Munsiyari, Johar pargana is the centre of Bhotia population. In Danpur pargana there is only a small number of Bhotias. There is rapid out-migration among the youth who do not find appropriate work at home.

The main rivers of the region are Kali, Gori and Dholi. Kali separates India from neighbouring country Nepal. Tawaghat is the confluence of Kali and Dholi and Jauljeewi is the confluence of Kali and Gori rivers. Johri, has simperingly noted the extreme poverty in Gori valley in his book. He states "I was shocked to see the poverty and ignorance of this tract . . . one has to visit the lower Gori valley to know that the poverty and ignorance is."

Due to the cold climate and high peaks of mountains and lack of availability of agricultural land, the principal occupation of the Bhotias is trade and services. From areas above 9000 feet Bhotias migrate during winter to the lower parts of districts. The valleys, two harvests in a year can be grown at ease while the upper areas yield 3 crops in two years rotation. Agricultural produce of the region is utterly insufficient for the support of its inhabitants. The region depends for its food supplies almost on the plains. Foodgrains, the prime necessity of the Bhotias, is catered by carrying food stuffs from Haldwani. They use rice in food but rice is not produced in the region because of cold climate. They grow rice in lower valleys. Jhungra and Phaphar grows in upper ranges also. The main products of agriculture in the region are Barley, Wheat, Uwa, Potato, Phaphar in Darma, Byans and upper part of Johar and Wheat, Maduwa, Jhungra, Barley, Potato in lower parts of the region. Some fruits are also produced such as apple, apricot, peaches, etc. but cultivation of fruits is not extensive.

Before 1962 Bhotias has the principal occupation of trade. They used to bring goods from Tibet to India and trade in Tibet. They possessed complete monopoly in trade in this region and had accumulated good lot of wealth. But due to Indo-Chinese War the trade came to an end in 1962.

The Bhotias of Johar or Munsiyari's are economically well off in comparison to Bhotias of Dharchula. The main cause of this difference is that in Dharchula the means of transport are very poor. Geographically hard location, lack of educational institutions in the region of Dharchula. There is little bit of smuggling of Tibetan wool to India via Nepal in Dharchula area.

Due to complete end of Tibetan trade Bhotias' dependency on agriculture increased. Now they are improving their fields and using more manures and even improved seeds. The agricultural implements and method are traditional in Bhotia agriculture. The climatic state does not allow good cropping for cereals in these areas. They spin and weave the wool. Raw material is the greatest problem since 1962. Some raw wool is supplied by Govt. stores but that is not sufficient and is also quite inferior in quality. They produce blankets, carpet, and woollen cloths. Womens also participate in the work very dedicatedly. Bhotias are alert and make use of facilities for them. In fact, their ancestral savings made through trade have now finished but and state aid has highly benefited them.

They wear woollen clothings in summer and winter both because the region's climate is very cold. They build their houses with stones and wood. Their houses are similar to other castes-houses in hills. House building cost is high because they do not know this work. They hire measons and labour for the house-construction. Bhotias are very sharp in business-like dealings and they seem to be prepared to catch-up any facility which filters to them under tribal welfare schemes.

Jewellery used by them is made of gold and silver. Mostly gold ornaments are found but a few of those are silver ornaments only due to poverty. Most of the Bhotia households are prosperous educated, cultured and ambitious and command a good foresight.

Their food habits are the same as that of other hill people. They take rice and pulses in morning and *chapati* and vegetables in night. Mostly Bhotias are non-vegetarians. The traditions and customs of Johar pargana of Bhotias are the same as those of Hindus but Darma Bhotias have different customs and traditions.

Introduction to Raji Habitat

Let us now proceed to discuss the situations, climatic conditions, food habits and traditions of Rajis. Kimkhola village is mostly inhabited by Rajis which is 35 km. far from Dharchula situated in the south-east direction. This is one kilometre at the side of Dharchula - Pithoragarh public road. Water is available for drinking purpose but not available for irrigation. Post Office, Primary School, Veterinary Hospital, Primary Health Centre, are at a distance between 2 to 3 kilometres. Education in the village is negligible. Only a very small part of population is literate. No person from the village is in Govt. and other services. No. of animals, milch and draught, was 225 in village. Out of 243 acres land, only 43 acre is used for cultivation, the rest is not fit for cultivation because the slope is very steep and on some land forests are grown. Author found that Rajis were living in caves and in temporary huts made from grass leafs and wood. They say that cave is very suitable for huts, because only one portion of the cave needs covering. Now Government has given them grant for constructing houses. During survey the author found that they are also constructing their pucca houses. Most of the Rajis villages are small. In a village only 10 to 18 families live. Between 2 to 6 members are usually found in a household. They are accustomed to hard conditions of life and manage within few belongings.

In past their main occupation was to cut wood and to make wooden vassels as Atkinson describes. "They manufacture wooden bowles for sale, live under temporary huts, frequently moving from place to place amidst the jungle of Chipula. They have dilect of their own." They also know some typical symbols which the community uses for their script but only few seem to be aware of these traditional ways of expression. The youngs use Hindi words. They exchange the wooden vassels with articles of their need such as cloths, food grains, jwelleries etc. but the exchange system was very unique. Majumdar wrote "They come with their products at mid-night and placed them in the courtyards of the agent and also keep some symbols to indicate what they want in exchange. The following night when all are asleep stealthily they enter the courtyard of the agent and take what they get in exchange". They are known locally as "invisible traders". Now this type of system is not found. Now they do not make wooden vassels in large scale and complain that for vassels there is a need of good wood, which is not available, and if available anywhere there is a ban on cutting trees. Now they mix-up easily, with the local public and work as labourers at various places specially with forest and P.W.D. contractors.

Now the principal occupation of Rajis is "manual labour" in forests or on roads. Agriculture is their subsidiary occupation because their holdings are very small in size. They produce wheat, Jhungra, barley, Maduwa, etc. in a very small quantity. The produce can not fulfil their needs. They eat boiled rice and cooked pulses at morning and *chapati* and vegetables at night. Bhat, Gahat, Moth, Beans are mainly cooked in pulses. Some Raji use non-vegetarian diets also. They go for fishing and catch birds. They eat many types of wild roots, fruit leaves and buds as their meal. Their art in killing wild animals and fish is praiseworthy. They are darker in colour and are perhaps the aborigins of Kumaon. By appearances they seem to be quite scared and hunted. The tribe of Rajis is perhaps an extinguishing wing and have only an academic significance as tribe. They are like the ordinary poverty striken scheduled caste population of wider plains of U.P. Raji are quite similar to the landless or marginal farmers in east U.P. who manage their livelihood by devoting to manual labour. The only difference is that Raji are proud of being the exiled prices and treat it a right to use the forests at their will.

NARAYANPUR MURIA

Genetic Structure

Here we will discuss the evolutionary position of the Narayanpur Muria with the help of demographic and anthropometric data: The present concept evolution, as we know, is the change in gene frequency of a particular allele of a population, and for which any of the factors like, non-random mating, mutation, sampling error or genetic drift, migration or hybridization and natural selection may be responsible. Since the present sample includes a part of the entire population of Narayanpur Muria, which is a large one and because of certain technical limitations of the present study, factors like mutation and sampling error responsible for evolution could not be discussed here. The non-random mating has been studied through assortative mating and inbreeding. While the former has been studied with respect to 13 anthropometric measurements, the latter is covered through consanguineous marriage and marriage distance. As in consanguineous marriage, there are also chances to increase homozygous allele in case of decrease in marriage distance. Among the other factors, selection and admixture have been discussed in this chapter.

Assortative Mating

The 13 anthropometric measurements through which assortative mating in the present sample has been studied are; maximum head length, maximum head breadth, head height, morphological facial height, upper facial height, nasal length, nasal breadth, minimum frontal breadth, maximum bizygomatic breadth, bigonial breadth, head circumference, weight and stature. Assortative mating means here, the mated pairs are more similar for some phenotypic trait than would be expected if they were chosen at random from the population. Since individuals with similar phenotypes will usually be somewhat similar in their genotypes, a population with assortative mating will increase the average homozygosity and total population variance.

The degree of homozygosity between husband and wife, has been measured following Pearsonian Product-moment Coefficient of Correlation (*r*). Due to lack of such information on any Indian population the present study has been compared with the data available from outside India.

TABLE 2.6

Assortative Mating with Respect to 13 Anthropometric Measurements

Sl. No.	*Characters*	*Number of Individuals*	*Value of 'r'*	*Value of 't'*
1.	Maximum head length	200	(-) 0.0581	0.8189
2.	Maximum head breadth	200	0.01044	1.4771
3.	Head height	200	0.2273	3.2844**
4.	Morphological facial height	200	0.1266	1.7959
5.	Upper facial height	200	0.2020	2.9022**
6.	Nasal length	200	0.1778	2.5424*
7.	Masal breadth	200	(-)0.0053	0.0746
8.	Minimum frontal breadth	200	0.1552	2.2744
9.	Maximum bizygomatic breadth	200	0.0902	1.2744
10.	Bigonial breadth	200	0.0896	1.2659
11.	Head circumference	200	0.0431	0.6070
12.	Weight	153	0.1132	1.4000
13.	Stature	153	0.0346	0.4254

* Significant at 5% level of Probability

** Significant at 1% level of Probability.

Table 2.6 shows that the range of correlation varies between .0053 to +0.2, correlation being highest in head height and upper facial height where the value is 0.2. Negative correlation is found in case of maximum head length and nasal breadth. Of the 13 measurements, the matric difference between husband and wife is significant at 5 per cent level for nasal length and at 1 per cent level for head height and upper facial height. On the basis of above exercise it can be concluded that degree of homogamy is very low for all the 13 measurements under study among the Narayanpur Muria.

Table 2.7 shows a comparative account of assortative mating of Narayanpur Muria and other world populations for all the 13 measurements. In respect of weight, stature and head circumference for a few samples and bizygomatic breadth and head height for one sample each the present sample differ considerably. The difference in *r* value of the present sample with the remaining one is not remarkable. The table 2.7 shows that out of 102 samples of the 13 characters, in maximum number of cases, the correlation value limits within 0.2. The *r* value between 0.2 and 0.3 found in two samples of weight, six samples of stature, two samples of head circumference and one each for maximum head breadth, head height, maximum bizygomatic breadth and upper facial height. In two samples of weight and four samples of stature the *r* value is between 0.3 and 0.5 while this value is more than 0.5 only in two samples; one in stature and one in maximum bizygomatic breadth. The table also reveals that out of 13 characters the *r* value is found to be comparatively more in case of stature and weight than other characters.

Coefficient of Inbreeding

The coefficient of inbreeding among the Narayanpur Muria has been studied to find out probability of any particular individual in a pedigree to be homozygous for a typical pair of allele; both of which are inherited from some common ancestor through different pathways of descent. Inbreeding, which does not bring change in gene frequencies but shifts in frequencies of genotypes effecting the genetic structure of a population, has four principal effects in a population i.e. the reduction in frequency of heterozygotes together with corresponding increase of homozygotes, changes in population variance, increases in correlations between sibling pairs and between parents and offspring.

TABLE 2.7

Assortative Mating with respect to Anthropometric Measurements in Narayanpur Muria and Other World Populations

	Character	*Population or location*	*No*	*r*	*Source*
	1	2	3	4	5
1.	Weight	American	46	0.32	Schiller, 1932
		American	107	0.30	Pmerat, 1936
		American	984	0.21	Burgess & Wallin, 1944
		American	100	0.13	Smith, 1946
		English	989	0.26	Pearson, 906
		Ann Arbor	205	0.08**	Spuhler, 1962
		Ramah Navala	76	0.15	Spuhler, 1963
		Muria, Narayanpur	153	0.11	Present Study
2.	Stature	English	774	0.09	Pearson, 1896
		English	100	0.28	Pearson & Lea, 1902
		American	46	0.36	Schiller, 1932
		American	107	0.63	Pomerat, 1936
		American	989	0.31	Burgess & Wallin, 1944
		American	100	0.38	Smith, 1946
		Japanese	533	0.07	Furusho, 1961
		Ukrainian	84	0.09	Nicolaeff, 1931
		Russian	80	0.07	
		Jewish	192	0.23	
		Bulgarian	148	0.27	
		German	112	0.25	
		Italian	270	0.14	Genna, 1931
		Sicilian	337	0.11	Willoughby, 1933
		Central Italian	269	0.17	
		Hungarian-Slovak	91	0.19	
		Bohemian	294	0.10	Willoughby, 1933
		Polish	64	0.08	Willoughby, 1933
		Hebrew	418	0.12	Willoughby, 1933

1		2	3	4	5
		Grotch	36	0.32	Willoughby, 1933
		Sari	665	0.20	Tomici, 1939
		Greek	177	0.14	Nicolaeff, 1931
		Ranah Navahe	77	0.18	Spuhler, 1968
		Ara Arbor	205	0.29**	Spuhler, 1962
		Muria, Narayanpur	153	0.03	Present Study
3.	Head circumference	Ukrainian	77	0.01	Nicolaeff, 1931
		Russian	68	0.24	Nicolaeff
		Jewish	179	0.24	Nicolaeff
		Bulgarian	148	0.02	Nicolaeff
		German	110	0.19	Nicolaeff
		Greek	168	0.03	Nicolaeff
		Ramah Navahe	71	0.01	Spuhler, 1968
		Sassari	639	0.07	Tomici, 1939
		Murja, Narayanpur	200	0.04	Present Study
4.	Maximum head length	American	319	0.05	Harris and Govaerts, 1922
		Ramah Navahe	77	0.07	Spuhler, 1968
		Ann Arbor	205	0.07*	Spuhler, 1968
		Sassari	649	0.04	Tomici, 1962
		Sicilian	337	0.04	Willioughby, 1933
		Central Italian	271	0.10	Willioughby
		Hungurian-Slovak	91	0.03	Willioughby
		Bohemian	293	0.06	Willioughby
		Polish	64	0.17	Willioughby
		Hebrew	618	0.12	Willioughby
		Scotch	37	0.14	Willioughby
		Muria, Narayanpur	200	0.05	Present Study
5.	Maximum head breadth	American	319	0.12	Harris & Govaerts, 1922
		Ramah Navahe	77	0.20	Spuhler, 1968
		Ann Arbor	205	0.20**	Spuhler, 1962
		Sassari	650	0.04	Tomici, 1939
		Sicilian	337	0.16	Willoughby, 1933

1		2	3	4	5
		Central Italian	284	0.12	Willoughby
		Hungurian-Slovak	91	0.05	Willoughby
		Bohemian	296	0.05	Willoughby
		Bohemian	296	0.05	Willoughby
		Polish	64	0.02	Willoughby
		Scotch	37	0.17	Willoughby
		Hebrew	618	0.09	Willoughby
		Muria Narayanpur	200	0.10	Present Study
6.	Head height	Ramaḥ Navahe	77	0.50	Spuhler, 1962
		Ann Arbor	205	0.18	Spuhler, 1962
		Muria, Narayanpur	200	0.22**	Present Study
7.	Minimum frontal breadth	Ramah Navahe	77	0.03	Spuhler, 1968
		Ann Arbor	205	0.10*	Spuhler, 1062
		Muria, Narayanpur	200	0.15	Present Study
8.	Maximum bizygomatic breadth	Italian		0.56	London, 1938
		Ramah Navahe	77	0.17	Spuhler, 1968
		Sassari	649	0.09	Tomici, 1939
		Sicilian	336	0.12	Willoughby 1933
		Central Italian	284	0.17	Willoughby
		Hungalian-Slovak	91	0.08	Willoughby
		Bohemian	294	0.16	Willoughby
		Hebrew	476	0.22	Willoughby
		Scotch	31	0.01	Willoughby
		Muria, Narayanpur	200	0.09	Present Study
9.	Bigonial breadth	Ramah Navahe	77	0.08	Spuhler, 1968
		Ann Arbor	205	0.13*	Spuhler, 1962
		Muria, Narayanpur	200	0.08	Present Study
10.	Morphological facial height	Ramah Navahe	69	0.06	Spuhler, 1968
		Ann Arbor	205	0.001*	Spuhler, 1962
		Sassari	636	0.06	Tomici, 1939
		Muria, Narayanpur	200	0.12	Present Study

1		2	3	4	5
11.	Upper facial				
	height	Ramah navahe	71	0.07	Spuhler, 1968
		Ann Arbor	205	0.10*	Spuhler, 1962
		Sassari	628	0.17	Tomici, 1939
		Muria, Narayanpur		200**	Present Study
12.	Nasal length	Ramah Navahe	77	0.09	Spuhler, 1968
		Ann Arbor	205	0.05*	Spuhler, 1962
		Sassari	648	0.10	Timici, 1939
		Muria Narayanpur	200	0.17*	Present Study
13.	Nasal	Ramah Navahe	77	0.01	Spuhler, 1968
	breadth	Ann Arbor	205	0.09*	Spuhler, 1962
		Sassari	649	0.12	Tomici, 1939
		Muria, Narayanpur	200	0.01	Present Study

* Significant at 5% level of Probability.
** Significant at 1% level of Probability.

The coefficient of inbreeding among the Narayanpur Muria has been calculated by Path Coefficient Method (Wright 1922) which is as follows:

$$F = \frac{Fe \cdot n}{N}$$

Where,

n = frequency of certain categories of consanguineous marriages;

Fe = coefficient of inbreeding for a particular category of such marriages;

N = total number of marriage investigated.

It is mentioned earlier in Chapter 3 that in the present sample only first-cousin marriages were recorded, which is 29.6 per cent of the total marriage. The coefficient of inbreeding among the Narayanpur Muria calculated on the basis of first-cousin marriages is. 018.

Table 2.8 presents a picture of coefficient of inbreeding on first-cousin marriages for Indian tribes studied so far. The *F* value on first-cousin marriages have been calculated by the present author from the five samples of Pingle (1975) and one sample of Ghosh (1972) which include other consanguineous marriages also. In rest of the samples the *F* value on first-cousin marriages are available separately. The table shows that out of the 18 tribes, for Kolam and Gond two different samples have been covered and two subsequent studies have been made on Kota tribe by Chakravarty (1968) and Ghosh (1972). The two different *F* value i.,e. .006 and .003 found in the two studies among the Kota by Chakravarty and Ghosh respectively might be due to the difference in time of study on size of the sample. The table also shows highest *F* value (.037) for Gond of Chindwara district of Madhya Pradesh (Yadav 1968). On the other hand Pawras of Maharashtra is the only tribe among whom *F* value is 0. In seven samples the *F* value found to be within .010, the samples are Agri, Kolam, Gond, Toda, Kota, Mathura and Pawras, whereas, in four samples; Kolam (Pingle), Pardhan, Katkari and Gond the *F* value exceeds .025. Alongwith the present sample the Irula, Kurumba, Paniya, Muthuvan, Rajgond, Andh and Bhil have *F* value between .010 and .25. The above picture reveals moderate F value in the present sample in comparison to other Indian tribes. When compared with other Gond groups the Narayanpur Muria shows a comparatively lower *F* value than that of the Rajgond of Andhra Pradesh and a Gond sample of Madhya Pradesh but its *F* value is higher than that of the other Gond sample of Madhya Pradesh.

TABLE 2.8

Coefficient of Inbreeding (*F*) based on first-cousin Marriage in Narayanpur Muria and other Tribal Populations of India

Tribes	*State*	*Sample size*	*First-Cousin marriages (per cent)*	*F*	*Source*
1	2	3	4	5	6
Agri	Maharashtra	520	7.7	.004	Sanghvi, et al. 1956
Kolam	Andhra Pradesh	680	15.0	.009	Chakravarty, 1968

1	2	3	4	5	6
Gond	Madhya Pradesh	200	14.0	.007	-do-
Toda	Madras	80	10.0	.005	-do-
Kota	Madras	112	10.7	.006	Chakravarty, 1968
Irula	Madras	290	20.7	.012	-do-
Kurumba	Madras	180	20.0	.011	-do-
Paniya	Kerala	300	30.0	.018	-do-
Muthuvan	Kerala	225	24.4	.013	-do-
Kota	Madras	449	5.6	.003	Ghosh, 1972
Rajgond	Andhra Pradesh	397	34.5	.021	Pingle, 1975
Kolam	Andhra Pradesh	283	45.2	.028	-do-
Pardhan	Andhra Pradesh	114	53.5	.033	-do-
Andh	Andhra Pradesh	21.2	99	.013	-do-
Mathura	Andhra Pradesh	93	5.4	.003	-do-
Bhil	Maharashtra	124	32.3	.020	Malhotra, 1978
Pawra	Maharashtra	80	-		Malhotra, 1978
Katkari	Maharashtra	97	42.3	.026	Malhotra
Gond	Madhya Pradesh	293	59.04	.037	Yadav, 1968
Narayanpur Muria	Madhya Pradesh	1,468	29.6	.018	Present Study

Marriage Distance

The study of temporal and spatial variation of gene irequencies of population is one of the major objectives of geneticl demography. Migration and marital movements are the main sources to bring integrity in the human populations distributed to a wide range which play a major role for such type of spatial variation in the gene frequencies. Local genetical structures are determined both by the amount of gene flow and the size of geopgraphical area over which genes are flowing. The geographical area of gene flow is determined by the marital distances of the sopouses. So marital distance is one of the important measures of population structure. The distance between the villages of the spouses i.e. marriage distance reflects and even predicts the nature of gene distribution; larger the marriage distance larger will be areas of spread of a gene, conversely smaller marriage distance will lead to localization of genes. People tend to select their mates within some limited part of their distribution and thus the genetic strucutre can be best viewed as a series of overlapping neighbourhoods. Mate selection decreases with increasing spatial distance.

In Narayanpur Muria 22.3 per cent of marriages took place within the same ancestral villages of husbands and wives. 70.5 per cent of marriages took place within the distance of five miles and 89.1 per cent within 10 miles. The mean marriage distance of the present sample is 4.9 miles with S. D. 6.6. These indicate that the marriage distance in the present population tends in localization of genes. In comparison to other Indian populations, as shown in Table 9, the present samples has lowest mean marriage distance (4.9 miles). The mean marriage distance of the present sample compare very well with Bhil, Pawra and Santhal while the five tribal groups of Andhra Pradesh reported by Pingle show fairly high mean marriage distance values. Though the present sample and Rajgond are considered as offshoots of the Gond tribe there is a large difference in mean marriage distance between them.

Admixture Rate

Admixture is a process by which genes from one population come into another population. It plays an important role in determining the genetic structure of a population, since gene flow between populations are influenced through admixture, but it does not produce new genes. Admixture had another effect on the genetic composition of a population. It can upset or reverse the effect of genetic drift. In a population where admixture is high, the genetic drift is low, the effect is reverse when admixture is low.

Though the Narayanpur Muria do not recognize any of their two neighbouring tribes namely, the Kondagaon Muria and Hill Maria as separate ethnic groups, earlier scholars like Grigson, Elwin Rakshit and some Census Reports have considered these groups as three different ethnic groups. The present exercise examines the admixture rate taking the views of the Narayanpur Muria as well as that of the scholars.

TABLE 2.9

Mean Marriage Distance in Narayanpur Muria and other Tribal Populations of India

Sample	*Place*	*Sample size*	*Mean Marriage Distance (in miles)*	*Source*
Santhal	Bihar,		6.7	Basu, 1973
Andh	Andhra Pradesh	117	33.9	Pingle, 1975
Mathura	Andhra Pradesh	104	16.7	-do-
Pardhan	Andhra Pradesh	128	16.4	-do-
Kolam	Andhra Pradesh	305	14.3	-do-
Rajgond	Andhra Pradesh	425	11.6	-do-
Bhil	Maharashtra	116	5.2	Malhotra, 1978
Pawra	Maharashtra	72	5.5	
Narayanpur Muria	Madhya Pradesh	1,351	4.9	Present Study

Admixture rate has been calculated by the method of Lasker (1952) as it has certain advantage as shown by Lasker and Kaplan (1964) in their following statement "When the birth place of parents is recorded, the same will be recorded repeatedly if more than one son or daughter appears in the same; those with most children born and living in the community will be counted most often. Thus, if for instance immigrants are less fertile, or leave some of their children in the places from which they came (the admixture rate as calculated according to the above method) will be automatically weighted for any such factor whether they tend to exaggerate or minimize the effects of immigration on the genetic constitution of the succeeding generations."

It was observed that out of 1,342 matings, there are 206 cases where one of the partners came from the neighbouring two tribes and in 26 cases both the partners are other than Narayanpur Muria. These 206 couples have 638 children and 26 couples have 81 children. Then the parental element is contributed from outside the population in 638/2 + 81 of the 5,393 individuals of the present sample i.e. admixture rate is 7.42 per cent. But when Narayanpur Muria and Kondagaon Muria are considered as a single group and its admixture rate with the Hill Maria is examined, the admixture rate decreases to one per cent. On the other hand if the Narayanpur Muria and Kondagaon Muria are considered as separate groups the admixture rate increases to 6.42 per cent. Sample has been compared with the four Scheduled Tribe populations (Northern Pahira, Southern Pahira I, Southern Pahira II and Kota) and two Scheduled Caste populations of India in Table 2.10. Out of these seven groups the maximum admixture rate is noted among Southern Pahira II (27.04%) whereas Kota has the minimum (0.29%) rate. Both the Scheduled Caste groups show very low admixture rate. Northern Pahira (6.31%) is found closer to the present sample (7.42%) in admixture rate which is moderate in relation to other populations. But the rate (1%) comes nearer to that of the two Scheduled Caste samples if Narayanpur Muria and Kondagao Muria are considered as a single group.

TABLE 2.10

Admixture Rate in Narayanpur Muria and Other Indian Populations

Population	*Place*	*Sample size*	*Admixture rate (per cent)*	*Source*
Tribes				
Muria	Narayanpur, Madhya Pradesh	5,393	7.42	Present Study
Northern Pahira	Ayodhya Hills, West Bengal	301	6.31	Basu, 1969
Southern Pahira I	Dalma Hills, Bihar	475	26.00	-do-
Southern Pahira II	Dalma Hills, Bihar	577	27.04	-do-
Kota	Nilgiri Hills, Tamil Nadu	1,203	0.29	Ghosh, 1976
Non-tribes				
Dula Bagdi, 12-village group	24 Parganas, West Bengal	1,998	0.90	Talukdar, 1979
Dula Bagdi, 9-village group	24 Parganas, West Bengal	1,202	1.83	Talukdar, 1979

Selection Intensity

Selection is one of the major evolutionary processes which can change the 'genetic equilibrium' of a population. By the genetic analysis of demographic data on fertility and mortality, the selection intensity of a population can be studied. For this application of two formulae are made; Crow's index of total selection and subsequently renamed as index of opportunity of selection (Crow 1966). In the selection, changes take place in the inheritable characters, depending upon its correlation with fitness. The index of total selection intensity measures the maximum potential rate of change by selection, where 0 indicates no change (Livingstone and Spuhler 1965), the utility of this type of study has been discussed by a group of scientists at Geneva (World Health Organisation, 1964).

Among the Narayanpur Muria, the mean number of livebirth per mother who have completed fertility (women who have completed their 45th year have been included considering that they have completed fertility) is 5.10 and its variance (V_f) is 6.37. Proportions of mortality before 15 years of age after birth (P_d) and embryonic death (P_{ed}) to total livebirths is 19.80 per cent and 2.46 per cent respectively. These proportions have been calculated on the mothers of all ages.

From the above demographic picture, index of selection intensity (*I*) calculated on the basis of Crow's earlier method was found to be 0.550 and this (*I*) according to Crow's modified method was found to be 0.589, as shown in Table 2.11 and Table 2.12 also indicates that index of fertility (I_f) and index of mortality (I_m) are 0.244 and 0.246 respectively, which are nearly equal in the present sample. The index of total selection intensity among the Narayanpur Muria is closer to the lower range (0.60-3.70) observed by Spuhler (1962) in the 10 tribal populations.

TABLE 2.11

Indices of Selection Intensity in the Narayanpur Muria

Sample	*According to Crow's earlier formula*			*According to Crow's modified formula*			
	I_m	I_f	I	I_{ms}	I_{mc}	I_f	I
Narayanpur Muria	0.246	0.244	0.550	0.025	0.246	0.244	0.583

TABLE 2.12

Indices of Selection Intensity in the Narayanpur Muria and Other Tribal Populations of India

Population	*Place*	I_m	I_f	I	*Source*
Kota	Nilgiri Hills, Tamil Nadu	0.79	0.83	2.25	Basu, 1972
Kota	Nilgiri Hills, Tamil Nadu	0.25	0.64	1.37	Ghosh, 1970
Pardhan	Adilabad, Andhra Pradesh	0.80	0.38	1.19	Murtny & Ramesh, 1978
Northern Pahira	Ajodhya Hills, West Bengal	0.81	0.18	1.13	Basu, 1967
Manne Kolam	Adilabad, Andhra Pradesh	0.54	0.47	1.01	Murthy & Ramesh, 1978
Southern Pahira I	Dalma Hills, Bihar	0.53	0.14	0.79	Basu, 1967
Hill Kolam	Adilabad Andhra Pradesh	0.35	0.38	0.73	Murthy & Ramesh, 1978
Rajgond	Adilabad, Andhra Pradesh	0.35	0.38	0.73	
Southern Pahira II	Dalma Hills, Bihar	0.48	0.14	0.69	Basu, 1967
Muria	Narayanpur, Madhya Pradesh	0.24	0.24	0.55	Present Study

The range of *I* value in other Indian tribal populations studied so far applying Crow's earlier formula, varies between 0.69 to 2.25 as shown in Table 12. In comparison to this the *I* value of the present sample show a lower value (0.550), indicating comparatively low selection pressure on the sample population. The index value (*I*) reported by two successive studies on the Kota tribe of Nilgiri Hills in Tamil Nadu are highest. These two estimates (2.25 and 1.37 respectively) suggest a decline in the index of total selection during the five years from 1961 to 1966. Kota along with three sections of Pahira population of Ayodhya and Dalma Hills of Eastern India are small demes and their indices of selection intensity range between 0.69 to 2.25 with an average of 1.24. Tribes, like Pardhan, Manne Kolam, Hill Kolam and Rajgond of Adilabad in Andhra Pradesh are large demes where (I) value range between 0.72 and 1.19 with an average of 0.91. So there is an indication of more selection pressure on smaller demes. Talukdar (1977) in a study has found out a similar comparatively less selection pressure on larger demes (non-tribal) than smaller demes (tribal and non-tribal). In the samples, Varendra Brahman, Varendra Kayastha, Tili and Tele are the larger demes, whereas, Dule Bagdi 12 - village group, Dule Bagdi 9- village group, Northern Pahira, Southern Pahira I, Southern Pahira II and Kota are smaller demes. Rajgond, like the present sample is considered as the offshoot of the Gond tribe shown as (I) value (0.72) nearer to the present sample (.55). Like the Narayanpur Muria, Rajgond, Hill Kolam and Kota have almost equal contribution of I_m and I_f component to their total index of selection intensity. The mortality component exceeds the fertility component by more than two times in Pardhan, sections of Pahira and slightly exceeds in Manne Kolam. The I_j value and I values in all these samples range between 0.24 to 0.81 and 0.14 to 0.83 respectively.

FAMILY AND KINSHIP

Family

Tribal India exhibits a colourful diversity of families because of varied rules and customs among different tribes. Two types of families may be distinguished on the basis of the number of family members: (i) simple or nuclear family, (ii) extended and joint family.

The first type represents the basic grouping of the mates and their children. Such families have very limited number of members. Many Indian tribes like the Birhor, Pariya, Korwa, etc., maintain this type of family. If this nucleus is extended by the addition of other closely related kins, then it is called an extended family. If this is still further extended by the principle of Kinship, then we get a family like the Hindu joint family. The Nairs of Kerala are taken as classical example of this type of family and the Nair's *Tharawad* is an important institution in itself.

A variety of families may also be distinguished on the basis of the number of marriage partners. Although most of the tribes have monogamous families, i.e., families consisting of a husband, a wife and children but polygamous families are also not very uncommon. Such families come into existence on the basis of two forms of polygamy viz., polygyny and polyandry. A polygynous family consists of a husband, two or more wives and their children. This is a condition of marital arrangement common all over tribal India. Then there are polyandrous families in which the husbands are more than one, as for instance among the Todas of Nilgiri Hills of Tamil Nadu and the Khasis (or Jounsaris) of Jounsar-bawar in U.P. where several brothers marry one wife without any exclusive right of cohabitation for any one spouse. The shortage of women was formerly due to the custom of female infanticide which tilted the sex ratio heavily towards the abundance of males. This does not imply, however, that sexual relations are promiscuous. Actually, strict rules are observed by the parties concerned; and when a child is born, its paternity is established by means of a social ceremony instead of biological considerations.

Several other forms of family are also found among the tribes of India on the basis of authority of father and mother. Who is more important in the family, father or mother? This determines the patriarchal and matriarchal nature of the family. This situation further leads to two more sets of situations: patrilineal/matrilineal and patrilocal/matrilocal. Most of the Indian tribes acknowledge the authority of father in family affairs and hence they have patriarchal families where descent is also traced from father, i.e., patrilineal and the wife leaves her parents' home and comes to reside with her husband, i.e., patrilocal. However, the Khasis of Meghalaya and the Nairs of Kerala are the classic examples of the rare matrilineal, matriarchal and matrilocal family. The Khasis live in the Khasi and Jaintia Hill of Meghalaya. They are famous all over the world as the best example extant today of a society which is nearest to being a matriarchy. They trace their descent from mythical female ancestresses. Their family consists of mother, her unmarried children, male and female, her husband, her married daughters and their husbands. The Khasis are matrilocal at the time of marriage, but later on, when a husband shows evidence of his ability to support himself, his wife and children, he may set up an independent household of his own. According to traditional law, men have no individual right to ownership, whether they are husbands or sons. Property is inherited from women to women. Majumdar aptly remarks that whereas the Khasi family grows round a nucleus of blood-related females who are surrounded by a fringe of males—unmarried brothers and sons, fathers and husbands—and whereas property, authority, religion, residence are all in the hands of women, menfolk also are respected and even exercise some authority. The all-powerful Khasi woman addresses her husband as her lord. The above description is the traditional situation and the Khasis are also changing with times.

Kinship

People in all parts of the world and in all the societies, irrespective of their technological level, are bound together in groups by various kinds of bounds. The most universal and the most basic of these bonds is that which is based on reproduction, an inherent human drive, and is called kinship, But social recognition is seen to override biological fact in the affairs of kinship, especially among the primitive societies all over the world.

The tribes of India are divided into lineages. While most of the tribes are divided into patrilineal lineages, Khasi and Garo of Meghalaya have matrilineal lineages.

Like other people of India, the tribal population too recognizes both types of kinship viz., consanguineous kinship and affinal kinship. While consanguineous kinship includes all the kins related through blood or biological ties, affinal kins consist of those recognised through marriage. But an interesting and significant fact, as mentioned earlier, is that the consanguineous kinship among them does not recognise only biological ties. The case of Todas of Nilgiri Hills following fraternal polyandry may be cited as an instance. Paternity is established among them through a social ceremony known as 'blow and arrow ceremony' in which the particular brother who presents the common wife a bow and an arrow before a congregation, is recognised as the father of the child and until another brother makes the ceremonial presentation, all children born to her of several brothers are regarded as the children of that brother who last performed the ceremony.

The most profound impact of kinship ties on the social life may be felt through *kinship usages* found in every society. Kinship usages among the tribes of India present very interesting and significant spectacle. Such types of behaviour pattern, verbal and non-verbal, explain many complex intricacies of kinship system.

It has been found among many tribes that many sets of kins avoid each other. The avoidance between daughter-in-law and parents-in-law is quite common. Likewise, though less universally and also less rigorously, a son-in-law's relations with his parents-in-law are found to be cramped by certain restrictions. Among the tribes of Andaman and Nicobar Islands, the elder brother does not talk with his younger brother's wife. Radcliffe-Brown has given one of the most plausible of contemporary explanations. He points out that avoidance is a social fact and must, therefore, have a social explanation. He says that whenever people come in contact with each other the possibilities of cooperation as well as conflict are always equally present. But there are certain kinds of kinship where hostility is regarded as against social norms. The best way to prevent such hostility from becoming manifest is to put restrictions on the growth of intimacy; and hence the kinship usages of avoidance. Freud's psycho-analytical explanation is based on sexual attraction and the need to prevent sexual intimacy between various kinds of relatives.

Another kinship usage which is just reverse of the avoidance relationship is an extreme degree of familiarity expressed through joking relationships. Such joking may amount to exchange of abuse, obscene and vulgar references to sex, ridicule and so on. Apart from joking relationship between sister-in-law and brother-in-law and between a wife and her husband's brothers, such relationships have also been reported between grandparents and grandchildren among the Oraons and the Baigas. The Ho tribe of Chotanagpur also indulge in a variety of joking relationships. Majumdar opines that joking relationships may be indicative of equality and mutual reciprocity. They may also be indicative of potential sexual relationship. Thus is explained the joking relationship between a man and his wife's younger sister. In each case the two may be potential mates. A joking relationship, when not mutual, assumes the role of social control. It becomes indicative of correction through ridicule.

Avunculate and amitate, as known in anthropological parlance, are two other kinship usages prevalent among the Indian tribes. Among the Khasis, Garos, Nairs, and a couple of other societies the maternal uncle enjoys a pre-eminent place in the life and affection of his nephews and nieces as a matter of convention. He has special obligations towards them which exceed those of their father and transmits his property to his nephew. This kinship usages is called *avunculate.* Obviously, this is a common usage among matrilineal societies. A special role, similar to that outlined in case of the maternal uncle, for one's father's sister is designated as *amitate.* This is explicable in patrilineal tribes.

Among the Khasi, Toda, Ho, Oraon, and a host of other tribes, a queer practice has been reported, called *couvade,* on the basis of a similar practice known among the Trobriand Islanders by the same name in their local dialect. The practice consists in "making a husband lead the life of an invalid alongwith his wife whenever she gives birth to a child. He refrains from active life, goes on sick diet and observes certain taboos". Thus, the Khasi husband, like his wife cannot cross a stream or wash clothes until the spirits connected with child-birth are propitiated. Sometimes, among some other tribes, this practice is extended to the extent of putting up the poor husband in an adjacent hut to his wife's where she intends to deliver the child, is made to cry and scream in agony like his wife and made to ape the actions of his wife. Malinowski believed *couvade* to be a cementing bond of married life and a social mechanism designed to secure paternal affection. Other anthropologists have sought to give a psycho-analytical explanation. They have attributed this usage to the husband's desire to lighten the wife's discomforts, in the absence or lack of proper modern medical care, by a process of participation through identification. Some scholars have attributed this practice to the matriarchal and matrilineal mode of social organisation but the prevalence of this practice, till recent past, among some patriarchal and patrilineal societies like the Ho, Oraon, etc., negates this assertion.

MARRIAGE

The institution of marriage is another point on which the tribal people throughout the world have been much maligned. Wild and baseless charges were hurled at them, fantastic insinuations were formulated and many pseudo-scholars, claiming to have an intimate knowledge of the tribal world, let their imagination run riot for the benefit of a receptive readership. Some degree of laxity regarding sexual liaison was taken to mean 'promiscuity' or free sex under which, according to such people, the institution of marriage could not exist. Such spicy phrases like 'sexual communism' were coined to describe a non-existent social situation. Interestingly no ethnographic data collected from any part of the world support this hypothesis. In India, too, the simplest and the rudest of tribal cultures we know, e.g., the Andamanese, the Kadar, the Paliyan, the Malapanthram, the Chenchu, the Birhor and others do not furnish us any evidence of promiscuity.

Indian tribes like tribes of other parts of the world practise several forms of marriage as a matter of convenience and social acclimatization in their respective cultural-ecological settings.

Monogamy

Monogamy is a form of marriage in which no man may be married to more than one woman at any one time. A majority of the Indian tribes practise monogamy. Just to refute the allegation that among the most backward and primitive tribes no clear-cut scheme of marriage exists, the example of the Kamar, a very backward tribe of Madhya Pradesh, may be cited. This tribe is monogamous.

Polygamy

Polygamy, that is, marriage to more than one person, is fairly widespread all over the world. Among Indian tribes, there are many who are following this type of matrimonial alliance. Polygamy has two aspects: (i) Polygyny, (ii) Polyandry.

While polygyny is the marriage of one man to several women, polyandry means the marriage of one woman to several men. Both types of marriages are referred to as polygamy in common parlance.

Polygyny is found among the Naga tribes, the Gond, the Baiga, the Toda, the Lushai and most of the other Proto-Australoid tribes of middle India. In most cases such form of marriage comes into existence as a result of disequilibrium in sex ratio. Obviously, in a society where the sex ratio is normal, such type of marriage may force many of the male members to remain bachelor. Hence, normally such a practice develops in a society where the number of females is quite larger than the males. In an otherwise normal situation it is the privilege of the powerful and rich who keep more than one wife as a symbol of prestige and status. Among the Indian tribes like Gond, Baiga and Lushai, this type of marriage is resorted to, facilitate a better division of labour.

Polyandry is, comparatively, much restricted in distribution. This type of matrimonial alliance is found in the Himalayan tract stretching from Kashmir to Assam and is popular among the Indo-Aryan and Mongoloid tribes. In its classical form it is prevalent among the Tiyan, the Toda, the Kota, the Khasa (Jounsari) and the Kadakhi Bota. It is also popular among the Tibetans.

Among the Indian tribes, two types of polyandry are in vogue. When several brothers share the same wife, as among the Khasa and the Toda, we have *fraternal polyandry*. Majumdar (1967) opines that in the general type, also found among the Toda of Nilgiri Hills, there need not be any close relationship between the husbands, and the wife goes to spend some time with each husband. So long as a woman lives with one of her husbands, the others have no claim over her. Nayar polyandry was of this type. Polyandry is not everywhere explicable with reference to a preponderance of men over women. In Ladakh it was actually the women who were more in number. Among the Toda, property considerations and sex-disparity explain this institution. Polyandry is found to lead to fewer children to every woman, more male children, and a high incidence of sterility among women.

The Khasa of Jaunsar-bawar have evolved a very practical mode of polyandrous matrimony. Among them, when the eldest brother marries a girl, she automatically becomes the common wife of the rest of the brothers. If a brother is minor, he may, on becoming adult, marry another girl to match his age. Hence this leads to a situation where a number of brothers have more than one wife which is not the classical mode of ployandry. Observing polygyny and polyandry mixed up, Majumdar coined an interesting phrase, *Polygynandry,* to describe this situation.

Till some time back the Todas of Nilgiri Hills used to observe an interesting ceremony called *bow and arrow ceremony* to declare the paternity socially. In this ceremony, all brothers and the common wife assemble amidst the rest of the villagers in the fourth or fifth month of pregnancy of the wife and as a result of consensus one of the brothers presents a set of bow and arrow to the wife. This is taken as declaration that this particular brother will be accepted as father of the coming child. In this way 'sociological fatherhood' overrides the 'biological fatherhood' in the bewildering mosaic of human affairs.

Beside demographic factors, an economic factor called *bride price* is also responsible for the prevalence of polyandry among Indian tribes. Under the system of *bride price* the husband/husbands are obliged to give an agreed amount of cash/kind to the parents of the bride as price which usually varies according to the physical beauty and utility of the bride. With the passage of time the bride price continued to soar and a stage came when it became almost impossible to arrange the bride price individually. Furthermore, the agricultural holdings in mountains are quite uneconomic and the pursuit of cultivation too hard to be borne by a single individual. Hence, to avoid further fragmentation of holdings and sharing the enormous labour, such a mode of marriage might have come into existence.

Another mode of polygamy, which may be called 'bigamy' , is also in vogue, though on a very restricted scale. Under bigamy a man is allowed to marry two sisters at one time. This type of polygamy has been reported from the Holiya and Medara tribes of Mysore.

Preferential Marriage and Prohibitions

It is observed that, on the one hand, the society prohibits sexual liaison or matrimonial alliances between particular kins or in the same clan or *gotra* but on the other hand, it encourages, matrimonial alliances between certain other kins. In such cases there is a prescription, or only a preference, expressed for marriage to a particular kin. The following are some of the popular types of 'preferential' marriages prevalent among the Indian tribes:

(1) *Cousin marriage*
   - (a) cross-cousin marriage
   - (b) parallel-cousin marriage

(2) *Levirate*

(3) *Sororate*

Both types of cousin marriage, viz., cross-cousin marriage are quite popular among the Indian tribes. The Gond, Kharia, Khasi and Nadar are some of the important Indian tribes practising cousin marriage. Anthropologically speaking, when the children of a brother and a sister marry, it is a cross-cousin marriage while it is parallel-cousin marriage when the children of two sisters or two brothers get married. A Gond is supposed to marry his or her cross cousin, and if one likes to have this prescription waived in one's case, a compensation has to be paid to the losing party. Cross-cousin marriage, as observed by Majumdar, is often explained to be a device for avoiding payment of a high bride price, and also for maintaining property in the household. The Gonds of Madhya Pradesh call this form of marriage *doodh lautawa* (return of milk). The implication is that the bride price paid by 'A' for his wife would be returned to his family when the daughter of 'A' marries her mother's brother's son. Claude Levi Strauss has said that preferential marriage has, for its main purpose, the strengthening of solidarity within a tribe.

Levirate and sororate are two other types of preferential marriages which are also said to promote 'inter-familial cordiality' by making certain linkages imperative. When a woman marries her husband's brother this is called levirate. It may be split into two types: (a) junior levirate, (b) senior levirate. When the woman marries her husband's younger brother, it is junior levirate while marriage with the elder brother is called senior levirate. When levirate occurs in non-polyandrous societies, it is of paramount importance because in the event of her husband's death, the widow finds a guardian, husband and patron while the children get a man as their father who has been loving them earlier too. Among some tribal groups, a degree of laxity is allowed in the matter of intimate social relations and sexual liaison between a woman and her husband's brothers as a prelude to the coming event. This situation may be termed as 'anticipatory levirate'!

When a man marries his wife's sister/sisters, it is sororate. It may occur after the death of his wife or even in her life. The death of a spouse is compensated by supplying a new spouse, generally a younger sister of the deceased. Levirate and sororate emphasise the acceptance of inter-familial obligations and the recognition of marriage as a tie between two families, and not only between two individuals.

Ways of Acquiring Mates

Nine important ways of acquiring a mate have been found to be popular among the Indian tribes:

1. Marriage by capture
2. Marriage by exchange
3. Marriage by purchase
4. Marriage by elopement
5. Marriage by service
6. Marriage by intrusion
7. Marriage by trial
8. Marriage by mutual consent
9. Marriage by probation.

When a man forcibly snatches away a woman from her village and marries her, it is called marriage by 'capture'. Many tribal societies give social sanction to this type of marriage which symbolises valour and chivalry. Marriage by capture has been most popular among the Naga tribes of north eastern region where Naga tribals of one village used to invade the enemy's village and capture grown up girls. This led to female infanticide. However, with the widening application of the Indian Penal Code and growing social consciousness as a result of culture contacts this practice is fast vanishing into oblivion. Cases of capture have also been reported from the Ho, who call it *Oportipi* and the Gond who call it *Posiothur*. Among some other tribes like Bhumij, Kharia, Munda, Santhals, etc., this practice has given place to mock capture as a 'survival' of the old practice in which after finalising the marriage the parents of the girl request the groom to come to an agreed place and 'capture their daughter'. In a mock gesture, the girl (bride) also puts on symbolic resistance. Among some tribes like Ho, it is the exorbitant rate of bride price that often leads to marriage by capture.

Majumdar reports that in Assam, physical captures take place during raids by one village on another. In middle India, the method is more peaceful, capture being effected on festival days at inter-village meets when there is much rivalry, drinking and intoxication. Such captures are given social sanction by requiring the gallant who has made the capture to pay a compensation and/or give a feast to the tribal brotherhood.

Marriage by *exchange* has primarily been evolved as a means of avoiding the payment of high bride price. Under such a marriage two households exchange women with each other and thus avoid the payment of bride price. This practice is found, in varying degrees, all over India in which a man gives his sister or any other woman of his household in exchange of his wife. Interestingly, the Khasi tribals of Meghalaya do not permit it.

Marriage by the 'purchase' is a highly prevalent mode of matrimony throughout tribal India. Bride price is the central theme in this type of marriage. This is paid either in cash or in kind or partly in cash and partly in kind. Lowie has emphasised that although the economic nature of this transaction cannot be minimised, it nevertheless would be wrong to regard the payment of a bride price as indicating sale and purchase. It may be only symbolic of the utility of a woman, and by way of compensation to her parent's family. Among the major tribes, marriage by payment of bride price is prevalent among the Munda, Oraon, Ho, Santhal, Rengma Naga, etc. The worst consequences of bride price are probably seen among the Ho tribals of Chotanagpur, Bihar. Their poor general economic condition has been made worst by the ever increasing amount of bride price. The amount is so high, and to accept a lower amount being against one's status and prestige, that many young men and women remain unmarried. These unfortunate youngmen often resort to marriage by capture and the spinsters have often to undergo further injustice by being identified with witchcraft and sorcery. In many cases their natural desire to marry lead them into the clutches of the cunning moneylenders and the consequent bondedness.

Marriage by *elopement* is also a peculiar feature of tribal India. As is well-known, child marriage is a new phenomenon in tribal India. They started adopting it as a result of culture contact with their Hindu neighbourhood. Previously, only adults entered into married life, and therefore, almost everywhere, marriage by mutual consent with parents' approval was the general rule. But with the changing times boys and girls started shedding their traditional submissiveness. In case the parents' consent is not forthcoming, an elopement is generally the way out. Of course, the indulgent elders receive back the over fond couple. This practice is often resorted to in the face of high bride price. The tribes of Chotanagpur are famous for one type of elopement or the other.

Marriage by 'service' is another way of avoiding the payment of bride price altogether or minimising it considerably through service rendered by the prospective groom at bride's residence. Thus, if a Gond or Baiga finds himself not in a position to pay the bride price, he goes to serve in his would-be father-in-law's house as a suitor servant and marries the desired girls after a lapse of some years. Purum of Manipur recognise it as the only traditionally genuine mode of matrimony. They have to work in the bride's household for three years and have to fulfil all the responsibilities of a son. The boarding and lodging arrangements are taken care of by the would-be-in laws during the entire period of stay. Among the Birhor, the father-in-law often lends money, which is returned in instalments to enable the son-in-law to pay the bride price. Till such time as the loan is repaid, the son-in-law is compelled to stay at his father-in-law's household.

The opposite of 'marriage by capture' is also found among the Indian tribes and is known as 'marriage by intrusion'. This is the case of a girl desirous of marrying an unwilling youngman. In such a case the girl thrust herself on the unwilling groom and his parents. She tries to serve the would be man in his life and his parents but is humiliated and tortured in return. If she persists in her intentions and her endurance lasts for a considerable period she is finally accepted as daughter-in-law of the household. The Birhor and the Ho of Chotanagpur are some of the major tribes who practise it. Ho call it, very appropriately, *anadar,* meaning humiliation or disrespect.

Marriage by 'trial' is another way of acquiring mate among some of the Indian tribes. It is the recognition of personal courage and bravery as highly desirable traits in a youngman. The prospective groom has to prove his prowess before he can claim the hand of the desired girl. It is most popular among the Bhil. During the Holi festival youngmen and women perform a folk dance round a pole or a tree to the top of which a coconut and *gur* are tied. All the youngmen and women are free to participate in the dance, locally called as *gol gadedho*. The girls make an inner ring of dancers round the tree. When a youngman attempts to break through the cardon to climb the tree to eat the *gur* and break open coconut, the girls resist his attempt with their full force. The aspirant may incur even severe injuries but it is taken in good faith. If in spite of these obstacles, a daring man succeeds in this drama, he has the right to demand any of the surrounding girls as his wife.

Marriage by 'mutual consent' is the result of the tribals' contact with the Hindus. This practice is similar to that prevalent among the Muslims, Hindus, Christians, etc., in which all the formalities of marriage are arranged by the parties concerned through the process of mutual consultation and consent.

Probationary marriage can be called as primitive version of modern practice of courtship before marriage. Under this practice the prospective husband and wife are permitted to live together for some time in the bride's house. If they like each other and decide to marry, elders arrange their early marriage. In case the couple do not find each other's temperament to be suitable and compatible they separate and the man has to pay cash compensation to the girl's parents. Such a practice is widely prevalent among the Kuki of Arunachal Pradesh. Some tribal groups of Chotanagpur also approve of this practice and call it *Raazi-Khushi.*

Pre-marital and Extra-marital Sex Relations

This is another area of tribal life which has been shamelessly exploited by many authors and journalists who have tried to enter into overnight fame by unthoughtful and exaggerated versions of the tribals' pre-marital and extra-marital sex life. When the imagination of others run riot, it is to the anthropologist's credit who skillfully avoids these pitfalls and makes a serious and objective study of all the aspects of tribal life, including his sex life.

Pre-marital sex relations, in varying degrees, are seen to be permissible all over tribal India, as with the tribal people of other parts of the world. Obviously the conception of virginity or chastity in a society plays the crucial role in this context.

Among the tribes of middle India, pre-marital sex relations are overlooked unless of course they lead to pregnancy which is generally regarded as shameful for the girl's parents. Also, for a girl to become pregnant is regarded as an extreme family disgrace. She is asked to name the child's father and he is forced to marry her. In this case the amount of bride price is either reduced considerably or it is waived altogether. Among the Koinyak Naga, the girl continues to live in her parent's house even after marriage where her conduct is overlooked by the parents and other village people. Usually after the birth of her first child, she moves to her husband's household. Among the Muria Gond of Bastar, young boys and girls are traditionally allowed a degree of permissiveness within the four walls of the youth dormitory. All the stages of courtship are gone through and they get married with the blessings and approval of their parents. Ao Naga, too, do not attach undue importance to the so-called virginity of the girls.

Extra-marital sex relations are not as common or permissible as pre-marital liaison. It has been reported that among the Maria, the main cause of high incidence of murder and suicide has been marital infidelity. But the Tharu tribe of Uttar Pradesh presents an interesting spectacle. The Tharu men are said to be so much overwhelmed and overawed by the beauty of their wives that they play only second fiddle to them. The wife may indulge in extra-marital sexual liaison and get away with it.

The Khasa or Jaunsari tribe of Uttar Pradesh has evolved a different value system regarding the extra-marital sex relations. Since most of the girls are married off at an early age, there is hardly any possibility of pre-marital liaison. Hence, their main worry is about extra marital relations. In her parental house, the wife is called *dhanti,* while in her husband's house she is called *rhanti.* These two seemingly ordinary words of native dialect carry a very significant connotation. When she is *dhanti,* a woman enjoys all sorts of freedom. She is a free bird. She can meet anybody. Allow anybody to take liberties with her. But the same woman is like a chained slave while she is *rhanti.* In her husband's house she has to work hard in the fields and in the house; she is generally frustrated and her conduct and movement always remain under the strict control of her husband/husbands and other affinal relations. For a little respite, she comes to her parents' house generally during local fairs and festivals. The strains which these women suffer by being wife to several men, who are mentally and physically unlike each other, are relieved by the unfettered life which she can lead in her parents' village.

This sort of dual role prompted some anthropologists and sociologists like Majumdar (1962) and Saxena (1964) to term it as "dual morality" which is quite a misnomer when viewed by an outsider who tries to measure the moral fabric of these simple folk with his own yardstick of puritan hypocracy and so-called morality.

Divorce

Unlike Hindus, marriage is not a religious sacrament among the tribes of India. Hence, divorce or dissolution of marriage is not only possible but widely practised. It may easily be obtained if the parties no longer wish to live in wedlock.

The ground for divorce, however, varies from tribe to tribe. The Khasis permit divorce for reasons of adultry, barrenness and incompatibility of temperament. In some cases, the party desiring the dissolution may have to pay compensation to the other party and remarriage between such people is not possible. The divorce, like marriage, has to be a public ceremony where the mother gets the custody of the children. The Lushai, however, allow remarriage between those once divorced. The Gond, Kharia and others also allow divorce freely on grounds of marital infidelity, sterility, laziness, etc.

Despite contacts with the Hindus, widow remarriage is still practised among almost all the tribes of India and there is little likelihood of its discontinuation. Since widow remarriage carries on stigma among the Indian tribes, the plight of a young woman falling widow is far from miserable.

REFERENCES

1. Pande, G.C.; *Economic Development Planning in India,* Vol. II, Anmol Publishers, New Delhi, 1978.
2. Pande, G.C.; Travails of Tribal Change, Ed. *Himalaya and Development,* Journal of H.R.G; S.C. Joshi *et. al.* Nainital, 1980, No. 2.

THREE

The Basic Unit of Social Structure: Family, Clan and Kinship

THOUGH family is the basic unit of social organization, the term itself remains one of the most loosely defined in the vocabulary. E.W. Burgess and H.J. Locke in their book *The Family* (1953) attempted a definition of the family in the following words:

> "The family is a group of persons united by the ties of marriage, blood, or adoption; constituting a single household, interacting and inter-communicating with each other in their respective social role of husband and wife, mother and father, brother and sister; creating a common culture".

The family is the basic and universal social institution. It fulfils needs and performs functions which are indispensable for the continuity, integration and change in social system. In one sense the whole social system begins with the family because the society is a living entity that must continually be replenished. In societies of all types the family is fundamental multipurpose organisation for many of the principal life functions of the individual and of society.

The nature and composition are important aspects of family in every society but more important in context of the tribal community. Family has been the very foundation from the tribal social structure. It plays a very decisive role in all aspects of their collective and co-operative living. The family is a "multi-functional" unit in the tribal societies. All the important functions, namely socialization of children, status assignment, economically productive unit, division of labour based mostly on sex and age, political, religious and educational functions are centered round this fundamental unit of tribal social structure. Therefore, any study pertaining to Tribal community cannot afford to leave out of consideration this most nearly universal human group, namely, the family. Historically, the joint family has been considered characteristic of Indian life. The large joint families have always existed in India. The nature and composition of family are generally embedded in the character of relationship and the nature of economic activities being pursued by a community. Tribal societies being simple in way of life with collective and co-operative economic activities, the large and joint family in its ideal form could exist.

Traditional Joint Family in India

In order to understand the nature and composition of the family structure in the tribe under study, it is necessary first to sketch the traditional attributes of joint family in Indian society. Sociologists and anthropologists have made a closed study of the characteristics of the joint family in India. They have noted the basic structural, psycho-social and functional features of the type of family in India. In order to do this we shall adopt here Iravati Karve's definition of the Joint family which is one of the most precise and comprehensive. "A Joint family is a group of people who generally live under one roof, who eat food cooked at one hearth, who hold property in common and who participate in common family worship and are related to each other as same particular type of Kindred."[1] I.P. Desai adds, common income as well as properties, and also stresses mutual rights and obligations.[2] On the basis of the above definition of the Joint family an outline of the attributes of Joint family will be as follows:

1. The members of the Joint family generally live under one roof. The traditional family household was composed of a number of separate family units living under one roof. The whole family used to share the common roof for all the living activities.
2. A common kitchen was another important characteristic feature of a joint family. Cooking was considered to be a common activity of the family. The whole family used to share the food cooked at the common hearth.

3. The traditional joint family was both producing and consuming unit. The production and consumption were familistic. There was also a common purse into which all members put their earnings. The senior male member of the traditional joint family usually manages the family's finances. Sometimes the eldest son, who takes over the management of the properties on the father's death, will be assisted by his mother. The property of the joint family passed down in a strictly prescribed way from father to son.

4. Participation of members in common family worship is one of the striking features of the Indian Joint family. Each family has its own Gods, which help to bind that particular family. All important family events and festivals are deeply steeped in religious rituals and ceremonies and daily family worship has always been a part of family routine. Religious and other ceremonies have for their object the security and prosperity of the family. Even the relationship between the Gods and Goddesses are familistic, they being related to one another as father, mother, brother, sister etc. In the traditional joint family religious and ceremonial rites are performed, when all the members of the family gather together and the eldest the 'Karta' has the controlling voice in the affairs of the family.

5. The joint family is far more homogeneous, stable, integrated and organically functioning group. The ties binding the members of the family, for instance, the husband and the wife, parents and children are stronger and last longer.

6. Joint families being homogeneous, compact unit, strengthen emotions of solidarity and co-operation among the family members. They develop more collectivistic family consciousness and less individualistic emotions. There is greater inter-dependence among the members of the family.

Therefore, ideally speaking, traditional family is a corporate group whose members act together to meet their common purposes.

Typically they live in the same house and eat food prepared in the same kitchen, they work together, put their income, expenditure and property and perform religious rituals as a family.

The large joint family is characterized by intimacy, mutuality of interest, strong, primary group controls mutual assistance in times of need. It is a system which strongly limits social mobility and social change because it binds the individuals to others on the basis of birth, and forces him to contribute to the support of a large group independently of their ability. In the joint family, affection as well as dependence are diffused among so many relatives. Each family and kin position is a complex of detailed duties and rights, attitudes, sentiments and expectations which must be carefully balanced if the whole unit is to function effectively.

The large family is eminently suited to a stale society in which life is relatively simple and there has as yet been no need to develop separate institutions to care for the needs of the group. It means the large joint families were best suited to such societies where the economic activities were collective and co-operative endeavours. As stated earlier the nature and composition of family are deeply embedded in the character of economic and social organization of the community, author will see how the large family norm was adequately suited to the tribe under study.

Traditional Family among the Pardhans

In the light of the nature of traditional joint family in the Indian society, a description of the traditional family among the Pardhans with its similarities and differences from the Indian joint family will not be out of context. Since the Pardhans traditionally lived as priests, Pujaris and musicians and consequently had nomadic way of life, joint families are very common among them. The large and joint families seemed to have worked effectively in the past owing to typical way of living and their traditional order.

The traditional economic activities of the tribe were based on solidarity among the members of the family as well as the tribe and it also involved risk. Therefore, joint families have become more or less common feature among the Pardhans.

The typical Pardhans joint family consists of a man and his wife, his sons and their wives and children, his daughters until they are married. The Pardhans are patrilineal and patrilocal in residence. The general practice among the Pardhans is that the sons after their marriage continue to live in the family of their parents with their wives and children. After the death of the father, the property can be divided, if they so desire, equally among the sons. Some of the respondents, during field investigations, have remarked that so long as the father (the head of the family) is alive, sons have no right to be separated, it is only after the death of the head of the family, the sons can think of separating themselves, if they so desire. A similar thing is also observed in the study of the Tikopian family by Raymond Firth. "The household in Tikopia usually includes more than one nuclear family. Sometimes two brothers with their wives and children live together each taking a section floor. More often the man will have his unmarried brothers and sisters or his father and mother, living with him. On the other hand more than two nuclear families live together since the rule is that brothers divide their property, if any, at the death of their father, specially if all are married."[3] Women among the Pardhans families do not inherit the property rights. As long as the family remains undivided it is regarded as joint in food, worship and estate. Family is an economic unit. All the members of the family including the aged and children participate in some kind of traditional economic activity and contribute to the maintenance of the family. Economically the entire family functions through the common pooling of resources and their utilization according to demands of all its members. As a result of this, each member has a share in the property and the expenditure. The father is the head of the family. He is the owner of property. The traditional joint family among the Pardhans approximates to a great extent the ideal model of traditional Hindu Joint Family. There are striking similarities in terms of the attributes of joint family as mentioned by renowned sociologists. The attributes such as common property and common participation in the economic activities are predominantly noticed among the Pardhans. All the members of the family eat food cooked at the common health. They have common cooking activity in which all the members (sometimes the male members) are seen engaged in it. All the members of the family, though separated for particular period of time for doing their economic activities, do participate in the rituals and ceremonies performed by the members of the family. During interview with some of the respondents it was remarked that the members of the family were expected as a matter of tradition to participate in the functions, social and religious of the family. Non-participation would mean that he had been separated from the parental family. This shows that common participation of members of rituals and ceremonies is one of the striking features of the Pardhans joint family. The Pardhans joint family appears to be a very diffused family in terms of intimacies among the members and mutual obligation of the members towards family. There is one striking difference between an ideal pattern of a joint family and the joint family among the Pardhans. Historically speaking, there was no concept of common roof as these people were in nomadic phase and had no houses of their own. They used to have a small tent which was being used for storing their belongings and all other activities centering around the family used to be performed in the open in front of those tents. It was more of a collective and community living. There was no clear-cut division of labour among the members of the family and it was basically an economic unit. The family activities were performed jointly or collectively. There seemed to be very little separation of family activities. It was only after the father became feeble and incapable of managing the family affairs, that the eldest son takes over the family affairs. Thus, the joint family affairs among the Pardhans represent an ideal model of the Hindu Joint family in terms of the common residence, common kitchen and common participation in the rituals. The joint family among the Pardhans is far more homogeneous, stable, integrated and organically functioning. The tribes in India still remain a cluster of joint families, though being influenced through the impact of industrial urban growth. The family structure among those people is composed not only of the members of the family but also frequently includes distant relations.

It has been stated that the traditional joint family structure of the Pardhans tribe is being subjected to the domination of developing urban economy of Vidarbha area being thrown into such unfamiliar situations that consequently there has been modifications in their social and cultural values. The traditional family structure of the Pardhans seems to be under transformation giving rise to new adaptive structures of adjustment. It is not therefore, surprising that the urban way of life is slowly but steadily pushing its way into the social pattern of life of the Pardhans of Vidarbha, replacing some of their characteristics of traditional family.

Prof. K.M. Kapadia has also shown that in modern times the circumstances are changing. This itself can be called a new factor to reckon with. He deals with the impact of urbanization on the Indian family. Urbanization in his view is an important factor in all social change. Adjustments have to be made quickly and there is the possibility that more concessions will be made to the circumstances than under the situation of slow change. New circumstances bring with them a new cultural element inimical to the traditional element. This new element is referred to by various names such as the Philosophy of individualism, nationalism etc.[4] The author task is to find out how far the situation in the institutions of the family can be described as the adjustment of traditional culture element to the new circumstances.

The Changing Family Structure

Anthropological and sociological analyses usually regard the structural components of societies as being so closely interrelated that the change in any part of the system would have repercussions in all other parts. Hoselitz and Moore have stated that, "If a model of extreme functional interdependence is adopted, the characteristic of any component of the system would determine the characteristics of all other."[5]

Sociologists might review a few major trends of structural changes in the family in India. The transition from extend family based society to nuclear family based society in essence is an example of structural family change. This involves systematic changes in the role structures through processes of differentiation. Compared to an extended family the combinations of the role structures in nuclear family are fewer. The networks of kinship relations are also different. A nuclear family is itself an example of structural differentiation from the more composite social structure of an extended family. Changes are now taking place in the traditional family forms. This bears significant relationship with the direction of social change and modernization in India. Wherever the economy expands through industrialization, family patterns change, extended kinship ties weaken, lineage patterns dissolve, and a trend towards some form of conjugal system generally begins to appear. Then the nuclear family becomes a more independent kinship unit. Modern commentators have reported this process from many parts of the world.[6]

The studies concerning the distribution of family types (structurally) in India show results which considerably fluctuate on the basis of criteria employed for the classification of jointness. The jointness among the members of the family has been defined in terms of residence, property and mutual obligation among the kin. It has also been explained with reference to the nature and quality of social interaction which involves in it sentimental bonds, ritual and economic obligations to other family units. The families may be functionally joint in obligational ties. Family jointness still continues to be a major sociological phenomenon in the Indian Social Structure. Greater degree of jointness was observed co-existing with agriculture as well as business and other occupations and it was found that the "longer urban stay did not dissolve jointness". The findings of K.M. Kapadia support the conclusions of I.P. Desai.[7] K.M. Kapadia found that the joint family pattern was not only predominant, but stronger in the towns. Kapadia concludes that "not only the total complement of the joint family is higher in the town but even its size is larger there than in the rural areas. In M.S. Gore's study among the Agarwals in Delhi, three fourths preferred the joint family but only 54 per cent believed that brothers should continue to live together after the death of the parents. It has been observed by I.P. Desai and other sociologists that nuclear family in India is merely a stage in the joint family cycle. S.C. Dube makes the following observations on this point,

> Simple families grow into extended families and then break up into simple families again. A simple family emerging out of this process may retain some adhesions from the former extended family. The changes from simple to extended and extended to simple are fairly frequent. Nevertheless, Indian values and attitudes are still generally in favour of the joint family and that a number of important structural changes in the joint family are occurring.[8]

A wider picture of the changes in the family structure in India can be obtained only by comparative regional studies. Kolenda analyses, "the factors which could possibly be associated with the predominance of joint family in one region or in one group and that of the nuclear in another. She concludes that neither economic explanation nor classical Hindu Law, nor caste identity nor ownership of land, nor the dominant or subservient status of castes has a universal association with preponderance of joint family types".[9] The basis for structural limitations are clearly recognised by Murdock and other Anthropologists who have made comparative studies of social structure, lies in the existential situations or the material and economic resources which could be commanded by social units with in and outside the family structure.

The changes have also been observed in the internal structure of families in India which A.D. Ross describes as the sub-structure of rights and duties, of power and authority and of sentiment and work. In her study of the upper and middle class urban families in Bangalore, Ross finds that with the increasing strain of new types of activities in urban context many traditional forms of family role expectations are changing. Children now often tend to be more independent on certain issues; traditional division of labour between man and wife breaks down in an urban nuclear family as the husband has to share some work which was traditionally the duty of the wife. From the point of view of authority, the family still continues to be the most important institution for enforcement of discipline and its authority remains strong. Transition from joint to nuclear families also alters the nature of affection and sentiments in the interpersonal relationships of family members, altering the very structure of traditional joint family sentiments. But changes in this sphere of the family are rather slow.[10]

> Changes in the structure of families have also been reported in the matrilineal Tarvada families of Kerala, where accumulation of private property, growth of business connections or higher education prompt a person of the younger generation to establish a separate home for himself, his wife and children, away from the traditional Tarvada from the joint family.[11]

In the light of the above mentioned studies, it was hypothesized that during the period of economic development "The multifunctional family structure changes into several more specialized structures" (Separation, differentiation and more specific role structures emerge).

As the family is stripped of its economic functions, there emerges a setting for institutionalization of relatively autonomous economic systems that exhibit a greater emphasis on values like universalism, functional specificity and rationality.

The joint family seems to give way to nuclear family but even that is not suitable to their way of living. But in the present context author may say that the husband, wife, and children type of family structure is emerging in terms of residential and compositional pattern. Thus, the structural transformation of large joint families of the Pardhans may be attributed to economic reasons as the members of the family are pursuing new economic activities in the area of occupations. It shows mere separation in terms of residence of large families into small units; but this does not imply that the jointness is declining. The separation may be due to occupational and economic exigencies.

To substantiate the above arrangement the views of I.P. Desai may be given here, "The phenomenon of structural changes in the joint family on the basis of incidence of structural differentiation from joint to nuclear families is rather vague. What matters more is not the composition of the residential family group but the nature and the quality of social interaction emanating from the supposedly nuclear family which inter links it in sentimental bonds, rituals and economic obligations to other family units in the same place".[12] Therefore the trends of neutrality among the Pardhans may be attributed to the reasons of occupational necessity. However, it was observed that the members of the constituents households consider themselves duty bond to meet on occasions such as the celebrations of Dussehra, Diwali and especially Holi festivals and marriage ceremonies.

Such occasions keep feelings for joint family activities. But it has been observed during field work that the occasions for such family obligations are decreasing in the changed context and joint family sentiments will be weakened in consequence.

In the light of the above, two probable conclusions are, that the majority as a whole still largely conforms to the pattern of joint family living in behaviour and attitudes. The second is, within this overall pattern of conformity, separation in residence and new occupations, do seem to introduce a slight trend towards small family from among the Pardhans of Vidarbha. The direction of this trend is indicated more clearly in the study on the position of the family structure. It also indicates the affirmation of traditional patterns of behaviours in the acceptance of family obligations, the continuance of the pattern of collective living on ritualistic occasions and in terms of mutual obligations and property.

Inter-personal Relations within the Family

Family relations are changing as a result of overall transformation in the structure of family. As described earlier that the Pardhans have large joint families having at least three generation depth, the family being basically the unity of interaction personalities, the observation were focused on certain set of relationships. The family in the context of tribal society is a multi-dimensional functional unit. It is a functional unit in the sense that all the significant functions are centred round the basic and fundamental institution. Conversations with a few respondents revealed that the people of the tribe are proud of large joint families because large families have been associated with more economic gains and domination over the members of the tribe. However, the structure of family is in the process of transformation as a result of the interaction of the Pardhans with other tribals and also non-tribals of the area under study in particular and with Vidarbha in General.

Husband-Wife Relationship

Husband-wife relationship shows variations according to the economic activities pursued by the family. However, the husband is generally the head and the master of the household. He enjoys the highest status in the family and he has by virtue of his position the major say in the affairs of the family. This is only due to the fact that the nature of the family among the Pardhans is patriarchal and patrilocal. The wife is expected to be submissive and to pay respect to the husband in the usual manner. Wives are expected to be faithful to their husbands. The husband is of course in a superior position. It should not be assumed that women are looked down upon but do enjoy a status in the family.

There appears to be no clear cut division of responsibilities between the husband and wife. The husband is responsible for the maintenance of family. Household duties are exclusively done by the wife and very little assistance is given in such duties by the husband. It is noteworthy here, that even though household duties are managed by wife, when the wife is outside for economic activities such as begging or any other petty economic activities, the cooking is managed by the husband or the young children under supervision and guidance of the husband or some male member in the family. Sometimes he prepares it independently when the wife is away on economic activities. This appears to be an internal adjustment among the members of the family, particularly the husband-wife relationship, as the women also contribute economically. Though the care of the children is primarily the responsibility of the wife, the husband must sometimes take a hand. There appears to be an adjustment on the part of the husband in connection with the household responsibilities of the wife. The relationship between the husband and wife appears to be quite informal and less reservations are observed in their personal and family relations. The wife has a sense of freedom in her relationship to her husband. However, wife takes the permission of husband in all important matters of the family including the economic activities being pursued by them. The power of the husband over the wife was clear in several cases when the husbands were seen abusing and even beating their wives in the locality. However, it should not be inferred that women have no authority in family affairs. They are observed being consulted on matters of family concern, wives are in a way an economic asset to the entire family even though the wives contribute to the income of the family. It has been observed that all the funds and expenses are controlled by the husband to a large extent. Drinking liquor is very common among the Pardhans, wives also join their husbands in drinking country liquor. There seem no restrictions regarding drinking in this tribe. If the wife is suspected of having illicit relationship with an outsider, or other than the husband, she is severely punished. It means adultery is considered to be a severe offence in this tribe. It is due to the fear of punishment or harsh treatment by the husband, that the women are submissive and obedient. The women are not shy; but free and frank with outsiders also. Women are observed gossiping about their contacts with outsiders particularly about the tricks used in befooling them while doing their economic activities.

Even though there have been changes in the structure of family organization of the Pardhans, they seem to have a traditional outlook on the husband-wife relationship. This traditional pattern of relationship between the husband and wife appears to be strong among the Pardhans.

Parents and Children

The relationship between the father and son appeared to be more intimate and affectional because he could help and protect the family from the enemies and the outside world. He would also be an economic asset. He not only brings income through his work, but he might eventually become the family's economic support. Field observations revealed that the birth of a son was a matter of happiness for the entire family. The members of the tribe also cherish certain superstition about this Russell and Hiralal in their book *Tribes and Castes of Central Provinces of India,* Vol. IV mention, "After the birth of a child the mother and another woman stood on opposite sides of the cradle and the former tossed her child to the other commanding it to the mercy of Jai Gopal, and waited to receive it back in like manner in the name of Jai Govind. Both Gopal and Govind are names of Krishna.[13] The relationship pattern within the family shows that the children are looked after by the mother. When the parents are out for economic activities, the children within the age group of 4-8 years are mostly left to themselves in the locality for their socialization. Many a time the children are left uncared for and unattended by the parents. The parents seem to have no concept of cleanliness and the young kids in the family are seen without adequate clothes on their bodies. The parents show no concern about this mainly due to their ignorance and typical tribal style of living. The parents appear to be not concerned with the education of their children. The nomadic way of living was an important hurdle in the way of children's education. Another reason as stated by respondents was the nature of their new non-traditional economic activities which required constant help of all the members of the family and consequently the children are not encouraged to go to school. Mostly the children within the age group of 8-14 years accompany their mother for their new economic activities, mostly begging and quarrying etc.

The relationship between parents and children appears to be extremely informal, free and frank. The children do not seem to be scared of the parents. They are also expected to participate in new-non-traditional economic activities. They are also found sharing with parents family matters very frankly without any reservations. In spite of such informality between the parents and children, the parents are highly respected and obeyed by them. when directed by parents for doing certain household duties, the children are expected to carry out household responsibilities ungrudgingly. Even the married sons consult their parents and refer to them all their problems. Thus parents seem to be chief advisors and counsellors for them. The children have been given freedom to pursue their economic activities independently. The head of the family still yields power in the family structure among the Pardhans.

The Clan Organisation

Although tribe, caste, sect, racial group and class are the various types and orders of social groups found in India, it is the tribe and the caste which dominate the scene, the former primitive communities and the latter the Hindu Society. Society is a web of social relationship and social organization is the particular system of social relationships. In this system of social relations, i.e., the groups are individuals. The mutual relationship between individual are controlled and regulated by institutions and associations. Hence institutions and associations, along with individuals and groups form a part of the social organization. Social organization may refer also to the sum-total of cultural institutions and their inter-relationships including the body of the unorganized activities characteristic of the group. Thus the social organization, "includes and comprehends the cultural institutions and their inter-relationships in addition to the unorganized activities of the group". To quote Reuter and Hart, "By social organization is meant the totality of cultural institutions and their inter-relationships together with the body of the unorganized activities".[14]

Elliott and Merrill describe "Social organization "as a state of being, a condition in which the various institutions in a society are functioning in accordance with their recognized or implied purposes".[15]

Social organization has usually been taken as a synonym for social structure. Thus social organization of a small group or a tribe is the organization of inter-related roles at a particular time within it as expressive of certain permanent or semi-permanent structural principles. As such social organization would consist of the inter-relations, between a particular type of groups viz. those groups which make social life possible. The clan, marriage and family are the examples of such groups. Groups of people engaged in economic pursuits comprise the economic organization of the tribe and groups like the Panchayats constitute its political organization. The former sustains,. the latter controls and regulates the social organization. The inter-relation between the three would present the total pattern of tribal organization. Religion and religious groups are both social as also regulative.

Indeed no aspect of the social and ritual life of the Tribal communities is explicable without an understanding of its basic structure. The invariable and permanent elements of this structure are exogamous patrilineal descent groups known in Gondi dialect *Saga.* The phratries or Saga are firmly rooted in Tribal mythology, and their establishment as the principal exogamous units is described in myth which form a part of the spiritual heritage of all the tribals in general and of the Pardhans in particular.

Tribal opinion unanimously regards *Kalikankali*[16] as the ancestress of almost the entire Gond people. The myths recorded in, *The Gonds of Andhra Pradesh* by Haimendorf in Chapter 11 about the origin of Gond and their Gods, and how the Gond Gods-emerged from the cave into four batches and this division into four groups laid the foundation for the basic structure of Gond and Pardhan tribe." The myths do not offer any explanation for the division of the original Gods into four groups but all Gonds and Pardhans agree that these groups consisted of Seven, Six, Five and Four brothers respectively and consequently the phratries, which have no names, are described and termed as, Yerwen, Sarwen, Siwen and Nalwen Saga i.e. Seven-wen, Six-wen, Five-wen and Four-wen phratries in the book *The Gonds of Andhra Pradesh* by Haimendorf and translated freely as Seven brother, Six brother, Five brother, and Four brother.[17] Dr. M.P. Buradkar in his thesis, *Social Organization of Gonds*, says, "The Gonds are among those aboriginals in India who have maintained their primitive clan organization. The clans among them are grouped into exogamous phratries. Each of these phratries is designated by the number of Gods, its members are supposed to worship such as Seven Gods (Yerung Penk) Six Gods (Sarung Penk) Five Gods (Saiyung Penk) and Four Gods (Nalung Penk).[18]

The social group wider than and next to the family in the social structure of the Pardhan tribe is the clan. The clan consisting families, members of which bear the same clan-name. Members of the clan believe that they have been descended from a common ancestor. The clan being patrilineal, a man passes his clan name on to his children. A woman keeps for her father's clan-name till she is married. The clan among the Pardhans are mainly of four kinds. They are totemic, titular, territorial and eponymous. The first two kinds constitute the majority. The other two are limited in number.

(a) A Totemic clan bears the name of an animal plant, fruit, a natural phenomenon or object such as Bāgh (Tiger) Gōha (Large Lizard) Tekām (Teak Tree) Loha (Iron) Tirgām (fire) etc.

(b) A titular clan derives its name from some personal peculiarity or adventure of the founder of the clan. The name of the titular clan may also refer to the office the ancestor of the clan is supposed to have held. Such clans for example are Khandēte (Swordman), Pedām (Village Headman) Subhedār (Military Rank) Lochantia (Salt Licker) etc.

(c) A territorial clan is known after some locality where the ancestor of the clan lived. It also sometimes refer to the early settlement of the clan, from where it has migrated to its present locality. Such clan are Māhānadiā, Jainpuriā etc.

(d) An eponymous clan bears the name of a famous ancestor, a saint, a legendary hero or a chief. Such clans are very few among the Pardhans.

The clan organization of the Pardhans of Vidarbha constitutes the first two kinds of clan.

Since the Pardhan economic and religious system depends on the community of clans between the Gonds and the Pardhans, the Clan organization of the latter closely resembles that of the Gonds, and in its main outlines is based upon it. In detail, however, and especially in the development of local sub-clans, there is considerable divergence. Hivale, in his book, *Pardhans of Upper Narbaba Valley,* has listed five groups of clans among the Pardhans of Patangarh. (Mandla District of Madhya Pradesh). There, as per the restriction on marriage i.e. exogamy, members of the each first four groups must marry outside their clans, and group of clan is observed strictly but there is some vagueness among the Pardhans about the matrimonial relations towards the members of the other group. The relations of the fifth group have not been determined. The group contains 17,10,13,7 and 15 clans respectively.[19]

In respect of the clan organization of the Pardhans of Vidarbha, it can be inferred that the Pardhans strictly observe the restriction of clan i.e. Saga system in respect of marriage relations.

The Concept of Saga

The concept of Saga i.e. God on which the clan system of the Pardhans is based has been given below.

In all there are five clan groups of the Pardhans in Vidarbha viz.;

1. Four 'Saga' group
2. Five 'Saga' group
3. Six 'Saga' group
4. Seven 'Saga' group and
5. Twelve 'Saga' group

The first group viz. the four God Saga contains 51 clans. The rest, five, six, seven and twelve contain 18 (Eighteen) 27 (Twenty seven), 28 (Twenty eight) and 7 (Seven) clans respectively. They are as follows:

First group of 'Saga' i.e. the 'Saga' of 4 Gods Having 51 Clans

1. Bādām	18. Kunjām	35. Pusam
2. Bhidām	19. Kusrām	36. Pusram
3. Chudām	20. Mādkām	37. Sedmka

4. Dāwām
5. Dasedām
6. Derām
7. Dhārnām
8. Dimdām
9. Dopām
10. Ghãtte-
11. Gushrām
12. Gudrām
13. Jārām
14. Kadpam
15. Keram
16. Kowe
17. Kudām
21. Madpachy
22. Mānldām
23. Māgām
24. Matte
25. Muchal
26. Nahakam
27. Naitam
28. Neti
29. Odam
30. Pacam
31. Parchaki
32. Patam
33. Peram
34. Pidpam
38. Sedmaki
39. Sidam
40. Sidkam
41. Sonam
42. Sudam
43. Taram
44. Talande
45. Tedam
46. Tekam
47. Udam
48. Varal
49. Vedram
50. Wasam
51. Watti

Second Group of 'Saga' i.e. Saga of 5 Gods Having 18 Clans

1. Ade
2. Anhak
3. Arka
4. Dhikram
5. Gawande
6. Ghodam
7. Iskapa
8. Istam
9. Jugnak
10. Kadti
11. Kinaka
12. Kumre
13. Kursange
14. Poreti
15. Poyam
16. Soyam
17. Surpam
18. Uram

Third Group of 'Saga' i.e. Saga of 6 Gods Having 27 Clans

1. Aahram
2. Atram
3. Gedam
4. Katlam
5. Kodape
6. Kohashale
7. Kohawade
8. Koram
9. Kotnak
10. Kudmethe
11. Kumre
12. Markam
13. Parteti
14. Pawale
15. Pendor
16. Salam
17. Todsam
18. Toral
19. Tumram
20. Udye
21. Uike
22. Urveti
23. Vadey
24. Valadi
25. Verkade
26. Wate
27. Yerme

Fourth Groups of 'Saga' i.e. Saga of 7 Gods Having 28 Clans

1. Alam	11. Katange	21. Sarate
2. Bhalavi	12. Kokade	22. Sayam
3. Dadanja	13. Korwati	23. Tadam
4. Dhurwe	14. Madavi	24. Vansidam
5. Inwati	15. Masram	25. Vedma
6. Irpati	16. Marskol	26. Velka
7. Jugnak	17. Pandram	27. Wadve
8. Kannak	18. Purkam	28. Wadiwa
9. Karpati	19. Pusnak	
10. Karsange	20. Ranwati	

Fifth Group of 'Saga' i.e., Saga of 12 Gods Having 7 Clans

1. Harekadapa	4. Marapa
2. Harekumra	5. Raisidam
3. Mandali	6. Tora
	7. Vedi

No clear division among the Pardhans of Yavatmal district is observed in their clan organization into phratries, although groups of clans regard themselves as saga i.e. as related to each other. But there does exist the classification of clans according to the number of Gods worshipped that has been recorded in area under investigation.

The following are the groups of clans together with few totems recorded by the author during the data-collection in Yavatmal district. Each of the groups consists of clans that are related to one another and cannot intermarry. Each member must marry outside, not only his own clan, but his own groups. The Pardhans of the Yavatmal District are not very clear about whether, he can marry a member of any of the clans in the other groups.

The main clan groups according to Saga in Yavatmal District are as follows:

Four (4) Gods Clan: Totem-Tortoise

	Name	*Totem*
1.	Chikram	(A species of hawk)
2.	Keram	—
3.	Kusram	—
4.	Kowa	(Monkey)
5.	Naitam	(Dog)
6.	Pusam	—
7.	Markam	(Mango Tree)
8.	Parchaki	—
9.	Shadmake	—
10.	Tekam	(Teak Tree)
11.	Talandi	
12.	Sidam	(Louse)

Five (5) Gods Clan: Totem-Crane

	Name	*Totem*
1.	Ada or Ade	—
2.	Kinake	(Leaves of Ki tree)
3.	Kumare	—
4.	Surpam	—
5.	Ghodam	(Ghode-Nil)
6.	Poyam	—
7.	Iskap or Iskape	—

Six (6) Gods Clan: Totem-Tiger

	Name	*Totem*
1.	Atram	—
2.	Rajgadkar-Gedam	—
3.	Kudmeta	—
4.	Kotnalika	(Leaves of Kot tree)
5.	Pendam or Pendor	(Anus)
6.	Salam	(Sai fish)
7.	Todsam	—

8.	Marappa	—
9.	Uika	—
10.	Tumram	—
11.	Yerma or Yarma	(She Buffalo)
12.	Toria	

Seven (7) gods Clan: Totem Procupine

	Name	*Totem*
1.	Alam	—
2.	Dhurwa	(Chief)
3.	Kanaka	(From eye)
4.	Karpati	—
5.	Kursange	(Deer)
6.	Maraskota	(Axe)
7.	Meshram	—
8.	Jugnakha	(Leavs of Jugai Tree)
9.	Soyam	—
10.	Madavi	(Tree)
11.	Bhalavi	—
12.	Purke	—

The principal function of the clan was to regulate and keep restrictions on matrimonial relations i.e. marriage on basis of Saga. Under modern conditions the importance of the clan in all respects (except to some extent other than those ritual and regulation of marriage) is clearly on the decline and the present system of land tenure combined with the state laws of inheritance leaves little room for the right of the clan to prevent the diversion of the property of any of its members to persons outside the circle of clan-members.

The survey of the clan organization of the various sections of the Pardhan community inhabiting the Vidarbha area, particularly in Yavatmal District discloses certain characteristics. Firstly, the organization of the clan survives among these people only for the purpose of regulating marriages. Secondly, the majority of the clans, found among the Pardhans and Gonds are identical in names.

Kinship Organization

Here we will describe those aspects of kinship, marriage and inheritance which are related to the political structure of the Jats. The main purpose is to show the close correlation and interaction between the kinship groups (i.e. the family, lineage and clan) and the political institutions (lineage and the clan councils). The kinship groups and the political institutions which are based upon them are complementary in that both tend to support each other and produce social cohesion within the Jat community. Knowledge of the principles underlying this complementary interaction will help us to understand how the total social structure is maintained. Marriage and rules of inheritance will be discussed from the same point of view.

Structure of the Clan

The Jats of Meerut Division are organized into patri-clans. Most of the clans have compact residential areas of their own, varying clan to clan from twelve to eighty-four villages. The clan villages are situated near one another.

The clans are patrilocal (virilocal), patrilineal, and exogamous. Descent is reckoned from the ancestors who first settled in the area.[29] Every clan has a leader called the *Chaudhry*. He is not reckoned as the descendant of the clan ancestor but as the descendant of the leader of that branch of the clan ancestors who first conquered the present area and settled in it.

A clan is divided into lineages of varying depths, namely, *thoks* or maximal lineages, sub-*thoks* or major segments of a *thok,* and *khandams* or minimal lineages. Like the clan, each segment has its own headman or Chaudhry, but unlike the clan his office is not always hereditary. Election and unanimous selection of the lineage headman is practised if the descendants of the lineage Chaudhry are not considered fit to hold the office or if a person from another lineage is more able than the sons of the Chaudhry. Nevertheless, once a Chaudhry is elected or unanimously selected he becomes the permanent head of the lineage for the whole of his life and cannot be removed from his office.

The lineage of the clan Chaudhry is considered senior among all the segments of the clan, and its members command more respect than the others, in diminishing degree from the minimal lineage of the chaudhry to his sub-*thok* and *thok*. He is the head of all the three segments.

The lineage segments are hierarchically structured, but the recognition of seniority in the lineage of the clan chaudhry is not of much importance in political matters, though in day-to-day life the standing of the lineage may be observed in manners of speech and etiquette.

The depth span of a maximal lineage (*thok*) may vary from ten to fifteen generations from living adults, a sub-*thok* or major segment from six to ten generations, and a *khandan* or minimal lineage from three to five generations.

The lineages of varying depth spans are named after the founding ancestors. The line of descent from such a founding ancestor is generally remembered, or in case of doubt—which only happens in the case of *thoks* which have many generations —can be ascertained from the genealogical tables of the bard. The suffix *ke,* meaning descendants, is attached to the name of the founding ancestor of a lineage group and this gives a clear indication which segment is referred to, or whether a segment belongs to another *thok* or sub-*thok*.

After the clan Chaudhry, it is the head of a *thok* who wields the greatest amount of prestige and influence. The sub-*thok* and minimal lineage chaudhries are expected to obey and accept the leadership of the *thok* chaudhry, just as he in turn is expected to accept the leadership of the clan chaudhry.

A *thok* is divided into sub-*thoks,* and a sub-*thok* is segmented into *khandans* or minimal lineages. A minimal lineage comprises various nuclear and joint-families. (See the diagram)

Like the clan, the *thoks* of a village each have a compact area, both residential and agricultural. Thus the ties of kinship are reinforced by ties of local contiguity both at the *thok* and the clan level. The *bhaichara* (brotherhood) system of land tenure and the rules of inheritance maintain this spatial compactness, since land

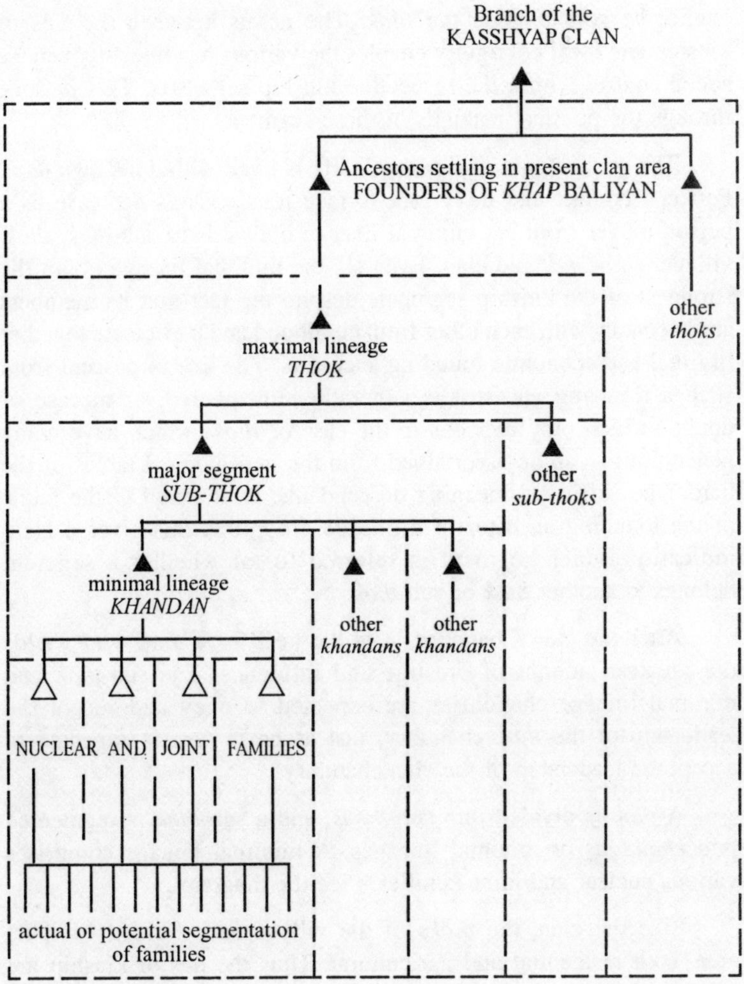

▲ Dead males

△ Living males

The broken lines indicate clan and lineage boundaries

No attempt is made in this diagram to show the actual numbers of ancestors, kinship units or frequencies of segmentation.

cannot be sold outside the *thok.* The nexus between the ties of kinship and local contiguity enables the various headmen to exercise social control within the respective kinship segments. This is done through the political councils of these segments.

The greatest part of a person's life is lived within his own *thok.* Personal contact and daily face-to-face relationships decrease as a person moves from his minimal lineage outwards to sub-*thok, thok,* village, *ganwand,* and clan. Even so, the minimal lineage is not the strongest of the kinship segments despite the fact that its members are in contact with each other from childhood and participate together in ritual and economic founding ancestors. The line of descent from such a founding ancestor is generally remembered, or in case of doubt—which only happens in the case of *thoks* which have many generations—can be ascertained from the genealogical tables of the bard. The suffix *ke,* meaning descendants, is attached to the name of the founding ancestor of a lineage group and this gives a clear indication which segment is referred to, or whether a segment belongs to another *thok* or sub-*thok.*

After the clan Chaudhry, it is the head of a *thok* who wields the greatest amount of prestige and influence. The sub-*thok* and minimal lineage chaudhries are expected to obey and accept the leadership of the *thok* chaudhry, just as he in turn is expected to accept the leadership of the clan chaudhry.

A *thok* is divided into sub-*thoks*, and a sub-*thok* is segmented into *khandans* or minimal lineages. A minimal lineage comprises various nuclear and joint-families. (See the diagram).

Like the clan, the *thoks* of the village each have a compact area, both residential and agricultural. Thus the ties of kinship are reinforced by ties of local contiguity both at the *thok* and the clan level. The *bhaichara* (brotherhood) system of land tenure and the rules of inheritance maintain this spatial compactness, since land cannot be sold outside the *thok.* The nexus between the ties of kinship and local contiguity enables the various headmen to exercise social control within the respective kinship segments. This is done through the political councils of these segments.

The greatest part of a person's life is lived within his own *thok.* Personal contact and daily face-to-face relationships decrease as a person moves from his minimal lineage outwards to sub-*thok, thok,* village, *ganwand,* and clan. Even so, the minimal lineage is not the strongest of the kinship segments despite the fact that its members are in contact with each other from childhood and participate together in ritual and economic activities. It is the *thok* which is the strongest and most effective kinship group in both the social and political fields. The minimal lineage segment is weakened by quarrels over the partition of family property and use of agricultural implements, cattle and irrigational resources. Personal ambitions, also, are disruptive in this segment. These quarrels often lead to hatred and account for the weakness of the joint-family system among the Jats, which tends to break up under the tensions they cause. The *thok* on the other hand, and to some extent the sub-*thok,* are free from such tensions. The benefits of local contiguity and kinship sentiment are therefore able to work unchecked and give them more solidarity and political effectiveness than the minimal lineage.

As the result of quarrels and rivalries, segmentation is more common within the minimal lineage and the joint-family than in the sub-*thok* or the *thok.* Minimal lineages grow up into sub-*thoks,* but the lineage of a sub-*thok* has never yet achieved the status of a *thok.*

From the point of view of its effect on the individual, the minimal lineage is the most important of all the kinship groups, except the nuclear or the joint-family. It is in this group that an individual grows up, is cared for, and learns his rights and responsibilities. In adulthood mutual interdependence and co-operation in ritual, economic and other matters are the keynotes of his relationships within the group. It is these same factors, of course, that produce the tensions and quarrels within the minimal lineage.

The recognition of seniority between the *thoks,* sub-*thoks* and minimal lineages determines rules of behaviour and etiquette towards the elders of a senior kinship group, but is not of great political significance.

Family Structure

A Jat's immediate family may be an independent nuclear family, an independent polygynous family or a joint-family. A joint-family may be in the form of either a joint household or several simple households where there has been a break-up of the residential unit but no formal partition of the property has taken place.

The authority of the father within the family is strong. As the head of the family he commands all the economic and other resources belonging to it. Even after their marriage the sons have to obey the father and conform to his wishes. Senior status is not achieved immediately after marriage; it takes from five to seven years before a married person is considered sufficiently grown up and responsible as a member of society. Till then he is not considered independent.

The relationship between the father and the son is a complex one, and is not free from strain. Economic difficulties or pressure of work may make a father irritated and bad tempered, and if anything goes wrong he generally takes it out on his sons. A father may beat a young, unmarried son; but after twenty years of age or so, a son is seldom given corporal punishment although he may be frequently scolded and reprimanded for minor faults. Even if a son is conscientious and hard working he is not praised by his father in his presence. Paternal love is not shown openly, although it may take indirect forms of praise in front of others. The apparent lack of appreciation may create resentment, and if this builds up over the years it may lead to a quarrel and possibly a demand for the partition of the property.

The situation becomes more complicated on occasions when the father has sons from more than one wife, though the Jats try not to favour the children from one wife over those of the others. All sons are treated equally by the father, except the eldest son who is generally somewhat favoured. He is the first to lighten the burden of the father when he comes of age. Because he is leniently treated in comparison to the others it is seldom he who asks for partition or wishes to separate from his father.[21]

If the father has children from more than one wife, the likelihood of a joint-family splitting is greater. Stepbrothers find it difficult to live together even during the lifetime of the father, quarrels among them often arising out of the allocation of work or when one or another of them gets married. The father's favouritism for the eldest son is a major cause of disharmony, especially when the son comes to have more authority and say in the joint-family matters, or comes to manage the family finances. Then a suspicion that the family income is not being equally distributed among the brothers becomes the basis for such quarrels. Over the years such disputes often lead to a partition of the property.

In the case of a joint-family containing stepbrothers, this process of partition is accelerated, and if it happens in the lifetime of the father, the other brothers may continue to live with him. The unmarried brothers may live with any married brother. If this happens, the elder brother also manages the share of his younger brothers.

A joint-family may consist of three generations, that is, the father's father, the father's unmarried brothers, the father and his married and unmarried sons, unmarried daughters, and, in a few cases, the father's widowed sisters or daughters. After the death of the father, the sons may attempt continuing to live together for some time. But increasing tension and quarrels between the brothers or between their wives will usually lead to a situation where partition of the joint-family property becomes inevitable.

In case of a partition between brothers, a widowed mother may go to live with any of the sons she likes most, and the son who takes the mother in his care is given a higher share than the others. After the death of the mother this share is divided equally among the brothers. The mother is not entitled to inherit her husband's property but she holds a right in it which lasts during her lifetime.

During the lifetime of the father or father's father the joint-family is patrilocal, but after their death it becomes fratrifocal; till it may, in some cases, split into independent nuclear families.

Khandan or Minimal Lineage

Kinship behaviour between the members of a minimal lineage is much the same as within a joint-family. The elders are addressed in the same terms as used for joint-family members, except that the terms 'father' and 'mother' are not used outside the family. Youngers or equals in age are regarded as brothers and sisters, and are called by their names. When referred to before a third person, relatives within the minimal lineage—as also within the sub-*thok* and the *thok*—are distinguished from real or primary relatives, and a descriptive prefix is added to the primary terms. Respect is expected and shown in daily behaviour to lineage elders just as it is in the case of joint-family elders. The minimal lineage elders consider it their duty to teach, guide or reprimand the younger members of the lineage.

In contrast with the practice in outside kinship groups, the unity of the minimal lineage is expressed by reference to the common descent from the founder of the lineage, by members calling themselves the descendants of such and such person. Outside interference in the internal affairs of the lineage, even by members of the sub-*thok* or *thok,* is strongly resented. In quarrels and disputes with other groups such as the other minimal lineages of the same sub-*thok* or *thok* or kinship groups outside the *thok,* the various families of a minimal lineage tend to support their own kind and stand with them as one group. Disputes with outsiders strengthen the unity and solidarity of the lineage group and personal differences are put aside for the time being.

Ideally the lineage elders have as much right to command obedience from the younger generations as the father, grandfather, or father's elder brothers. Furthermore, persons of the same generation within the group regard themselves as brothers and sisters. But whereas kinship behaviour within the group is more or less uniform and follows the same pattern as with primary relatives, kinship sentiment is not so strong, tending to decrease as it moves out of the primary kinship group to the minimal lineage and then to the sub-*thok* and *thok.*

The minimal lineage, like the joint-family, presents a picture of internal tensions and ambivalent feelings. On the one hand there is close social intercourse and daily contact between its members. Kinship and territorial proximity, and dependence upon each other in economic pursuits (e.g. borrowing agricultural implements, using the same cane-crusher and taking each other's produce to the market) being them closer to each other. Recreational activities also are carried out mostly within the minimal lineage. Further, the head of the minimal lineage is equally respected by all its members. Generally he keeps himself from taking sides with any of the constituent joint-families, and the family heads and other members of the lineage go to him for advice and help. Thus, in its Jural and political aspects, the unity of the sibling groups is extended to the minimal lineage, as also to the sub-*thok* and the *thok.*

Tensions, quarrels and suspicions, on the other hand, are common between the families and members of a minimal lineage. They arise out of the partition of the property, misuse of agricultural implements, attempts to buy land from another family by lending money against land as security, personal aggrandisement and undue political influence or victimization by one family over another. Dishonest or selfish behaviour by an elder brother who has taken over the joint-family funds after the death of the father, and when the other brothers are still young, may lead to quarrels which will last a lifetime, causing the formation of two cliques permanently opposed to each other within the minimal lineage. Some differences become so deep that they lead to permanent hatred and to quarrels which the lineage council fails to resolve, and which ultimately split the minimal lineage.

Such factors render the minimal lineage the weakest political unit after the joint-family. Its elders are seldom considered neutral when their own families are involved, and even in other cases they are generally not sufficiently influential, and command insufficient prestige, to be able to iron out differences within the lineage. In short, the presence of many tensions coupled with the absence of strong political leadership expose the minimal lineage to frequent fragmentation. This is not the case with the other two lineages, which are of greater lineal depth.

Sub-Thok or Major Segment

The tensions which beset the minimal lineage are generally absent at the sub-*thok* level. Kinship behaviour is the same as within the minimal lineage, as is the use of kinship terms; but the sub-*thok* elders, excepting the chaudhry, do not expect to command total obedience from the younger members of the group, nor are they obliged to control their conduct or reprimand them.

Daily face-to-face contact and interaction is less at the sub-*thok* level than in the minimal lineage. Similarly, borrowing of agricultural implements or asking for other kinds of help, economic or otherwise, is less common. Such help as is given is the result of mutual friendship and understanding rather than of kinship obligations; though some sentiment of kinship proximity also exists. Members of the same sub-*thok* may form themselves into an economic group if they possess agricultural lands near one another, or get on well together, particularly if quarrels within the minimal lineage compel a family to seek economic help and friendship outside it.

The strong point of the major segment is that it has the advantage of proximity of kinship and local contiguity while avoiding the tensions from which the minimal lineage suffers. Quarrels resulting from personal aggrandisement and the partition of property are not frequent in the sub-*thok* ; they take place mostly at the joint-family or the minimal lineage level. Nevertheless, kinship sentiment and behaviour at the sub-*thok* level is more formal and impersonal, unless accompanied by ties of friendship and mutual understanding. It is also more optional than within the minimal lineage, depending more upon individual choice.

Yet kinship affinity in the sub-*thok* is strengthened by the pride of common descent from the founding ancestor, who is not far removed genealogically. Common lineage gods and propitiation of common ancestors, keep kinship sentiment fairly strong. The principle of unity of the lineage group is extended to the sub-*thok*, which regards itself as one group in the face of outside groups. Disputes within the sub-*thok* are regarded as its own business, and the *thok* elders do not interfere in its affairs unless invited by the sub-*thok* elders to do so. Sometimes the *thok* elders feel strongly that a certain dispute should not be allowed to go on within a sub-*thok*, but they seldom interfere.

Thus the threat of segmentation within a sub-*thok* is much less frequent than in a minimal lineage; and the degree of social control exercised by the sub-*thok* council is correspondingly greater. Perhaps the reason why there is no specific term for the sub-*thok* in local parlance is because unity in their codes and statutes, and in their co-activities, is sufficiently evident not to need the pointer of a special name.

Thok or Maximal Lineage

Kinship behaviour in the *thok* is the same as in the sub-*thok*, but kinship sentiment is more diffuse. Members of a *thok* are considered related only in comparison with those of other *thok*. On account of the numerical size of the *thok*[22] and its settlement over a wide area of the village, close social intercourse in daily life is more infrequent than is the case with a sub-*thok*. There is little sign of specific kinship behaviour in day-to-day life.

The kinship terms that are used for members of the sub-*thok* and minimal lineage apply in the *thok* also; but the use is restricted to those elders who are either considerably older than the speaker or command prestige and influence within the whole kinship group. Other *thok* members are addressed by name, and scant regard is given to kinship behaviour in these cases.

The factors which lend solidarity to the group are the sentiment of common descent from the founding ancestor, physical proximity and common residential and agricultural area, and the confinement of most social, economic and religious activities within the *thok*.

The *thok* is a property-holding descent group, as land cannot be alienated outside it; and its members have a common interest in the land which has not yet been divided. The tensions which are frequent within the minimal lineage, and to some extent within the sub-*thok*, are absent at the *thok* level. Social interaction is generally by individual choice rather than by the compulsive factor of kinship obligation.

Such religious practices as the worship of common ancestors, who are remembered and can be genealogically identified by the members, emphasize kinship sentiment within the group and help to make it the strongest political unit. This is in spite of the fact that kinship sentiment within the *thok* may still be more diffuse than in the minimal lineage or sub-*thok*. The feeling of *thok* affiliation is strong.

In the village and in the wider area of the clan, a person derives his political status by virtue of his *thok* affiliation. It does not wholly depend upon his economic power or other social status. Politically a person is of no consequence unless he has the support of his *thok*.

The power and political prestige of a *thok* depend upon its depth span, numerical strength and economic resources. Large *thok* carry more prestige than smaller ones, both in inter-village organization and at the clan level.

Kinship ties and behaviour between the members of a *thok* may not seem to be conspicuously operative in the everyday life of the community; but on all important occasions such as births, deaths, marriages and religious ceremonies, they come to the fore and are seen as obligatory. The duties and obligations imposed by such ties must be carried out according to the social norms of the community. Failure to do so is unforgivable and may lead to a permanent cleavage which may endanger the unity of the lineage group. Therefore any such failure in kinship obligation within the *thok* is frowned upon by everyone and may bring down the wrath of the lineage elders. Differences are forgotten on social and religious occasions, or at least are kept in the background. Opportunity is taken of such occasions to settle disputes or differences of opinion, under the general influence of happiness and gaiety or grief, as the case may be.

The *thok* is the most politically effective kinship group. It can exercise sanctions and other methods of social control which the sub-*thok* or the minimal lineage cannot apply.

Religious Aspects of Kinship Solidarity and Lineage Organization

During the festival of Kanagat (September-October) the Jats propitiate their ancestors for fifteen days. Oblations of water are offered to the spirits of the deceased ancestors. Every remembered ancestor is propitiated in this manner on the *tithi* (lunar day) on which he died, during the course of the festival. The head of a family offers *pindas* (ritual offerings given to the manes), assisted by a Brahmin priest who performs certain rituals and recites Sanskrit hymns during the course of the ceremony. On the last day of the festival a final offering is made to all the remote manes whose names are no more remembered.

The ancestors worshipped and propitiated are the *thok* (maximal lineage) and clan ancestors. The *thok* ancestors are more important than the clan ancestors, who are seldom now remembered by name. But a final offering of the *pindas* to the clan ancestors is necessary. It is believed that if the remembered ancestors are satisfied (they are mostly the *thok* ancestors), all others who are further removed must also be satisfied.

The spirits of all ancestors are believed to look after the welfare of their descendants. The offerings of the *pindas* intend that the spirits may live in peace in another world and may not feel neglected; therefore, that they may not bring misfortune upon their descendants. These spirits are the guardians and must be propitiated so that their benevolence may be ensured. Failure to propitiate may enrage the spirits, who may become malevolent and bring down misfortune in the shape of illness, economic or other kinds of loss, or physical harm. But they are also propitiated because of the sentiment of filial piety and to ensure their peace in another world.

The worship of ancestors constitutes a religious charter for the lineage and clan organization of the Jats. In most cases the deceased ancestors are common to minimal lineage (*khandan*), sub-*thok* or major segment, and the *thok* or maximal lineage. The majority are genealogically remembered. Their propitiation provides an opportunity for the emphasis of one of the most important structural principles, namely the kinship bond, the proximity of blood relationship between the members of the lineages of various depth spans, and the duties and obligations that go with it.

There are no common propitiatory rites at the *thok* or clan level. Common ancestors are propitiated individually by the head of a joint- or a nuclear-family. Some of the clan ancestors, whose names are well known and remembered for one reason or another, are also propitiated by name on the last day of the festival. The *thok* ancestors, by virtue of their nearer genealogical proximity with the living descendants are considered more important than the clan ancestors. But a final offering of the *pindas* to them is also necessary.

This rite not only makes the structural principle of the community explicit on the festival of Kanagat, it also leads throughout the year to 'a considerable clan feeling and not unfrequently much pride of descent from some noted ancestors' among the Jats.

This practice of ancestor-worship runs counter to the ideology of reincarnation, the cycle of re-births. It is strongly criticized and discouraged by the Arya Samaj movement.[23] But the Jats manage to continue the rites while remaining faithful adherents of the movement. The reason why they have not abandoned ancestor-worship when they have discontinued several other religious practices discouraged by the Arya Samaj should have emerged from the foregoing discussion.

An unmarried youth, dying at the age of eighteen or so, may under certain circumstances become a *devata* or godling. If, for example, the spirit of the deceased appears in the dreams of a member of the family and complains that it is unhappy or uncared for, the family members may build an abode for it at a corner of a field belonging to the family. This abode is in the shape of a mound about two feet high. It used to be made of earth and plastered periodically with cow-dung; but nowadays it is generally made of kiln-baked bricks built in the shape of a square, about one foot high and with a niche in the centre in which to put an earthen lamp. When this lamp, filled with mustard oil, has been lit a prayer is made to the spirit to rest in peace and not to harm the family members.

Another circumstance which necessitates the building of the abode is when the spirit causes harm of any kind soon after the death of the youth. If any member of the family experiences illness or misfortune within the first year of the death, it is believed that the spirit of the departed is disturbed or feels neglected, and thus has become malevolent. Therefore, to placate it and to set it at rest, an abode is built.

Once an abode has been built to such a spirit, it must be propitiated and worshipped at regular intervals to keep it placated. The spirit is also credited with supernatural powers of granting fertility to barren women and young wives of the family. Thus it becomes a godling, wielding both benevolent and malevolent powers. It is worshipped and propitiated during the festival of Kanagat, at the time when a male member of the family gets married, or when a woman married into the family fails to have children in the first few years of the marriage. In the main it is worshipped by women married into the family or the lineage, except on the festival of Kanagat when oblations of water or the *pindas* are offered to it by the male head of the family. It is also worshipped after the marriage of a boy, when his bride is taken to the abode where she prays to the godling to grant her fertility and to look after the health and welfare of her children.

Such a godling grows in status as the family grows into a minimal lineage and further into a major segment (sub-*thok*) or a maximal lineage (*thok*). However, the creation of such a godling is fairly uncommon, depending on the frequency of the special circumstances mentioned above under which it comes into being. In the absence of such circumstances over a long period of time, a sub-*thok* or a *thok* may have only one godling worshipped and propitiated by the whole lineage. More commonly the minimal lineages have their own separate godlings. The setting up of a new abode for a godling may, sometimes, signify the breaking away of the family from the parental lineage. Cases of such a godling being common to the sub-*thok* are not frequent. There is only one such case in the village of Shoron. Cases of a godling worshipped by the whole *thok* or maximal lineage are even more rare.

The belief in, and worship of, this godling is another factor that emphasizes the unity of the lineage group. Thee is a direct correlation between this kind of religious worship, i.e. of ancestors, and the strength of the social structure. These beliefs and practices tend to produce social cohesiveness within the lineage groups, and this forms the basis for the political functioning of these groups in the socio-political life of the Jat community.

A word with regard to clan gods and goddesses. Mayer reports the presence of the clan goddess and the importance of worshipping her as a test of common clan membership among the Rajputs of Central India. The Jats of the *khap* Baliyan do not have a clan god or goddess.[24] Neither do they have any religious festivals or rites in which the whole clan takes part. All that Jat religious beliefs and practices provide are common symbols and a common ideology which may, in certain circumstances, lead to a sense of unity among them. The unity and solidarity of the clan is based upon kinship and the political system rather than upon common religious rites and offices at the clan level. Even the various lineages do not participate in worship as a group; it is performed independently by the heads or members of the nuclear-or joint-families.

On account of the influence of the Arya Samaj movement, belief in black magic, exorcism, or the mystical power of the evil eye, are not common among the Jats—although such beliefs may be held by a small section of the community which, on account of illiteracy or similar factors, has not been able to imbibe the teachings of the Arya Samaj. Any such cases as exist are confined to the minimal lineage.[25] No cases have been cited outside this kinship group, either in the kinship groups of greater depth span or in the wider social or political field. The reason for its existence in the minimal lineage group is probably that the tensions within the group lead to charges of black magic and the like. But even so a joint-family or minimal lineage has seldom been known to break up following such accusations; fission is far more likely to take place on account of the causes which are inherent in these kinship groups.

Even after the partition of property, enmity and hatred may persist between brothers or parallel cousins over the years, and both the parties may continue to harm each other. The Jats have a saying: 'A brother can be either the best of friends or the worst of enemies'. Accusations of black magic have a cathartic effect where such emotionally charged relationships exist; and they do, without doubt, help to canalize the forces of disruption.

Personal misfortune or the failure of crops is not attributed to black magic, for it would be very difficult to prove such an accusation since there are no diviners to verify it. I have not come across a single council case where such an accusation was an issue.

Inter-Thok Relationships

The relationship between different *thoks* is marked by mutual regard and courtesy in behaviour and manner of speech, particularly between *thok* elders and leaders. In certain cases, the *thok* founders may have been very closely related to each other, or the ancestors who conquered or founded a village and after whom the various *thoks* are named, may also be very closely inter-related. Although the genealogical relationship between the founders of various *thoks* may not be wholly remembered, the sentiment of kinship proximity is generally present. Common ancestry, past history, and physical proximity within the village, binds *thok* leaders together and ensures that disputes and differences of opinion are not allowed to come in the way of gracious behaviour. In disputes with *thoks* of other villages, the various *thoks* of a village tend to unite and lend political support to each other.

No doubt there is factionalism and competition for political power between *thoks* at the village level; but on account of certain social customs[26] the members of two politically opposed *thoks* are obliged to present a picture of unity. Efforts are made to keep all differences within the bounds of the village, and any attempt to flout this norm is considered in bad taste and an act of irresponsibility. Open acts of hostility are avoided. Any political factions formed with outside *thoks* as against one's own village are generally on an individual basis rather than on the *thok* level as a whole. Moreover, this is done secretly and is not admitted publicly.

Kinship ties between the *thoks* of a village are reinforced by ties of friendship between the individual *thok* members. These ties are based upon mutual help and common participation in religious and social ceremonies.

As an extension of *thok* solidarity, the villages of a *ganwand* may unite against another *ganwand* or at the *khap* council level, particularly if the *thoks* in the *ganwand* are related to each other.

Importance of Some Uterine and Affinal Relationships

For a Jat, the most important kinship group outside his own lineage is that of the mother's brother and his family. For economic and other kinds of help, if not forthcoming from his own lineage, an individual turns to this kinship group. His relationship with his mother's brother is marked by affection and intimacy. All kinds of help from the mother's brother are expected as a matter of right and obligation. A local saying which epitomizes the relationship is that 'a mother's brother cannot stop his sister's son even from taking away his only buffalo', the milch animal which symbolizes the economic resources and general prosperity of the family.

The next closest kinship group after the mother's brother's family, is the father's sister's husband and his family. Although the relationship is marked by respect for the father's sister and her husband, it is intimate and affectionate. A strong bond exists between an individual and his father's sister, and also between the cross-cousins. Close kinship ties are maintained by frequent visits to each other's villages.

Affinal relatives are not generally approached by an individual for help, as this may lower his prestige in the eyes of the members of his own lineage group. But if they come forward with help it is not refused, and may further cement the affinal ties between the two groups.

Help from one's younger sister's and daughter's husband's families is out of the question, even if forthcoming, and is politely refused by means of various excuses. One is expected to give them help whenever possible rather than receive anything from them. In the case of an elder sister and her husband's family, help is welcomed, though seldom asked for.

In political matters, however, these kinship and affinal ties are to little importance, because all such relatives belong to other clan areas and are not in a position to be of much help in intra-clan affairs. At the inter-clan or the *sarv-khap* (all-clan) council meetings, such relatives are not recognized as judges where individual behaviour is concerned. By the customary code of council conduct they are expected to form an opinion (as the attendant members of the council) on the basis of the facts of a dispute at issue, without allowing kinship ties to colour their opinion. But even if they speak in favour of the relative who is involved, their voice does not carry much influence: it is considered prejudiced by the fact of kinship ties. Nevertheless they may be invited by the council judges to exercise their influence upon the individual and appeal to him, by virtue of kinship ties, to accept the decision of the council.

Therefore, in political matters, one can only expect support from paternal relatives and one's own lineage groups. These tend to take the side of the individual and to adopt his cause as the cause of the whole lineage group. The influential elders and heads of the larger lineage groups are, however, and exception. They do not allow themselves to become involved unless they are sure of the justice of the cause of their lineage member.

The fact that the lineages are involved greatly reduces the chances of open fights between members of different groups. There are few cases of such fights between the members of two lineage groups, outside the minimal lineage. In a dispute between the members of two *thoks*, the matter is promptly taken up by the elders of the two lineages who try to settle the dispute before it can assume serious proportions. Retribution and vengeance, though rare, are considered the duties of the *thoks* acting on behalf of the individual member or family.

Within the *thok,* political factions run along sub-*thok* lines, and within the village, inter-village (*ganwand*) and clan, along *thok* lines.

Rules of Descent, Succession and Inheritance

Descent among the Jats is strictly patrilineal. The son takes the name of the father irrespective of the caste or community of the mother.[27] Adoption outside the clan and caste is totally unknown. It is illegal according to the customary law of the Jats, and is so recognized by the public law courts. All adoption, especially outside the *thok,* is strongly resented and may even lead to serious disputes between brothers. Normally any attempt to adopt a child from outside one's minimal lineage will lead to a quarrel. Adoption is usually restricted to a brother's child or, failing him, a parallel cousin's son from within the minimal lineage.

In the absence of any male issue, a father may appoint his daughter's son as his successor to the property. In such a case the daughter's son may come to live in the village. He and his descendants are called the *bhānja,* sister's sons, by the villagers. The lineages founded by daughters' sons invited to the village have a separate kinship identity and clan name, but by the *bhaichara* (brotherhood) concept their members are recognized as *bhānja* by all the *thoks* of the village. In political and other matters, these lineages side with the lineage groups of their mother's father. They cannot marry within the clan of their present settlement.

Sometimes, in the past, the daughter's son was invited to live in the village when land was plentiful and there were too few hands to cultivate it; but now, with the population multiplied and pressure on the land increased, such cases have become rare.

The members of *bhānja* (sister's son) lineages still enjoy more or less the same privileges which characterize the relationship between the mother's brother and the sister's son. The relationship is marked by joking and teasing to offset the tensions arising out of the fact that they are regarded as outsiders and appropriators of ancestral property.

Hereditary office, and any property connected with it, is also transmitted unilaterally and patrilineally. Other kinds of movable and immovable property are divided equally between the male issues, with the exclusion of sisters. A share is given to the widow as a

Genealogy of Qabul Singh, the khap Wazir

Pacchumal (*C.* A.D. 1560-1621)[28]
- Bhanichand
  - Jadorai
    - Tekchand
      - Kishanrai
        - Sheolal
          - Gulab Singh
            - Surajmal
              - Tejram (no issue)
              - Diwan Singh (no issue)
              - Khushiram
                - Sanwant Singh
                  - Mulchand
                    - Qabul Singh (the present wazir)
          - Siiram[29]

matter of right. It is intended only for her subsistence and lasts only her lifetime. It cannot be bequeathed by her to anyone; after her death it is again divided equally among the sons. But she has the right to give her share to any one of her sons with whom she decides to live after the partition of the family property, though only for her lifetime. She has the further right to give her own personal property like jewellery and other kinds of movable property which is her *streedhan* (presents, including cash, received during her lifetime) to anyone whom she chooses. Generally she gives it to her daughters or daughters-in-law, or both.

A woman's position is subordinate to a man's. After the death of her husband she does not manage the affairs of the family independently, but only under the care of the eldest son or husband's brother. Nevertheless, after the death of the husband her influence in family matters increases.

The office of the clan and *thamba*[30] chaudhries, and that of the *khap* wazir, is hereditary and passes from father to the eldest son. If the eldest son is incapable in body, mind or character, of holding such an office, it passes to the next son or failing that to the closest parallel cousin within the minimal lineage, provided that the clan council has decided unanimously to appoint such a person in preference to the eldest son.

The office of the heads of the various lineages also tends to be hereditary, passing in the same manner; but in these cases the choice of the eldest son has to be accepted first by the respective lineage council. The eldest son does not automatically succeed to the office of his father as in the case of the clan and *thamba* chaudhries. His behaviour and social conduct is watched closely by the members of the lineage. If it is considered satisfactory according to the norms of the society, he is chosen as the successor long before the lineage head dies. The chaudhries—whether of the lineage groups or of the clan and *thamba*—cannot actually appoint anyone to succeed to office, however. The successor is only considered as accepted when the constituent *thoks* of the clan or *thamba* have performed the ceremony of 'presenting the turban' to him after the death of the incumbent. The same is true of the various lineages. The ceremony of presenting the turban signifies the acceptance and recognition of a person as the head of a kinship group. In the case of joint families the ceremony is performed by the uterine and affinal kin.

The principle of hereditary succession from father to eldest son does not operate automatically. Although it is true that the eldest son stands a better chance than a younger brother or an outsider, sometimes he will be passed over if a candidate is found who is better qualified in head and heart and is approved by the lineage members. Even so, such cases are not common because they may lead to the formation of two factions, which may ultimately result in splitting the lineage group.

Once a person is accepted as the head, he cannot be removed from his office during his lifetime. In cases where the new head is other than the deceased chaudhry's son, the office tends to be hereditary in the new line.

Rules of inheritance are as follows: from father to son to son's son, failing that to brother's sons or more distant parallel cousins or their sons within the minimal lineage, major segment or maximal lineage, as the case may be. Nowadays, property does not go out of the maximal lineage except in the few cases where the daughter's sons are invited to the village and the property is given to them either in the absence of male issue or because the land is too extensive for the sons to cultivate the whole of it. As has been said, this custom is now rare; and in the absence of male issue pressure is put upon the landowner, by his brothers and other members of the minimal lineage, to adopt a brother's son. Some of the forms of marriage described in the following section also help to keep the property within the joint-family or the minimal lineage.

Forms of Marriage

Until recently, the Jats often practised polygyny. Several Jats of the older generation have more than one wife; but among the younger generation the tendency is towards monogamy. The Hindu Marriage Act of 1955 declares polygyny illegal and a cognizable offence punishable by law.

Four types of marriage are practised among the Jats. First is the marriage proper, in which the father or head of a girl's family looks for a boy and settles the engagement with the father of the boy. The engagement ceremony is completed by the girl's father presenting a rupee to the boy. There is no bride price among the Jats, though under the influence of Hindu castes they have adopted the custom of dowry, given by the bride's father. But this custom is on the decline on account of resolutions of the *sarv-khap* council of 1950.

The second form is widow marriage. The widow, soon after the death of her husband, may start living with either his elder or younger brother or, failing them, any of the parallel cousins within the minimal lineage. (See Table 3.1). After some time, if any such brother agrees to take her as his wife, her father comes and presents a rupee to him. No other ceremony is performed and she is then considered legally married. In such a case the sons from the previous marriage are not adopted by the second husband and do not inherit his property; but children of the new marriage have as equal right to property as any children resulting from their father's marriage with a previous wife (who may be still alive). This form of marriage is called *bithana* by the Jats, or 'asking the woman to sit in his house'. It implies a modified version of the Hindu institution of widow inheritance, in that the sons of the deceased brother do not inherit the property of the mother's second husband.

If no one within the joint-family or the minimal lineage wants the young widow as his wife, and if she is not happy in the family and wants to get married somewhere else, she goes to her father's house and he marries her at another place. But she is not allowed to go if she has children, unless she is willing to leave them behind.

It is considered the duty of surviving brothers to look after a widow and her children by taking her as a wife, and generally a brother does come forward to marry her. The widow's father with try to persuade one of the brothers to take her, for he will not often wish to marry her elsewhere. Any attempt by the father to marry her outside the patrilineal kin group of the deceased husband is felt to be an attack on the prestige of the deceased husband's lineage. If the widow is young and without children and is married outside the maximal lineage of the deceased husband, no marriage rite or ceremony is conducted. A rupee is given to the prospective husband and he takes the widow to his home. This type of marriage is called *karao*.

The third form of marriage is called *mol-lana*, or buying a woman. The woman is bought for cash from her parents or guardian and may be of any caste or community. This form is comparatively rare, particularly with women who are in the possession of a man who traffics in them; for girls of untouchable or very low caste are not taken as wives. Cases of buying women of Brahmin and Muslim castes are not infrequent, but if the caste of a woman is known to be low, this fact is kept secret and she is passed off as belonging to some high caste. That women are bought is admitted by many Jats, though the members of the lineage concerned fight shy of owning up to specific cases.

Children raised from *mol-lana* marriages are considered legal heirs to the father's property, for a married man seldom goes out to buy a woman. Although the buying of a second wife used sometimes to be practised by the Jats on account of the scarcity of women, created probably by the custom of female infanticide[31] which was prevalent among them about sixty or seventy years ago, it is now most uncommon. Infanticide itself has completely died out.

Generally speaking a woman who has been bought is not at first accepted in the joint-family, and her husband will live apart in a separate house. But as she bears children and they grow in age, she comes to possess some prestige among the women of the minimal lineage and may take part in social and religious ceremonies, more or less as an equal.

The children from such a marriage find it somewhat difficult to attract spouses from good families. The sons may have to remain unmarried, except where they themselves take a deceased brother's wife. The girls are married to the poorer Jat families, usually with some difficulty. The Jats never marry girls outside their own caste whether higher or lower. There is no hypergamy.

Neither do the children from *mol-lana* marriages enjoy the social status of children from the previous two types of marriages, although they are not segregated in social and religious ceremonies. As the generations multiply this distinction in social status decreases, and by the time of the fourth generation the descendants from such a marriage acquire full social status.

TABLE 3.1

Exceptional Jat Marriages Recorded in Genealogies in Shoron

Total number of Jat households now in Shoron: 280
Total number of Jat marriages recorded in genealogies: 1,140
Persons dying unmarried at an old age: 102

Widow marriages	
With late husband's married elder brother	18
With late husband's unmarried elder brother	9
With late husband's married or unmarried younger brother or parallel cousin	30
Outside *thok* or clan (*karao* marriage)	4
Marriages by purchase (*mol-lana*)	
With a woman of high caste	5
With a woman of low caste	0
Marriages by elopement (*bhaga-lana*)	
With a woman of higher caste than the Jat	4
With a woman of lower caste than the Jat	9
With a Jat woman	8
Women bringing children from existing marriage	5[32]

The accent of the society is on the paternity of the child rather than on the maternity and this helps a great deal to obliterate such differences in the social status of the children from the various kinds of marriage.

Mol-lana marriages are not common. Even in previous generations only the poorer sections of the community, who found it difficult to get married on account of the scarcity of women, bought wives. And *Mol-lana* marriages are found only in the older generations of the community. There are about five such marriages in Shoron village. There is no instance of this type of marriage among the younger generations below the age of thirty-five or forty.

Finally, Jats have also married by elopement (*bhaga-lana*). This form of marriage also is confined mainly to the older generation, and has the same reasons behind it as that of buying a woman. In *bhaga-lana* marriages a woman is abducted and brought to the village where the person sets up house with her. The woman must be from another caste and *Khap*. Sexual relationship with any woman of the *khap* area, irrespective of caste or community, is considered incestuous by extending the principle of *bhaichara* to all castes living within the *khap* area. Any default of this rule may be promptly taken up by the *khap* council and may lead to a bitter dispute between the *thoks*, thus jeopardizing clan solidarity and *khap bhaichara.*

Children from *bhaga-lana* marriages are considered legitimate and are entitled to the property of the father. Nevertheless they will suffer from the same handicaps with regard to social status as the children born of the woman who is bought.

When a woman brings children from her existing marriage with her, they are not adopted by the stepfather and have no right to his property. But he may agree to bring them up, and before he dies he may give a share of his property for their subsistence, a gift which is generally accepted by his legal heirs, i.e. his brother's sons. The share is only a fraction of his property. The rest of it must go to the next of kin (see Table 3.1).

Most of these persons find it very difficult to get married, and may have to remain single throughout their lives. Further, their descendants cannot acquire social status even after the lapse of several generations, for they lack the economic, social and political backing of affinal kin. Though they are considered members of the lineages of their stepfather, the lineages fight shy in supporting their cause in disputes with others, particularly in the case of disputes within a lineage group. In a dispute with outside groups, the *thok* of their stepfather, of which they are considered members even if of the second degree, may ultimately decide to stand by them, though it may take some time.

Mol-lana and *bhaga-lana* marriages both impose handicaps. In spite of the tolerant attitude of the community towards such marriages, they lead to some lowering of the social status both of the persons concerned and of the children born to them. Some of the educated Jats have strong objections to such marriages and hold that they are not the proper customs of the community but the actions of wastrels. These views run counter to the ideal of tolerance generally found in the community and perhaps are due to a conscious desire to raise caste status.

These two types of marriages lend support to Barth's hypothesis that a strongly patriarchal and patrilineal structure serves to make matrilineal and matrilateral kinship irrelevant to status and authority ascription and obviates the need for caste endogamy. The property-holding group does not suffer on account of such marriages.

Access to Brother's Wife

In Jat families, younger unmarried brothers are allowed access to their elder brother's wife. In some cases the elder unmarried brother may have access to his younger brother's wife, though such cases are not so common as the former. In any case, access is only allowed if the unmarried brother is living with the married one, works with him, and gives his share of the property to the married brother's family. The unmarried brother, if he stays unmarried, may finally adopt one of the sons of the married brother with whom he has been living for a long time, and bequeath his property to him. Or he may name the married brother as inheritor of his property. It is a considerable economic gain for a married brother if an unmarried brother comes and lives with him and gives him his share and income from the family property. This is one of the reasons why married brothers seldom object to such sexual access to their wives. In some cases they even ask their wives to try to gain favours of their unmarried brothers so that they can come and live with the family.

Thus the Jats show traits of fraternal polyandry; though it is limited only to the privilege of sexual access. Wives are not shared among the married brothers, nor are they called the wives of the unmarried brothers. The husband remains the legal father of the children irrespective of the biological paternity. Father's brothers are distinguished terminologically, depending whether they are older or younger than the father. The term 'father' is not used of anyone except the legal father. Therefore the term 'polyandry' cannot strictly be applied to the Jat way of life.

Divorce

Cases of divorce among Jats are not common. If a person turns out his wife without sufficient reason, it leads to a dispute between his and the wife's lineage. Her father takes the case to the inter-clan council; and pressure is put upon the husband and his lineage group to keep the wife, unless there are serious charges against her like adultery and insanity, or proven charges of cheating by her parents. A woman is not divorced if she does not bear children. The husband marries another woman with the consent of the first wife, who will even persuade him to marry again if she becomes sure that she cannot have children of her own. After the second marriage, the first wife remains senior in the house and has more say in family matters than the second wife. She takes a close interest in her step children, who are mostly left in her care while the second wife looks after the household work.

If a person leaves his wife without sufficient reason or refuses to keep her in his house, the wife's parents canvass against the person in their own *khap* and neighbouring *khaps*. If they hear that a certain family has approached the man's family for another marriage, they go to the girl's village and persuade her parents not to marry their daughter into that house. The wife's parents may also request their own *khap* council to put pressure upon its clan members to desist from marrying their daughter to such a person. Thus it becomes difficult for a man who has left his wife to get married again. The divorced woman is married by her parents somewhere else.

Marriage is considered sacred and inviolable rather than a mere contract between husband and wife or between two lineage groups. There was one case in Shoron village in the *thok* Natthawara here a person divorced his wife because he found out that she was having sexual relations with his father. He has not married since then, and does not allow his younger brothers to get married while his father is alive.

Prohibited Degrees of Marriage and Preferred Marriage

Marriage within one's own clan (*gotra*) or *khap* (with lineages of another clan but living within the same *khap*) is prohibited. Similarly, marriage in either the mother's clan or *khap* is prohibited, on the principle of lineal and clan-cognatic kinship.

Formerly, the father's mother's clan and *khap* were also among the prohibited degrees, but now this prohibition is not observed with rigidity on account of the difficulty of finding a spouse from neighbouring *khaps* without going too far. But marriage in the father's mother's *khap* is still avoided if possible.

Also, there is no cross-cousin marriage among the Jats even if the cross-cousins belong to different clans and *khaps*. There is no evidence that it was ever prevalent among them.

No particular preference is given to any particular clan or *khap* when choosing a marriage partner. But there are certain neighbouring *khaps,* for example Salaklain (sometimes called Desh), Gathwala, Chaugama, Meerutwasa, Battisa and Badanu, with which *khap* Baliyan marriages are common on account of territorial proximity and common customs and outlook. The Jats do not like to marry their daughters far away, even though a proposal coming from a better family of a clan farther away than the neighbouring clan areas is given preference over a proposal from a family which belongs to a nearby *khap*. Marriages outside the *khap* areas of the Meerut Division are not yet common, although there is an increasing tendency towards them on account of improving facilities of communication. The reluctance to marry outside the *khap* areas of the Division, apart from consideration for the girl who may find it hard to adjust herself to a different culture and dialect, also has political motives. These are that such a marriage does not establish affinal ties which can be used in the local political arena. The factions in the *sarv-khap* council sometimes run along inter-*khap* lines (between *khaps* having affinal ties), and these tend to join forces against other *khaps* with whom there are no close marriage ties. (For example, the *khaps* of Baliyan and Desh have such ties and tend to act together on the *sarv-khap* council). Further, if the girl lives far away from her parents, they cannot bring the political pressure of the *khap* and *sarv-khap* councils, in case of divorce or any other trouble, to bear upon the husband's family.

In area where the Jat clans are not organized into *khaps, khap* exogamy is not possible; but in such areas the *gotra* or clan name is avoided in marriage. This rule is observed without exception.

Marriage information runs along kinship channels, and families find it useful if they are associated with each other through a common relative and know each other's social background.

Incest Taboos

Sexual intercourse is prohibited with the mother, father's mother, father's sister or her daughter, sister, sister's daughter, brother's daughter, mother's brother's daughter, wife's brother's daughter, daughter and daughter-in-law. Any infringement of the rule prohibiting these relatives is considered immoral and the person may be punished by the panchayat or compelled to perform expiatory rites. Infringement may lead to temporary ostracism of the person till he had gone through the expiatory rites and has apologized for his misconduct. Outside these relationships the Jats are tolerant of sexual laxity.

The abhorrence for incestuous relationships is based on a rational code of ethical behaviour rather than on a belief that physiological or supernatural harm will result or that misfortune will befall the culprit or his family. In particular, no connection is drawn between witchcraft and incest.

Incestuous misconduct on the part of a person has adverse effects upon his social and political status. It is considered that he is not to be relied on for any office of leadership, e.g. the headship of a lineage group or a judicial seat at the council meeting. He is looked down upon by his own kinship group, although the good name of the group itself does not suffer on account of misconduct by an individual member.

Incestuous relationships between members of different *thoks* or villages of the same clan are not infrequent: but if they are found out the persons concerned may be punished. The girl, if unmarried, is at once married somewhere else. A case of incest may well lead to a dispute between two *thoks*.

So long we have tried to discuss some of the aspects of the Jat kinship system which are relevant to the political organization and have practical implications. The clan and the lineage structure is the basis on which the whole political framework of the community is based. All the kinship groups have elaborate functions which are exercised in their councils. The head of a kinship group is also the head of the corresponding political unit of which the clan council is constituted.

Possessive rights over the children belong entirely to the lineage, and it is within the lineage that the individual has his most important duties to perform and also his most significant rights, such as the right of support in economic, social and political matters, and rights of inheritance over property.

Laxity in observing marriage customs is tolerated because the strong patriarchal and patrilineal system of residence, descent and inheritance does not allow such laxities to affect the system adversely. In spite of close kinship ties and sentiment with the mother's lineage, matrilineal kinship and matriarchal influence does not disturb the patriarchal and patrilineal structure of the community. The same reason explains the absence of rigidity in sex morals.

But laxity in sex morals and marriage conduct does affect an individual's social and political status and prospects. Responsible persons in the community, who may be the actual or potential leaders of it, must be above such lapses of character. They have a jealous regard for their reputation, and this tends to make them more orthodox and more idealistic in their general behaviour and outlook than the rank and file of the community.

PATTERN OF SOCIAL TRANSFORMATION: MYTHS OR REALITY

Tribal People

During past few decades several works on tribal social structures of North-East India are published, but in no work do we witness the impact of new theoretical developments taking place within social anthropology. North-East India, for example could have been fruitfully made the focal point for testing componential analyses, conceptual conflicts centring on descents, kinship, and filiation; and for re-viewing the themes of bilaterally, ambilineality and double descent. On double descent system, however, the work of D. Danda (1978) is worth mentioning here. Concerning published material on matrilineal social structures this author has made elsewhere attempt towards re-interpretation of such material in the light of bilaterality and filiation. A brief summary of the same is provided here with some additional comments. Danda (1978) has provided an analysis of double descent system among the Dimasa of Assam. She has observed that among the Dimasa "the patri and matri clans, called as *seng-fong* and *jaddi* (or *julu*) respectively, are exogamous non-totemistic and non-localized" (Danda, 1978). There are altogether 42 particulars and 42 patriclans found today among the Dimasa, but originally they had "only seven patriclans and no matriclans" (Danda, 1978). The blood relationship among the Dimasa is traced through both the male and female ancestors, and male agnates and female agnates are called by distinct terms. But since the "clan solidarity is over-emphasized by the Dimasa, the lineage as such has no specific function in their social structure" (Danda 1978).

In Social Structure in South East Asia, Leach attempts to refute the traditional axioms of structural functionalists, who have concerned themselves primarily with the internal social problems which social structures meet. Eggan, in Murdock volume (1960: 49), states, "Social structures have jobs to do; they have to provide orderliness and continuity in human relations". Leach also noted that "Social structure reflects and is constrained by the economic order, by technology, and by numerous other components of culture" (1960: 123). Sahlins (1963), in concurring, notes that "Social structure functions not merely to organize human relations, but to sustain human existence". Most scholars have thus emphasized the relationship between abundance of resources, adequate exploitative techniques, group stability, and unilineality: and between poor habitat, rudimentary techniques of exploitation, unstable settlements and non-unilineality. In case of many North-East India tribes, as author's review of existing literature suggests, these particular relationships are not strictly applied. With the help of few examples (both from patrilineal and matrilineal systems) we shall try to review below the 're-distributive' mechanisms such as 'segmentation", alternate residence, adoption, dual inheritance and complementary filiation (matrifiliation and patrifiliation). We shall start by examining the existing material on matrilineal tribes of North-East India such a Khasi, Garo, Lalung and Koch, and then the partilineal example shall be taken up.

There are two different ways of looking at the kinship system, representing two dominant trends in the study of kinship in social anthropology. These two approaches are conveniently named as Descent and Alliance theories. Descent theory follows Radcliffe–

Brown's formulation and deals with actual relations between persons and lineages. Fortes (1949, 1959) makes this position clear and distinguishes between descent filiation and complementary filiation. Decent according to Fortes is fundamentally a jural concept in that it provides the connecting link between the external and internal aspects of these groups. Since descent confers attributes of status relating to a person's place in the external social structure it is bound to operate by placing person in categories or groups

In contrast to descent filiation is universally bilateral and does not depend on the recognition of descent or the existence of descent groups. That means, in a patrilineal society, and individual's tie of filiation with his mother is not lost and as a result of this he retains some rights. Fortes says 'in a segmentary patrilineal descent system matrifiliation endows a child with attributes of jural status submerging claims and obligations to its mother's lineage, without which it cannot be a normal jural person'. Fortes refers to this as complementary filiation, *i.e.,* the ties of an individual through the parent who does not give him his descent status. The concept of descent, so central to the structural analysis of kinship organization, has been a subject of controversy for a long time. Firth (1963) lists a number of criteria of recruitment for formation of viable descent groups: (1) transmission of name; (2a) title of specific resource, (2b) participation in a specific occasion; (3) generational depth defined by cultural rules, agreement of participants, or a combination of the two, (4) lineality of descent, (5) point of attachment of ego to the descent group, (6) residence rule, and (7) marriage rule. However, in considering unilineal and bilateral descent groups together Firth recognizes a great deal of similarity between them. The particular issue in the concept of descent, with which we are concerned, is it's distinction form filiation, to which topic Fortes (1963) addresses himself in his analysis of the Ashanti Kinship system. Whereas Seligman once regard Ashanti as having a "submerged patrilineal descent line" in addition to full-fledged matrilineal descent, Fortes considered it to be a case of 'complementary patrifiliation with mastrilineal descent.'

Another important question which has not received much attention is the issue of kindred. This is because the anthropologists, in general, are preoccupied in describing "unilineal descent system".

Mitchel (1963) grants that the kindred is generally limited to cognatic societies, if it is defined in terms of ego's equal filiation to paternal and maternal kin. Lounsbury (1964) suspects that there are not very many truly 'non-cognatic' systems, in the sense of their lacking a bilateral genealogical reckoning of personal kinship (original emphasis).

Since 1930 British Social Anthropology has embodied a well-defined set of ideas and objectives which derive directly from the teaching of Malinowski and Radcliffe-Brown . . . this unity of aim is summed up in the statement the "British social anthropology is *functionalist* and concerned with the *comparative analysis of social structures*" (Leach, 1961): But most of the anthropologists, according to Leach, are giving up the attempt to make comparative generalization; instead they have begun to write impeccably detailed historical ethnographies of particular peoples. He believed that to understand what is happening in social anthropology we need to "go right back to the beginning and rethink basic issues . . . really elementary matters such as what we mean by marriage or descent or the unity of siblings . . . ." (Leach 1961). Radcliffe-Brown's instructions were that it is necessary to compare societies with reference to one particular aspect . . . the economic system, the political system, or the kinship system. A serious objection, in Leach's view is that the typology makers never explain why they choose one frame of reference rather than another. Of many frustrations of this kind one is the category opposition patrilineal/matrilineal. Ever since Morgan began writing of the Iroquois, it has been customary for anthropologists to distinguish unilineal from non-unilineal descent systems, and among the former to distinguish patrilineal societies from matrilineal societies.

The categories of patrilineal and matrilineal societies are so obvious that it is extremely difficult to break out of the straitjacket of thought which the categories themselves impose. Because the type-finding social anthropologist conducts his whole argument in terms of particular instances rather than of generalized patterns, he is constantly tempted to attach exaggerated significance to those features of social organization which happen to be prominent in the societies of which he himself has first-hand experience Leach's view is that while the consideration of mathematical and logical models may help the anthropologist to order his theoretical arguments in an intelligent way, his actual procedure should be non-mathematical. The same structural pattern may turn up in any kind of society . . . a mathematical approach makes no prior assumption that unilineal systems are basically different from non-unilineal systems or patrilineal structures from matrilineal structures. On the contrary, the principle of parity leads us to discount all rigid category distinctions of this kind. As we know Fortes' concept of complementary filiation was devised to describe double unilineal element in the matrilineal Ashanti and the patrilineal Tallensi societies while rejecting the notion that these societies actually possess double unilineal systems. Leach argues that from one point of view complementary filiation is simply an inverse form of Malinowski's notion of 'Sociological Paternity' as applied in the matrilineal context of Trobriand society. We find that the concept became necessary to Fortes precisely because he had decided that the more familiar and more obvious notion of double unilineal descent was inappropriate.

Comparative Analysis of Matrilineal Systems

In the major ethnographic studies on matrilineal societies of North-East India such as Nakane's (1967) work on Khasi and Garo; Burling's (1963) work on Garo; and Syamchaudhuri and Das (1973) work on Lalung no specific analysis is provided to the theme of inherent, internal weakness of the unilineal systems. At the same time no ethnographer paid attention to the subject of *cognatic elements* in these societies. The segmentary structure, which is so basic to these societies, is rather unaccepted to these authors as an organisational principle. A remarkable feature of this regions that at different stages of historical development some sections of a 'tribe' are found to have become patrilineal; although in the past they had a strict matrilineal emphasis, such as the Koch of Meghalaya and the Rabha of Assam. The ethnographic material on the whole is uncritical as far as the process of disintegration of corporate structure of matrilineal societies of this region is concerned.

The purpose of the comparative analysis of some prominent features of social organization here is to show how far the descent groups emerge or do not emerge as functionally and structurally viable groups as also to show the different levels of involvement of cognatic elements in matrilineal societies of the Khasi and Garo Hills. Author shall also discuss in brief the politico-jural domain such as juristic dimension of corporateness and succession in support of author's basic argument.

Here we may describe in brief some prominent features of social organization of the Khasi, Garo, Koch and Lalung tribes. The review and re-interpretation presented here is based mainly on the material provided by Nakane (1967), Burling (1963), Syamchaudhuri and Das (1973) and Majumdar (1967). We shall focus on structure and composition of descent groups, and the various ways in which relatives may be aligned. Function of descent group is examined in relation to residential patterns as well as norms and behaviour at different circumstances. The subject of marriage, postmarital residence and family life is also considered. An attempt is also made at last to test the utility of Gluckman's (1950) concept of Father Right.

Nakane (1967) has shown that the social structure of the Garo and the Khasi differ greatly. Similarity is found only in the basic succession rules of mother-daughter, and mother's brother sister's son. In fact the property is owned by the woman, but the controlling power and authority over it are in the hands of the man. The main structural differences between the two lies in the composition of a property group: the property group of the Khasi is formed by a descent group at a shallow generation depth, while that of the Garo is maintained by the cooperation of the two local lines, each of which represents a localized lineage group. Hence the Garo descent group tends to be weakened in its solidarity. In matrilineal systems the ownership of property and the authority over the property group never rest in one person, and the succession to these two offices follows the female line (mother-daughter) and the male line (mother's brother-sister's son) as shown in line A and line B in the following figure, which is reproduced here from Nakane (1967).

As we shall later discuss in detail this duality of office-holding individuals within the succession rule is the intrinsic cause of complications and variations in matrilineal systems. Among the Garo, for example, the office of *Loskor* appears gradually to have accumulated power, probably at the expense both of the *Nokmas*

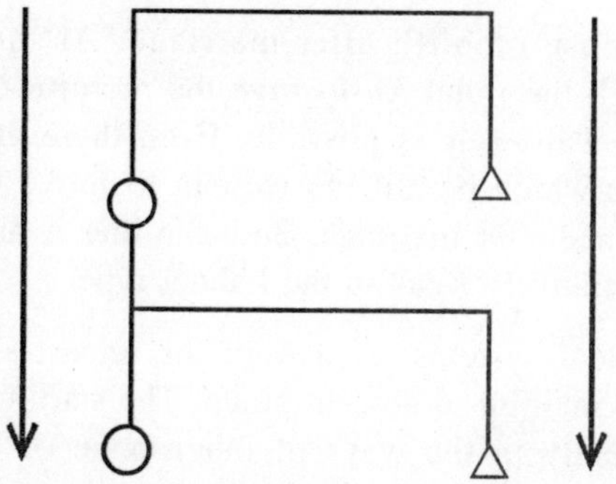

and of the matrilineal descent groups (Burling, 1963). Moreover the settlement of disputes among the Garo certainly does not depend on "matrilineal descent groups" (Burling, 1963). Thus we see that in politico-jural domain as well as in other contexts the relative importance of matrilineage has considerably declined. The difficulty of preserving in function both lines A and B is caused by residential problems - individual marriages which contradict the sibling cohesion. Different tribes resolve such contradictory factors in alternative ways as follows:

1. *The Garo Type:* The co-residential type is 'husband-wife' instead of 'brother-sister'. The function of both lines A and B is equally strong. This is kept by the marriage contract between two local lines, so that it is possible to keep the function of each line against the residential separation of the two lines in one descent group.
2. *The Khasi Type:* The ideal co-residential type consists of a woman with either her husband or her brother. The function of line A is much stronger than that of line B. This type is also found among the Hopi, the Zuni, the Trukese, the Negri-Sembilan Malay, the Yao, etc. However, the *Syiem,* the Khasi Chief, does live with his wife after marriage in the residence of his wife.
3. *The Lalung Type:* The ideal pattern is matrilineal inheritance and uxori-local residence. However, among certain clans from which kings (or chiefs) were selected the royal succession did not allow the clan-men to leave

> the house of birth after marriage. At the same time through the ritual *Kush-singa* the recruitment of a child into patrilineage is possible. Even there are obligatory rituals which permit the woman to move to husband's residence after marriage. Both the line A and line B are thus relatively weak in the Lalung type.

In matrilineal systems, as a rule, the ancestral property is inherited by the matrilineal descent group. The starting point of the difference is really in the ways of inheritance of the *acquired property* particularly by the husband.

In the Khasi type, if a man builds an independent house in which to live with his wife and children, that house and his acquired property during his matrimonial life automatically belong to and are inherited by his wife and children. In Garo society, because of the presence of cross-cousin marriage, a Garo prefers his son marrying the daughter of his sister, who has inherited the property of the family of his birth. Thus perhaps we find that in succession to offices and the settlement of disputes the links of 'matrilineal descent groups', among the Garo, are immaterial. The relative importance of Garo matrilineage is, therefore, bound to be weak.

The Garo and Khasi, in Nakane's view, follow a unilineal system but they do not have what is called segmentary lineage' system. My argument is that when a society has a lineage clan-organization it must have some kind of segmentary organization. The lineage, in both the Garo and the Lalung societies, certainly emerges as an exclusive corporate unit, although it is not so obvious among the Khasi. But author believes that both the processes of fission and fusion have been dominant features of all hill tribal societies of North-East India including the tribes such as Khasi, Garo and Lalung. For a discussion on segmentary system among patrilineal people one may refer to Das (1985).

The processes of segmentation of descent groups into distinct groups as well as spatial movement and grouping of descent groups into phratry-like cluster such as *Mahari* is clearly observable in Lalung society. The Lalungs believe that their clans have descended from twelve sisters. Fusion of clans was mainly caused by wars and feuds in Lalung, Khasi and Syngteng societies. Gait (1963): observed that from time to time some ambitious chief would conquer and absorb some of the adjoining communities, and the kingdom thus formed would continue to exist until the weakness of his successors gave an opportunity for the prevailing disintegrating tendency to assert itself, when it would again dissolve into a number of small independent communities.

This situation thus demanded an institutionalized arrangement in politico-jural domain to provide stability to several 'Independent' social systems. We will take up this point again in the following pages to clarify the argument. Turning to descent group formation, while among the Garo the localized lineage is expressed in terms of the village whose land bears the name of the localize lineage, among the Khasi on the other hand, the lineage is found only on a household scale . . . within the unit of *iing*. The clan is considered only as a ritual conception implying exogamy, but not as an organized body of kin such as we observed among the Lalung. Among the Garo the village theoretically consists of the members of the two localized lineages, as represented in the headman and his wife respectively. In Nakane's own interpretation we find a little contradiction in the analysis of Khasi lineage. She observed that in societies of the household lineage type, i.e., the Khasi, a functional unit is demarcated in the first place by common property and residence, which cut off clearly other members who may be included by the descent principle. This demarcation is so clearcut that the wider group, which may be recruited by descent principle, can hardly have a function in itself. The lineage, in the sense of wider descent units, may be vaguely seen . . . Again she agrees without any elaborate discussion that the bilateral characteristics of household-line-age type (of Khasi) correspond functionally to the scheme of a bilateral system such as the Maori. The property group is thus not always composed of a matrilineal descent group, nor has it any institutionalized organization with a matrilineal principle of inheritance, such as we observed among the Garo.

To sum up, the unilineal principle (matrilineal system) works differently in each given society, producing different structures. Descent principle and residence (with landholdings or property) are equally important criteria for the analysis of social organization. As different degrees and levels of different factors are involved in each given society we, the anthropologists, should not emphasize the prominence of a particular factor.

It is in hill tribal societies of North-East India that certain unique social processes are responsible for drastic social change which need urgent investigation. The change of matrilineal system to patrilineal system, through important economic and cultural changes or through Sanskritization and migration, is one such example. Author shall describe below, in brief, the process of gradual merging of the matrilineal Koch of Garo hills into the Hinduized patrilineal social structure.

The Koch of the Garo Hills represent a tribe with various degrees of Sanskritization. The Koch who are found in the western and south-western borders of the Garo Hills, are permanent cultivators, but they practised shifting cultivation also. According to 1961 Census the speakers of Koch language in Garo Hills is 4,560. The Koch are basically organised on the basis of matrilineal clans, known as *nikini.* Some clans claim a common ancestry and marriage between their members are prohibited. The male is regarded as the head of the household and he controls the activities of his wife and children. Divorce is very rare, and so there is no hard and fast rule about the division of the household at the time of divorce.

The interesting feature of Koch social structure is that it represents a stage of transition from the norms of a matrilineally-biased society to that of a patrilineally-biased society. This is due to (1) their attempt to elevate themselves on the social ladder by gradual adoption of Hindu practices, and (2) due to their shift from a *jhum* (slash-and-burn) economy to permanent agriculture. The Koch village predominantly consists of a core of related males, the females mostly belonging to other village. Cases of grown-up male children staying with their parents after marriage are very common. Such sons are given share of the property also. As regards kinship terminology we find that mother's brother's children are termed siblings and behaved as such. In Koch kinship terminology the only term showing affinity with Garo kinship terminology and divergence from Indo-Aryan kinship terminology is the term for sister's children (female speaking), which is the same term she uses for her own children.

As regards the stratification within the tribe we find that the Chapra section of Koch utilize the services of the Brahman priest and they consider themselves superior to other sections of Koch tribe. The Wanang section of Koch do not employ Brahman priest and they preserve a number of their own spirits. It is, therefore, that the Wanang Koch are considered to be most inferior. Thus the Koch draw a sharp line of division between their own sections and between themselves and neighbouring non-Hindus such as the 'beef-eating' Garo.

Let me now take up the case of the matrilineal Lalung tribe of whom very little is known to us. Author shall, therefore, start with a historical background of the people and their territory. The Lalungs, now-a-days, are mainly found in Assam but a section of these people live in Khasi and Jaintia Hills of Meghalaya. In Khasi and Jaintia Hills their census figures were recorded in 1891 and 1951 as 1505 and 298 respectively. The Lalung territory has a intermediate position between the patrilineal Kachari of the plains and the matrilineal Khasi of the hills. Grierson (1903): believed that the Lalungs are the autochthones of the Jaintia hills. Historical evidence of 'independent Lalung states' are not many. Dimorua, a Lalung state in the southwest of Nowgong was 'independent' till the 15th century. Later this and several other Lalung states were brought under the Ahom or the Jaintia Kingdoms. In 1835 the British marched to the Jaintia state and forced its king to surrender. In the same year the Lalung state of Gova was also annexed by the British. Local administration was, however, not taken over by the British and no revenue was demanded. Petty cases were allowed to be decided by the Lalung chiefs known as Dolois.

The Lalung clans, which are said to be descended from twelve sisters, to author, appear as based on a "segmentary system". A phratry-like unit, *mahari,* consisting of a number of individual clans, *Khul,* exists in the society, although Syamchaudhuri and Das (1973): have avoided the use of the term phratry. There are as many as thirty-one individual clans traced by these authors. One clan in each cluster is regarded as the dominant one. Formation of multi-clan *mahari* is effected in two ways the usual process is the splitting of a clan as it grew in size, and the other factor was the forcible induction and integration of new groups into a numerically dominant and powerful clan. We find that the number of clans in a cluster ranges from two to four. In Nambor village there are thirteen clans but only eight of them are grouped into four clusters. We are told that in this village there is no social hierarchy in the status of a clan of any cluster nor between the clusters themselves and thus we see that these authors contradict their own earlier statement about the undefined dominance of one clan in the *mahari* unit. In each *mahari* of Nambor village one clan is found to have descended from one of the twelve ancestresses, while the remaining clans are descended from a female sibling in the generation next to one original ancestress. The *mahari* solidarity is expressed in the belief that different clans in a *mahari* have descended from different female colaterals of the same womb.

The Garo also have a *Lalung-mahari* type unit but with a little difference. Even the same term *mahari* is used among the Garo. Several Gamo *maharis* constitute an unit called *machong* but structurally each *mahari* here is an unit within a *machong,* which is a wider territorial unit. Thus the descent and territorial principles are combined in Garo society through *machong* which refers to the *maharis* who live together in one territory.

In the past the Lalung tribe came into war-fare with a number of contending powers, namely, the Dimasa Kachari, Jaintia, Koch and the Ahom. It is quite possible that during these wars the original alliances of several clans had to be shifted leading to a change in the old formation. Unlike the Lalung the Khasi were less affected from alien intervention in the past. Probably due to these circumstances the Khasi did not require to form multi-clan units headed by a dominant clan, such as we observed among the Lalung. The territorial basis of the clans in Khasi society is thus better-defined. Comparatively the Garo *mahari* emerges as a more rigidly defined unit, both structurally and territorially. As all *maharis* share the same *machong* territory all kinsmen of a village live together. The Garo *mahari* which consists of kins of three generations, is, therefore, comparable to the smallest division of Lalung *mahari* and the *shi-ing* of the Khasis. Despite migrations to distant places, the Garo belonging to the same *machong* are regarded as close relations, though they may be living hundreds of miles away.

The economic system of the Lalung village is based on the interdependence between the households and the dormitory boys. When a Lalung marries he does not want to leave the economic environment with which he is familiar. As regards postmarital residence we see that among certain Lalung clans from which chiefs were selected the clan members did not leave the house of birth after marriage. Because of warfare in the past a large number of Lalung clans lost their integration and thus they were re-organised by some influential members of some old dominant clans. This group of dominant clansmen bring their wives to their own villages. There are thus enough evidences to show the inherent weakness of Lalung system.

An immediate or classificatory mother's brother, *borjela,* plays an important role in the marriage ceremony. When a man goes to live with his wife after marriage, it does not mean that he severs of all social relations with his parents. His first born child is accepted and recruited into his natal house. Of course this social obligation can be redeemed by performing a ritual called *Kushsinga.* In the same way when a woman takes her residence in the house of her husband, she is also required to sever her membership from the clan of her birth, by performing *Kushsinga.* If this ritual is delayed the woman's first-born child is taken by woman's parents to their house. This recruitment process is known as *jontana,* which means, one who has been pulled in. Thus we find that the Lalung do not necessarily loose a member by way of marriage and, on the other hand, by way of compensation through *jontana* they retain the particular matrilineal/patrilineal identity of a group. Moreover the position of *borjela* is interesting for our analysis. The *borjela* among Lalung is not a relationship term. It signifies a particular structural position of the first-born male of a family unit, which has descended from the original ancestress of a clan. In the context of consanguine relationship he is distinguished by the term *Khai* and in relationship with the children of his brothers and sisters he is *nomai.* Conversely, the siblings in the lower generations are *pagin* to him. The structural position of the *clan-borjela* is different from the *family-borjela.* The *clan-borjela* as the senior male colateral represents male lineality of matriclan. In the structuring of matrilineal consanguinity the Lalung stand between the Khasi and the Garo.

The Khasi and Lalung do not approve cross-cousin marriage, while the Garo prefer it. A Garo prefers his son marrying the daughter of his sister, who has inherited the property of the family of his birth. Thus among the Garo the idea of consanguine solidarity of the sibling born of the same womb is not present, but there is a certain kind of structural solidarity built upon the basis of a dual control over the immovable economic possessions between the siblings of the opposite sexes. Thus the difference in the extension of the degree of consanguinity through male element in these three societies also confirms the weaknesses of the systems.

A Garo always maintains a strong interest in the property of the family of his birth as his son marries his sister's daughter. Thus the male lineality is here supported by control of property also. This also presents a threat to matrilineal kin solidarity. Likewise, as we have earlier noted, the lineal emphasis of consanguinity in the male line is stronger in Lalung society than in the Khasi society. Perhaps due to this kind of in-built structuring that the Lalungs of the plains now show drastic change in the pattern of residence after marriage.

Matriliny: Myth or Reality

Let author now examines and tests the analytic utility of Gluckman's (1950) concept of 'Father Right'. Father Right as such is not necessarily associated with patrilineal descent. In Garo society, for example, authority within the co-resident extended family (*nok*) is vested in the senior husband in the group, the *Nokma.* It is he who exercises control over his wife's property and disposes of his daughters in marriage. A man has only marginal influence in the affairs of the households of his married sisters. The Garo thus seem to be a Father Right society. In the same way we observed that the Koch are also a Father Right society. Leach (1961) observes that Gluckman, who formulated the hypothesis of Father Right, in his argument presupposes that the descent structure of any particular society can be given a position on a continuous scale, the markers of which might read: Marked Father Right-Moderate Father Right—Bilateral (cognatic)––Moderate Matriliny—Extreme Matriliny. The general thesis seems to be that as we move along this scale from Marked Father Right towards Extreme Matriliny the probability of frequent and easy divorce increases, while the probability of quantitatively large bride-wealth payments decreases, the causal factor being the type of descent structure. Although author has not taken into consideration the subjects of divorce and bridewealth among these people, author's little and inadequate information on these people does support the contention of Leach. However, author believes that he has otherwise provided ample data to show the relative position of each of four matrilineal societies on the proposed scale from Father Right towards Extreme Matriliny. Divorce which is found to be rare among the Koch must have been a result of their shift to the patrilineal norms and behaviour. The Koch, in the above scale, thus belong to the position of the Marked Father Right and the Khasi belong to the position of the Extreme Matriliny.

Fortes (1969) accepts that in defining descent by contrast with filiation, rather than in abstract, externally descriptive terms or by reference to some intangible quality such as "lineality", we may define it by reference to a feature of internal structural differentiation and opposition that makes "unilineal descent" only a variety of the general category. He also stated that whereas filiation is the relation that exists between a person and his parents only, descent refers to a relation mediated by a parent between himself and an ancestor, defined as any genealogical predecessor of the grandparental or earlier generation. We may emphasize the importance of a "pedigree" as 'the charter of its' bearer's descent' for some social purposes, in particular societies, take a "unilineal form" but might elsewhere, or for other social purposes, be constructed by the social combination of mixed forms of filiation. Descent, in the context, serves as an actorcentred instrument for assignment of rights and status or for establishing interpersonal or intergroup connections, and can vary from actor to actor in a "group" constituted by other criteria (such as co-residence) as in the Hapu. The statement that an Ashanti lineage constitutes a "descent group" implies the precise information that these groups are made up of persons whose genealogical relations with one another are exclusively and exhaustively specifiable both by any member and by an informed outsider. The critical features of politico-jural alignment and a number of rights and duties can be deductively predicted for the actor. The lineage membership, in a system of unilineal descent groups, regulates only a part of person's nexus of statuses, defines only a selection of his rights, duties, and capacities and endangers only one sector of his total social identity. Yet we still find anthropologists who think of unilineal descent as a device for neatly sorting all the members of a society into discrete "groups". Thus misled, they are apt to fall into the trap of thinking of "cognatic groups" as sorted by contrast into "overlapping" compartments, difficult as it is to imagine such an arrangement. The fault lies again in the analytical ambiguity due to failure to distinguish internal structure from external context and to the fallacy of interpreting genealogically phrased relations as classifications of individuals, not as designations of status.

To be sure, in lineage based polities, lineage membership forms the indispensable foundation for a person's social existence; but there are components of personhood and areas of social action that are independent of lineage regulation. In these contexts of social relations and normative rules, there is ample scope for freedom of choice, as in patrilaterally ordered relations and activities among the matrilineal Ashanti, and in matrilateral and local contexts among patrilineal people like the Tallensi. There are even possibilities of choice within the limits of unilineal and other descent group constraints, as studies in the developmental cycle of domestic and family groups have shown. The principle involved is stated by Leach in these words: "In all viable systems there must be an area where the *individual is free to make choices so as to manipulate the system to his own advantage*".

We touch another undecided issue when we attribute the forms of kinship and descent institutions found in a particular society to the influence of exogenous parameters such as the ecological or the demorgraphic or the technological conditions and demands to which the society must adapt. However, new research among people with "bilateral" kinship systems has shown how doubtful is the validity of the above generalizations. I.M. Lewis' comparative analysis (1965) of six well-known patrilineal systems brings this out cogently. On reading the ethnographic works, both old and new, on the tribes of North-East India we find that it is not only the particular ecological conditions which are prerequisite for formation of large and successively segmented clans (and lineages) but other factors such as pre-existing cultural values and the political pressure of external groups also affected this process.

The people such as Khasi, Garo, Lalung etc., may think, act, and believe in terms of "dogmas" of matriliny, and that is what the ethnographers of these people have shown. What these ethnographers have not critically examined is the juristic dimension of corporateness. The juristic model is derived from Maine's as well as Weber's formulations. Whereas Weber's analysis is concerned with modern, capitalistic, and industrial forms of corporate organization as his primary data; Maine's analysis deals with institutions and norms that closely resemble those of contemporary tribal societies. There is also the functionalist model, which fits with Radcliffe-Brown's 1950 position. The fourth model is related to the property theory. Author understands that each model is relevant for the type of analysis we are making here. However, author shall discuss, in brief, relation of some models with his data. Distinguishing between unilineal systems with complementary descent groups and "full double descent systems" Goody takes the "division of property" as "the fundamental feature around which other differences... revolve" (1961).

Among several studies that bear directly on the property theory the most important is Good-enough's analysis of the Trukese lineage and property system (1951). The Trukese conceive of a property holding group as composed fundamentally of siblings (1951). In short, the corporation in Truk is an organized kin group of a martrilineage whose core and prototype is a group of own siblings. The corporate property of the lineage is administered by its most senior male member as its head.

Author thinks that the picture is not dissimilar to our Garo-Khasi-Lalung pattern. There are analogies, also, in the political level of the "district". The presence of "male heads" and its perpetuation explains the utility of the principle of "complementary filiation" in politico-jural context. We must see how for does it counterbalance the intrinsic separatism of the component descent groups. We must also see how far the matrilineages among these tribes as corporations are an important unit of politico-jural structure. Author personally believes that lineage or clan among people such as Garo, Khasi and Lalung is constituted by the perpetutation by matrilineal descent of the cross-sibling bond; and this is a politico-jural principle, not a function of property relations. The notion of a descent group as constituting "one person" takes many forms. The group is one by physical perpetutation and moral identity. Thus we discover that sibling group is commonly regarded as the nuclear, "one person" corporation. For siblings are both a plurality in themselves and by co-filiation an unity. Siblings are equal to one another in jural status and thus the sibling group is he perfect model.

Succession is of key importance in corporate group structure as well as in the continuity of corporation's sole in our case. In fact, it is the ambit of the authority, both politico-jural, vested in the office of the chief and priest (such as *Syiem* and *Lyngdoh* in Khasi system) that constitutes the boundary of their corporateness. The best evidence for this is the fact that in external relations with other units of the same kind, or with superior political authorities, citizens of these communities can only act in their capacity as citizens (not in private capacities) through their chief. But it is also important at the same time, particularly talking of Khasi or Lalung chiefs, to lay emphasis on the specification of the rights and duties and responsibilities, for behind each corporator in a corporate group these is still an individual, man or woman; behind the king or the priest there is still mortal man or woman bound by ties of relationship and loyalty of a personal kind that can at times conflict with the politico-jural and related statuses that pertain to him as a corporator in a particular aggregate, or as holder of an office. In the available ethnographic works on matrilineal tribes of this region no such contradictions are reported. This is because no ethnographer is concerned with distinguishing consistently between social relations and structural configurations, on the one side, and the innumerable and protean contexts of action, belief, and practice, as well as the natural environment, in which they become manifest.

Fortes (1969) has demonstrated that the social structure of every society has two basic and irreducible dimensions, or more concretely, that it comprises two basic orders of social relations, institutions, and norms. Familial domain and politico-jural domain, kinship and polity, moral order and legal order are alternative ways of designating this dichotomy of structural features, depending on which aspect one wishes to emphasize. The important point, however, is that these two orders of relations, institutions, and norms are, as author has tried to show, analytically distinguishable in every society, although they may be so fused together in the actualities of conduct and behaviour as to the superficially indistinguishable. Fortes has thus rightly stressed the complementary association of kinship and polity in social structure. He believes that the elementary components of patrifiliation, and matrifiliation, and hence of agnatic, enatic, and cognatic modes of reckoning kinship are, like genes in the individual organism, invariably present in all familial systems. The institutional patterns that emerge in Khasi, Garo and Lalung systems can be understood as resulting from or reflecting the balance of inter-dependence and integration, on the one hand, and of divergence and segreation, on the other, arrived at in the tasks assigned to each of these elements. Shifts of structural balance may be shown to be consistent with shifts in patterns of government or economic organization, or world-view and to fit the developmental cycle of the family. But as to what lies behind variations can only be understood by conducting prolonged and careful investigation.

Discussion on Patrilineal System

After having described the involvement of cognatic elements in some matrilineal societies as shall now take up the example of the patrilineal southern Angamis, who are also called as "Zounuo-Keyhonuo". During 1977 and 1982 this author studied the Zounuo-Keyhonuo people in Viswema village for a total period of six months. The brief discussion that follows is based on data collected from this village.

In Zounuo-Keyhonuo society the descent remains the most important principle of grouping in politico-jural matters as well as the source of rights and liabilities of the individuals. The analysis of the smallest social groupings such as the family units, within the wider descent groups, reveals their more important status and roles in the context of jural and political claims. Reliance on agnation as an organizing principle enables individuals and groups, and the titles they possess, to be systematically combined or divided at various structural levels with an almost mechanical ease and regularity.

The actors, or the individuals are thus within the purview of law of the lineage. Lineages are placed within the jural framework of clanship. While most disputes between the members of the same lineage are settled by the *sarra-pithi* (the lineage elder), disputes over property, etc., amongst the local hierarchy of social groups can frequently be settled without prolonged disruption of social relationships. Whenever two component units are in dispute the degree of their agnatic relationship automatically defines the superordinate group that should exercise its residual rights to the property in question by intervening to halt the quarrel. These patterns and consequences of a thorough-going employment of agnatic principles are of great functional value.

In Zounue-Keyhonuo society the elaboration of the descent group structures provides a scaffolding for organizing the relationships of territorially divided segments. A single genealogical chart encompasses the whole population of the 'tribe' and the villages are the products of a segmentary process going on over generations. Patrilineality receives recognition but then this is not mainly to defend the tribal interest based on a fixed territory. Although members distinguish in various ways between agnates and non-agnates and relate the distinction in some form or other to enduring social groups, descent groups are not necessarily everywhere organized patrilineally. Not only that cognates are permanently recruited to form "group-members", non-Zounuo-Keyhonuo, non-Naga persons could also be absorbed easily into social groups, without experiencing any economic disadvantage.

The fact that a woman inherits property shows that patrilineality is not the only organizing principle, and that only on the basis of the land ownership and utilization pattern that no strict classification could be offered. Although cognatic elements are inherent in patri-social groups of these Naga people but the 'complementary filiation' is not the only decisive factor, though, (agnatic) siblingship and (matri)-filiation serve equally to recruit the local groups. Different modes of inheritance and succession reveal very clearly the intrusion of jural regulation into the doman of family and kinship relations. These facts also reveal that the structural and functional status of women in politico-jural context is equally great.

The transfer of rights of a woman at the event of marriage is never absolute of permanent in true jural and economic sense among the Zounuo-Keyhonuo. Important aspects of her ritual, economic and jural rights remain permanently vested in her patrilineal group.

Although a woman is drawn closer and closer to her husband's lineage over time, she can never become a member of that lineage. Not only that she always retains definite property rights in her patrilineage and her natal home, at the annual clan festivals she also takes part along with her children as representative of her patrilineage.

The issue of married woman's jural rights and agnatic status may be discussed in the context of dissolution of elementary family through death and divorce.

The break-up of an elementary family through death or divorce has important consequences in relation to discent groups, for such an event may re-define the position of the offspring of the marriage in regard to those groups. If a woman dies, her unweaned child is taken by her mother or close uterine kinswoman, who looks after it until strong enough to return to the father's house. A widow may either continue to live in the husband's house or she may be allowed to re-marry preferably outside the husband's lineage without any ritual and bridewealth transactions. The death of a father in majority of cases results in a child being raised among other than agnatic kin; this death generally leads to a redefinition of lineage affiliation of the offspring. Such offsprings generally reside in the compound of their mother's agnates, where, by the time they become adults they are recruited permanently as "cognates"; such cognates acquire full jural status in their adopted matrilineage.

At divorce a woman returns to her father's home until she finds another husband. If she leaves her husband of her own accord all her 'gift-property' including land jurally become the property of her husband. In most such cases the children, particularly the grown-up ones, remain with the husband. Residence of such children in their father's compound is necessary to acquire the full jural status of a patrilineage member, which is a crucial aspect of the social structure.

The Zounuo-Keyhonuo Pattern of the Dual Inheritance

A woman's position in the total jural context of the society may be viewed by discussing the *pozuopu* and transaction. A *pozuopu* land is essentially a matrilineally inherited property which is transmitted only in the female line, i.e., from mother to daughter and daughter to grand-daughter, on their marriages. The case of Kezevinu, sister of this author's interpreter Shri Pukron, may be cited here. Kezevinu married in Zherima *thenu* (clan) of Viswema village. Her husband works in Kohima so she permanently stays in Kohima. When she left for Kohima she gave her *pozuopu* land (the terraced field) 'for use only' to Daniel (elder brother son). Daniel worked that land for sometime and then he gave it to Vizeho (Father Brother Son). Kezevinu could not sell her *pozuopu* land because that land is customarily to be given to Kezevinu's daughter at marriage, following the principle of matrilineal inheritance.

At marriage a woman not only brings her *pozuopu* land but also a lot of other articles such as cattle (cow and pig), ornaments, clothes and paddy. All these articles are called as *tenumishiephro. Pozuopu* land are not evenly distributed among the daughters, eldest daughter being entitled for a larger share of land. The daughters are generally also given a part of father's own (agnatically inherited) land. Such land is called as *tepumi-kitsa.* If a couple dies without a child and no child is adopted by them then the land inherited from paternal (agnatic) line goes back to the corporate patrilineage *Kayie* estate, and the *pozuopu* land goes back to the affinal kins (*omuni*). In such case the daughter may be asked to live in her parental house, even after her marriage. It is, therefore, we find that among the Zounuo-Keyhonuo a complex system of dual inheritance system prevails whereby women are palced in a highly advantageous position, particularly in terms of jural rights.

Recruitment of Cognates into the Agnatic Core

In Zounuo-Keyhonuo society the *matrifilisation* provides an alternative framework for recruitment of cognates with full economic and jural status. This dual patterns of filiation in Zounuo-Keyhonuo society gives rise to the bilateral extension of kinship ties, but, in fact, the two lines of unilineal descent are not recognized equally to very great extent. The Zounuo-Keyhonuo live at the point at which the inheritance follows the patrilineal and matrilineal principles and lines. But still unilineality is emphasized in male line only and ultimately it is between male agnates that the holder-heir situation falls. A man has only residual claims on the property of his mother's brother and ideally the relationship of the mother's brother and sister's on derives from the fact that the indiviuals concerned are the members of different property holding groups.

Thus from ego's point of view there are two aspects:

(*i*) his relationship with the members of his mother's descent group, and

(*ii*) his relationship with the offspring of his "sisters".

Ego's roles as sister's son (*otso*) or as mother's brother (*omuni)* are distinctly defined in Zounuo-Keyhonuo society. What is important to be noted is that these terms are widely applied to all lineage (*sarra*) members and indeed these are used without distinction of sex. While discussing these relationships it is necessary to do so in the context of the "descent" groups to which the individuals belong. Kinship relations are viewed by the people in terms of descent groups; the limits for the application of a particular kinship term are the boundaries of the descent group. The terms *otso* and *omuni* are thus lineage based terms applied both to the individuals as well as to the whole lineage or *sarra* groups.

To ego, the whole of his mohter's patrilineage emerges as his "mother's brother", generation differences being of less relevance outside the mother's natal homestead. In a *segmentary system* such as this, a true exogamous group has to be recognized (bride giving/ receiving group) to determine the jural status of individuals. This is particularly because the marriage involves not only the exchnage of the women but also transfer of the land. Significance of both the woman and land are sharply recognized in customary laws related to them. There are many lineages in Vishwema who have incorporated 'cognates'; such cognates now enjoy *total jural status* of a lineage member with claims on their mother's agnatic corporate *kayie estate*. Such rights as we stated earlier are granted by virtue of the residual claims which women possess on the property of their patrilineage.

Right from his early years through regular contacts, such as through his mother's visits to her natal home, a person knows fairly well most of the members of his mother's patrilineage. Mother's natal home remains an alternative home for him should be run into difficulties with his own agnates, or should his parents' marriage end by death or divorce. In the past warfare also caused complete death of whole lineages; one or two surviving individuals from such unfortunate lineages taking refuge in maternal descent groups.

The descent principle is thus invariably counter-balanced by the principle of complementary filiation. This is further revealed in the fact that a person's passage through life cannot be managed in customarily proper ways without the collaboration of his kinsfolk on both sides. This is indeed a strong binding force. We find that in every significant matter such as birth of a child, a marriage, a feast, or a death, patrikin and matrikin are both distinguished and equally involved. Mother's brother (own and classificatory) and even mother's, mother's brother, alongwith one's agnates, are co-responsible and have complimentary rights and duties in several jural and ritual contexts. At the occasion of feast giving ceremony (*Zhotho*), 'gifts' are received by a man from several groups of close kin of "patriline", "matriline" as well as his wife's "patriline".

Fortes had originally defined filiation as "the relationship created by the fact of being the legitimate child of one's parents" (1949). Originally Fortes contrasted filiation with descent in the context of a review of the theory of *unilineal* descent group structure. He was interested in the function of "complementary filiation" — that is to say, filiation with the parent who does not transmit membership of the unilineal descent group— "as the primary mechanism of segmentation within the group". Fortes defined descent as "fundamentally is jural concept . . . (representing) the connecting link between the external that is political and legal aspect of . . . unilineal descent groups, and the internal or domestic aspect". Thus viewed descent could be regarded as a principle and mechanism of social structure operative in the extra-familial domain of political and jural institutions, whereas filiation and complementary filiation could be regarded as the two components of a mechanism operative primarily within the familial and kinship domain. But at the same time, since cognates could be premanently recruited through 'matrifiliation' into the mother's lineage we find that the full jural capacity of a person could also be maintained without consideration of descent or descent group unilineality, particularly among this Naga group of people.

SOCIAL FORMATIONS IN NORTH-EASTERN FRONTIER REGION

The North-Eastern Frontier Region of India is said to be unique in many ways. Scholars have endeavoured to show its links to south-east Asian lands on the one hand, while on another, strenuous efforts have been made to prove that this region had been the part of India since mythical period. We propose to accept the region with its present specificity and structural generality within the process of the political economy of the present Indian political system in which professed state ideology of socialism and planned economy permit almost unrestrained expansion of capitalism. In this *note* we take the British period of over a century as a backdrop and try to identify the dominant trends of social formation evident in the lives of the communities in the region during the last four decades of the Indian Independence. We frankly acknowledge our lack of originality at the outset. The issues discussed elsewhere and on other forums are being examined within a view to meaningful academic dialogue. They are taken as indicative and not exhaustive. Though we may refer Assam time and again, our intention is to examine the social formations in the hill areas. We feel it will be advisable on our part to limit ourselves with the dominant trends rather than cases even from the hills. In the final analysis, we the academically alert and concerned citizens, may take stand on some of the disturbing trends threatening the professed pattern in our national life.

A serious analyst of the contemporary Indian social scene such as Srinivas stops his examination of Indian social transformation on the eastern border of West Bengal.[33] Perhaps historians, Raychaudhury and Habib, tried to rectify the wrong done in this North-Eastern region by putting the medieval history of Assam in the appendix of their celebrated anthology.[34] In fact, the geographers have been much fairer to this region. Spate identified it as one of the 34 regions of India with three-four Sub-regions.[35] In this recognition itself lies its diversities. One must hasten to add that besides the geomorphological consideration for regionalization, Spate and his colleagues also recognized the human factors, by that they meant technological base of human endeavour leading to various social formations.

In the aftermath of the sepoy mutiny of 1857, the British consciously felt the need to examine the nature of the Indian society. Alfred Lyall, an important colonical functionary, prevailed upon others to depict the Indian scenario as a confused conglomeration of caste and tribes, religions and sects, language and dialects, races and regions held together by the British imperial presence.[36] And that is how Dalton's *Ethnology of Bengal* and various volumes on caste and tribes were compiled. In their mercantile and strategic policy for the defence of the empire, it were the British strategies, who referred to the Indian mainstream (or *core*) against the distant frontier regions to be defended. On this distinctly colonical approach a series of books were written and published in course of time. In many ways, this trend still continues, which baffles an alert mind from the frontier region.

The historians inform us that there were various principalities before the Ahom could establish themselves in the Brahmaputra Valley. The way they organized their water-managed economy through an intricate system of *pyke* on the basis of *khel* and *mel*, was reminiscent of Wittfogel's *Oriental Despotism.*[37] Though the plains were ruled with a heavy hand, frontiers were secured through the payment of *posa* and institution of *Kakoti*. Many of these distant communities were loosely linked with the Ahom State and at times their services were requisitioned. There was a limited social intercourse, at times Ahom princes used to marry beyond their limits for political alliance. Though there was an economic hierarchy, Ahom Hinduism was largely free from social disabilities experienced in other Hindu kingdoms. At the cultural level, early Assamese was emerging as a lingua-franca for the entire region.

At the formal political level, there were three dominant models available in the region: (i) Hindu and Hinduized kingdoms such as Manipur, Ahoms, Jaintias etc., (ii) Buddhists like Chakma, Khamtis, Bhutanese etc. and (iii) tribal polities such as Khasi Syiemships.[38] Then there were a number of insipient state formations such as Mizos (Lushais), Angamis, Konyak and others. The basically subsistence hill economy generated an extremely limited surplus, which was too insufficient for the maintenance of a state structure. On the other hand, the region was on a difficult and agriculturally unsuitable locale, where possession of a plot of land was not preferred to an extensive topographical niche for hunting, grazing or transhumance. The basic character of a hill man is that of defiance and struggle against the natural obstacles and human intrigues.[39] Thus, if a surplus was not generated locally, it was considered imperative to a acquire such articles of necessity and luxury by force leading to raid, feud, invasion and even war.

After 1824-1826 Anglo-Burmese War, Lakhimpur district which touched all the sub-regional variations to a great extent, was considered an ideal location for colonization of the white settlers. As luck would have smiled on them, a stray and insignificant vegetation of the region—tea,, caught the imagination of the then technologically advanced British entrepreneurs. This resulted in an organized expansion of the plantation economy on an entirely technologically primitive base. The natural resources—land, forest, minerals, and wild life were considered inexhaustible. The key word was expansion—through adventure, intrigue, trade treaty and treachery. Among the *posa* articles, bottles of rum, opium, tobacco, were the items gifted to the hillmen.[40] Still the hillmen were referred as barbarians, savage, uncivilized, wildmen, headhunters and what not. In this way, while the valley land in the region was being transformed into one of the most progressive plantation economy in the world, the newly emerged formation was causing havoc to already stagnant indigenous economy.

In case one makes very broad generalization on the pre-British hill formations, the scenario presents relatively simpler contour. The hill communities possessed too extremely crude technology with their sparse population and abundance of natural vegetation, were engaged in hunting of the wild animals and collecting of the forest products of their subsistence. A secondary formation was taking shape in the form of family community based subsistence farming through slash and burn and less type of rotational cultivation (*jhuming*) often described as the 'Asiatic mode of production'. Ethnographers have described the economy in which there were no roles for the specialists. A few of them were engaged in barter trade in wild products for exchanging them with salt, threads, iron and other necessities. As their legends of migration indicate, hills witness incessant human movements leading to feuds, raids, repraisals and even wars. It appears by the middle of nineteenth century the entire hill tract was closely identified with various ethnic groups. Thus, there was hardly a patch of land in the region, which was 'no man's land'. However, the hills with their almost impregnable forests were no 'isolates'; in fact, there were trails across all the significant ranges.

It is a fact that the British did not directly administer the hill districts as they did in the case of the Brahmaputra valley. But an overall British control on the regional economy and inter-tribal relations led to the freezing of the tribal situation as if their natural process of growth was clipped off. A far reaching process was introduced in terms of capital and house taxes. Slowly and slowly, the entire hill region barring the upper ridges of Arunachal Pradesh was brought within the British capitalist economy. This was secured through introduction of cash economy. This was secured through introduction of cash economy, petty blue coat jobs, elementary education through the Christian churches and creation of administrative, market and urban centres.[41] What resulted in the process was the scenario in which subsistence farming tribes were exploitatively linked to the world metropolitan market in which they were reduced to suppliers of the raw materials and consumers of the industrial goods. To the extent that even the *Jhumias* were induced to cultivate some minor crops for cash transaction which were channelled through markets to the urban industrial centres. However, with the carving out of the scheduled districts in the hills the British appeared to be reluctant rulers to some of the naive tribesmen. Though even their paternalistic caring for the tribesmen did not stop inroads of the private commercial establishments, such as Rajasthani wholesalers, timber merchants etc., to the tribal areas.

With the Indian Independence, the tribesmen were induced to participative politics. The electoral politics created a situation in which tribals had to identify their representatives at various levels from the villages to the parliament. This resulted in an emergence of a new category of tribal elite, distinct from the traditional leadership, articulate enough to interact with the larger Indian community. Because of the constitutional safeguards to the tribal property and provision of investment for the planned development of the backward tribal areas, the newly emerged tribal elite in many areas began to appropriate the given resources as their private property. Provisions of bank loan to farmers for improved agriculture, horticulture, animal husbandry, cottage industries etc., have largely gone in the hands of these newly emerged power brokers. Studies have shown extensively how private ownership was introduced on the communal landholdings in various districts of the region resulting in absentee landlordism, sharecropping, landless agricultural labour. In this context, it may be pertinent for the concerned tribesmen to ask themselves whether the constitutionally guaranteed rights are adequate enough to stop these disturbing developments.

The traditional dominant mode of farming i.e. *Jhuming* is slowly giving way to settled agriculture in which various symptoms of agrarian relations found elsewhere are emerging. Collection of forest products and hunting the wild animals as a way of meeting the economic needs are no more viable, because of increased population and dwindling forests. Still forests are cut in such a way as if they are inexhaustive and timber is supplied to the saw mills. Invariably the timber depots and saw mills are owned by the non-tribal outsiders. The concerned tribals should ask themselves whether depletion of forest in connivance with the non-tribal timber merchants is not a denial of the traditional rights and privileges of the common tribal folk. Possibly there is a need for a grassroot movement of environmental awareness and preservation.

The tribal's genuine apprehensions against the non-tribals, lack of infrastructure and skilled manpower are some of the main reasons for the lack of industrial enterprise in the hill regions. However, industrial establishments are required for a healthy economic development of the region. With the reduced role of the primary sector of production and absence of the secondary sector, are the hill States willingly and knowingly not encouraging the service sector, which is non-productive and parasitic? What type of manpower planning do they vizualize in the years to come for their future ? Are they not deliberately short-sighted and over dependent on the federal exchequer for managing their administrative structure? Perhaps it is time for them to re-examine their priorities in the light of four decades of planned development and work out a future-oriented industrial policy for their people.

To sum up, the 150 years of tribal exposure to the capitalist *laissez-faire* economy presents a scenario in which a number of formations co-exist in the North-Eastern region. We have a well organized capitalist plantation economy on the one hand and extremely primitive subsistence hunting and collecting one on the other. In between there are various phases of agricultural practices, mercantile and industrial enterprises and a state controlled service sector. In case one looks at the region from the classical evolutionary vantage point, it provides various aspects for formations indicative of various stages of development. However, path of regional development provides enough evidence to the dominant role of the State—the British or the Indian Union in the lives of the people. It is a tribute to the State that the tribal structure continues to be viable and resilient enough inspite of all the demands on it. It appears that the basically community-oriented tribal leadership has no alternative, but to decide whether to strengthen the institutions and structures of age-old communal existence or go to an easy option of capitalist path of development.

Polyandry and Cicisbeism

For the successful functioning of social structure certain norms and values are adopted by all societies. Some of these values become the standard mark of a particular community. The institution of marriage has, among all societies, been the means to smooth social relations and social cohesion since early times. Different communities follow different ways for conducting their marriage system and relations. We come across monogamous union where one man marries one woman. Then there is polygamy which is reported in two forms. One is polygyny where one husband keeps more then one wife at a time. The other form is polyandry where a woman keeps more than one husband at a time. When the husbands are all brothers, it is termed as fraternal polyandry, and when they are not the brothers, the marital alliance is non-fraternal polyandrous. Polyandry has been reported among many tribes of India. In Himalayan range polyandry is reported among the Ladakhis, Jaunsaris, Kinnauris, Gallongs, Pailibos and Tangams. This interesting custom of polyandry is also reported among the Todas of Nilgiri hills. The focus, in this analysis, remains on the tribes of Arunachal Pradesh. Fraternal or adelphic polyandry marks the Gallongs and Pailibos and Arunachal Pradesh.

The institution of polyandry among the Gallongs could be prominently reported. Under the system the eldest brother gets formally married and the younger brothers have sanction for access to the same woman as wife. It is interesting to note that sometimes younger brother-in-law to wife enjoys right of sex upon her even if he is born after she is married to one of the brothers. The Gallong wife has to satisfy each husband of hers. She cannot show aversion to any particular brother. AT the same time the unmarried brothers are free to marry other woman. But again this wife will be shared by all the brothers. A wife is not the sole property of any single brother but is considered as common property of the family.

Among Pailibos too the fraternal polyandry is practised. Two or more brothers can share one wife and their children are born in the same house. The term *'Abo'* signifies the practice of adelphic or fraternal polyandry among Pailibos. According to Kumar (1979) they have to share one wife because of their poor economic condition. As such they are unable to pay the bride price for separate and many wives.

It may be mentioned that polyandry is not a general rule among these tribes, but is practised to some extent. Among other reasons in support of polyandry, the high bride-price is more prominent, especially in case of the Pailibos and Gallongs Due to exorbitant bride-price it becomes difficult to procure separate wives for all the sons or brothers, hence they share one wife. Though polyandry adds to the importance of woman as commodity, she equally exerts more influence upon her husbands especially the younger ones who dare not annoy her. The woman is pampered by all and consulted on all the household matters, big or trivial. She has her say in all matters relating to the children born of such wedlock. Children are recognised by the respective father as his own. All the husbands love the children equally. The relationship between wife and husbands is very cordial and affectionate. She is zealously looked after by all. Though the wife is supposed to work in the household and field, she is helped in her day-to-day chores by the menfolk.

Not exactly polyandry, but a practice closer to it is reported among the Hill Miris. A wife of one brother is under obligation to satisfy the sexual urge of the unmarried brothers of her husband till they get married. The woman is bound to obey this practice if, due to economic hardship, all the brothers are not in a position to procure separate wives. Under such a system the biological fatherhood has no importance as all the children born of such alliances belong to the social father. The actual husband cannot object to such extra-marital relations. The Hill Miris, thus, grant freedom for extra marital alliance to the woman. She can have sexual relations with the brother of her husband or any other man who stands in the same relation. A man who is from amongst the collaterals is, thus, privileged with sex access to the wife.

A wife in polyandrous union is looked after very well by all the husbands. This, at times, even goes to the extent of pampering as is noted among the Gallongs. Though a woman is dutibound to oblige each husband equally but it is her prerogative to attend, more or less, any one of them and she may have her reservations in this matter.

Among the Gallongs the marriage age of boys and girls is not fixed. A young girl can be married to a minor boy also. In such a case a wife is free to sleep with any of the grown-up brothers of her husband. As soon as her real husband comes of age she forsakes the previous relation. As the bride-price is very heavy the period between betrothal and marriage takes longer time. The boy to be married takes time to manage for the bride-price. Without paying the settled amount of bride-price the husband cannot take away his wife. The period between betrothal and marriage sometimes stretches unusually long because of the meagre economic resource. During this period the betrothed girl is free to have extra-marital relations to whom nobody, even her would-be-husband, can object. This type of freedom mostly ends up in adultery but it is sanctioned by the Gallong society.

Factors giving way to polyandrous unions may be many. For the Todas of Nilgiri hills the scarcity of women is one of the contributing factors to polyandrous marriages. Among Gallongs it is the heavy bride-price (many a times three to four Mithuns) which supports polyandrous alliance. In case of Ladakhis the ecological and economic factor, in collusion with social security, form the more important factors. Due to economic hardship and ecological requirement the Ladakhis have to take their flock of sheep and yak to far away pasture lands, and they may be away from home, continuously, for months together. In their absence a woman should not be neglected and be socially and economically secured. For this reason one of the brothers should be there to look after the woman. This requirement, as per the Ladakhis, is better met in the polyandrous setup.

Polyandry among tribal people is attributed to many factors such as economic, ecological and demographic. Among Wanchoos of Arunachal Pradesh polyandry is practiced as a means to check further fragmentation of the family land property, and to check the unwanted population which will increase if each son has a separate wife. The common practice, in case of Wanchoos, is that son, after marriage, settles his separate family and cultivates his own land. He builds his separate house and separates his land from the family of procreation. This way the family land keeps on fragmenting with each marriage in the family. To check this fragmentation an alternative could be adopted by the people of Longphong village. To keep the family land together, only the eldest son gets married and the land and family property remain in his name only. Other sons live in the same house with the elder brother and have access to his wife as their own. The children of such union belong to the eldest brother who is the social father to all the children. This arrangement has positive consequence to population control also which would, otherwise, be increasing if all the sons are having separate wives. For one wife they have to pay the bride-price only once, which is not very taxing on their already meagre economy. Polyandry, that way, is an adjustment with the hard economic conditions. On the other hand to do away with the surplus of unmarried females, polygyny is resorted to by the chiefs and the well-to do people of the Wanchoo community. Here we find a sort of social ambivalence and imbalance. On one hand meagre economy does not permit all the sons to get married and on the other hand polygyny is devised to adjust the unmarried daughters which is again economy resultant. This type of combination of polyandry and polygyny is one community is not the general rule but a rare case of adjustment to the tribal requirement and their socio-economic setup.

In polyandrous family a woman enjoys fairly higher status. She prevails in the arena of policy-making pertaining to various household matters including rearing of the children. But she has some handicaps due to the patriarchal social set-up. A woman in patrilineal society cannot inherit property as it goes to the males along. Among the Gallongs a woman is not entitled to inherit any property which is mostly bequeathed to the male members of the family. As the household set-up is patrilocal, a woman, after marriage, has to shift to her hushand's house and her clan is distinguished only at the time of marriages in the family. In polyandrous marital alliance a woman is married to one husband, and other husbands come to her automatically. But a woman head of family, clan or village is never heard of as headship or leadership is the prerogative of males only. Among Gallongs the women are segregated for certain reasons. The woman, even as a new bride, uses new ladder to enter the bride groom's house as she cannot use the entrance to the house meant for males. She has to use the back entrance throughout her life. Any neglect to this imposition will affect the hunting yield adversely. There will be no fishes in rivers, it is presumed, and the males have to come back without any game if women start using the male entrance. Among the Todas the women are said to be the most pampered but the females are debarred from touching any milk or milk products as it will pollute it and may not be worth consuming; yield will also become less. However, they enjoy considerable freedom in running the household chores.

In matters of social control also the woman is a sufferer among the polyandrous tribes. She cannot participate in *'Kebang'* (traditional Panchayat) among the Gallongs. She can be called for if she is involved in some case. But she cannot pass any judgement. She has to submit to the male judgement, as the leaders are all males, though she is given a careful hearing. The religious sphere too is mostly a male show. A woman cannot become a priest who offers sacrifice to the supreme deity. However, case of Ladakhis is rather notable in this respect. Among Ladakhis a woman is allowed to become *'Chomo'* (nun) and remain in *'Gompa'* (monastery), where the other monks stay, but she is inferior to a male monk. Though she is accorded more respect than the other females (married) in society but still she is inferior to male monks. Among the Gallongs a woman is not considered fit for offering sacrifice though the female puts the ritualistic rice paste on all the participants and the Mithun, which is to be sacrificed. As far as Todas are concerned the woman is treated polluted and is not allowed to participate in any ritual pertaining to much religious significance.

Thus, we find a woman taken as an economic asset, who toils hard in tribal economy and earns as much importance as to demand a very heavy birde-price, on one hand, but on the other she is treated not more than a chatel for the enjoyment of menfolk. We find heavy bride-price as one of the factors of polyandry. Women are very hard workers in fields and forests but their economic participation, too, does not add much to higher status. The higher status, enjoyed by the women in polyandrous union, is highlighted by her social security and in pampering her with lots of jewellery, of her choice, and clothes. But the other handicaps cannot be ignored which may be attributed to the patrilocal, patriarchal and patrilineal social set-up. The latter are so conspicuous in polyandrous set-up that they minimise the privileges enjoyed by the women otherwise. Though polyandry is a remarkable adjustment to the ecology, economy and social set-up it should be taken as a contributing factor to the enhancement of woman's social status. A woman should not end as an expensive commodity only but should be able to use the polyandrous set-up as one of the best means to achieve the status of woman at par, if not lighter than menfolk. The freedom in selection of mate by the womenfolk can be channelized to utilize the male chauvinism as the means to procure freedom and position in other fields also. Polyandry, however, does give tribal woman a comparatively better position in family.

In the event of fast-growing culture contact the customs of polyandry has received a set-back. Those who found this custom curious, and who assessed other cultures in the framework of their own cultural milieu, denounced it with derogatory sense. Such a trend has adversely reflected on the position of women in these far-flung communities. Because of unpalatable criticism of the custom of polyandry by the out-siders, the tribals are heading to an aim hurting to woman's better status. They were already denied a reasonable place in the arena of social control and religious structure, and the recent trends have started directing them to the same, as their better position in family, and the great deal of social security, are being eroded.

If we seriously intend to champion the cause of tribal development, we need to see their social-cultural matrix from within and adjust our efforts as per their requirement. In the name of progress, if we destroy the best elements and patterns of tribal culture, it would be an irreparable loss. This would ultimately reflect adversely on the happiness, genius and sentiments of tribal people. There is need to resolve, at operational level, that the tribals are not to be made second rate copies of non-tribals whosoever they are. They have to be helped to live a healthier, economically and socially speaking, life best suited to their local environments and social organisation. Let us preserve the best, not only as an ideology but as reality, among the tribals to meet the requisites of planned integration. In this direction the change agents, planners, anthropologists, social workers and other cultural specialists have to go a long way. If the opportunity is missed now, the best of the tribal value system would be lost for ever.

REFERENCES

1. Karve, Iravati, *Kinship Organization in India,* Poona, 1953, p. 5.
2. Desai, I.P., *Some Aspects of Family in Mahuwa: A Sociological Study Jointness in a Small Town,* Asia, Bombay, 1965.
3. Fifth, Raymond, *We the Tikopia,* 1957.
4. Kapadia, K.M., *Marriage and Family in India,* Oxford University Press, Bombay, 1966.
5. Hoselitz and Moore, *Industrilization and Society,* 1963, p. 136.
6. Goode, W.J., *The World Revolution and The Family Patterns,* Free Press of Glencoe, New York, 1963. p. 6.
7. Singh, Yogendra, *Modernization of Indian Traditions,* The quotation I.P. Desaid, 1973, p. 177.
8. Singh, Yogendra, *Modernization of Indian Traditions,* the quotation I.P. Desaid, 1973, p. 178.
9. Kolenda, P.M., (Ed.) Regional Differences in India Family Structure, Quoted by Yogendra Singh in *Modernization of Indian Traditions,* 1973, p. 179.

10. Ross, A.D., *Hindu Family in its Urban Setting,* Oxford University Press, Bombay, 1961.

11. Singh, Yogendra, *Modernization of Indian Traditions,* 1973.

12. Singh, Yogendra, *Modernization of Indian Traditions,* Quotation by I.P. Desai, 1973. p. 177.

13. Russell R.V. and R.B. Hiralal, *Tribes and Castes of Central Provinces of India,* Vol. IV. 1916, p. 192.

14. Reuter and Hart, *Introduction to Sociology,* McGraw Hill Book Co., New York, 2nd Ed., 9th impression, 1935, p. 143.

15. Elliott and Merrill, *Social Organization,* (4th Edition), Harper and Row Publisher, London, 1950.

16. Fürer Haimendorf, Christoph Von, *The Gonds of Andhra Pradesh,* Vikas Publication House, Bombay, 1979, pp. 180-84.

17. *Ibid.,* p. 80.

18. Buradkar, M.P. *Social Organization of Gonds,* unpublished Ph. D. Thesis. Nagpur University, Nagpur.

19. Ferreira, John V. *Totemism in India.* Oxford University Press. 1965. p. 144.

20. There are other branches of the same clans, with the same *gotra* or clan names in the Punjab, Madhya Pradesh and other parts of Uttar Pradesh. These branches do not come under the jurisdiction of the *khap* councils of Meerut Division, but marriage between them is prohibited.

21. This is different from some other societies where the youngest son is most favoured by the father. Among the Jats, the youngest son is the favourite of the mother rather than of the father.

22. The numerical strength of a *thok* ranges from 800 to 1,200 persons.

23. Lewis also reports the influence of the Arya Samaj in his Jat village near Delhi (1958), pp. 72-5.

24. Neither is the presence or worship of a clan god or goddess among the Jats reported by Oscar Lewis (1958) or McKim Marriott (1955), or by any earlier writer.

25. Among the Ashanti, 'it is only within the lineage that amity and solidarity are binding in virtue of absolute sanctions, and the inevitable inter-personal hostilities and jealousies thus aroused are expressed in the belief about witchcraft'. As among the Jats, witchcraft among the

Ashanti operates only within the lineage; though accusations of witchcraft are not so common among the Jats as among the Ashanti. Cf. Fortes (1950), third impression (1956), pp. 258-75.

26. For example, the ceremony of thanks giving (*badhai*), in which persons of all *thoks* present and accept money and sweets at the opening of a well. Another customs is rising the house of the husband of the 'daughter of the village' if one happens to be in his village, and presenting a rupee to the father or head of the family of the daughter's husband. This is done even for the daughters of the *kamin* castes, including the untouchables, when the head of the family is called and a rupee is given to him.

27. The Jatsalso take wives from other castes; in some cases they may buy a woman and her caste or clan may not be known. But such cases are rare among the younger generation.

28. Founder of the *thok* Pacchuwara (Shoron village), and the first *khap* wazir to be recognized by the emperor Akbar.

29. After Gulab Singh's death his younger brother Saiiram became the *khap* wazir, as Gulab Singh's son Surajmal was a minor at the time of his father's death.

30. A *thamba* is a political unit of the *khap.* It is a council of a group of villages, based on kinship and territorial proximity.

31. For the customs of female infanticide and buying women from other castes, see Crooke (1896), p. 29.

32. The children of 4 of these marriages received only a subsistence share of the stepfather's property; the children of the remaining marriage got full shares of the property.

33. Srinivas, M.N. 1977, *Social Change in Modern India,* (Second edition). Delhi: Orient Longman.

34. Reychaudhury, T. and I. Habib, (*ed*), 1982., *The Cambridge History of India.* Volume I. Delhi: Orient Longman.

35. Spate, O.H., et al., 1967, *India Pakistan and Ceylon: The Regions.* London: Methuen & Co.

36. Owen, R., 1973, Imperial policy and theories of social change: Sir Alfred Lyall in India. In *Anthropology and Colonical Encounter.* Edited by T. Asad, London: Ithaca Press.

37. Wittfogel, K.A., 1962, *Oriental Despotism* New Haven: Yale University Press.

38. Sinha, S.C. (*ed*) 1987 *Tribal Polities and State Systems in Eastern and North-Eastern India.* Calcutta: K.P. Bagchi.

39. Lattimore, O., 1962, *Studies on frontier History, Collected Papers 1928—1958*. Paris: Mouton Publishers.

40. Sinha, A.C., 1986, Social Frame of Forest History, *Social Science Probings.* 3, 2.

41. Aeir, L.T., 1986, *Contemporary Naga Social Formations and Ethnic Identity: A Case of Development or Decay* (unpublished Ph. D. Thesis) Shillong: North-Eastern Hill University.

FOUR

Plans, Policies and Development

Socio-economic Condition Amongst Tribes

SINCE Independence much endeavour has been made to focus on the problem of the Scheduled Castes and Tribes of the country. Some practical suggestions have been put forward for the eradication of different problems of these communities. Theoretical ideas have also emerged in this constructive process. But we all agree that the stumbling block which stands as a barrier to the desired social change has not yet been removed from the path of progress. Reasons may be many. And the administrators, social scientists and welfare workers have strived hard. At this juncture it has become our prime duty to review the balance-sheet of performance and formulate and prescribe ways to reach the expected goal.

The problems of the Scheduled Tribes thought uniform to certain extent throughout India have their own characteristics in different parts of the country due to varied ecological and demographic situations and historical traditions. In the case of the Scheduled Castes they almost follow a uniform pattern throughout the area of their dominance.

The eastern and north-eastern region of India also reveals the role of the said story in general. But here the problems and prospects of development widely differ from area to area due to the uniqueness of its colourful environmental set-up, ethnic background and psychological make-up of the people.

Keeping all this in view this section has been designed to focus on the following points:

(a) Socio-economic situation of the Scheduled Castes and Schedule Tribes of the area with particular reference to the development activities undertaken for bringing them on a par with the general mass.

(b) Prevailing gaps, problems and prospects in the developmental process and the emerging situation which calls for integrated approach from the social scientists in general and anthropologist in particular and also administrators, social workers, etc., for tackling the situation in the right perspective.

Out of 22 States and nine Union Territories the following nine States and two Union Territories form the Eastern and North-Eastern Region in general and have been taken into consideration for the purpose of the paper: States—Assam, Bihar, Manipur, Maghalaya, Nagaland, Orissa, Sikkim, Tripura, and West Bengal; Union Territories—Arunachal Pradesh and Mizoram.

Of the total population of India (54,79,49809) the eastern region shares 26 per cent (14,24,01,934). Further, the Scheduled Castes (2,12,13,137 persons—14.90 per cent) and the Scheduled Tribes (1,68,83,870 persons—11.86 per cent) jointly contribute 26.76 per cent of the total population of the eastern region. This indicates a significant impact of the Scheduled Caste and Scheduled Tribe population on the socio-cultural and economic life of the eastern region of India. Therefore the problems and prospects concerning the development of the people cannot be overlooked. Table 4.1 will give an idea of the Scheduled Caste and Scheduled Tribe population of different States and Union Territories in this part of the country.

Of the total Scheduled Tribe population of India 44.41 per cent are found in this region. The Scheduled Castes Constitute 26.52 per cent of the total Scheduled Caste population of India.

The population strength of the Scheduled Caste and Scheduled Tribe characteristically appear with more than 25 per cent jointly in most of the States and Union Territories of this region. Thus, in the Union Territories of Arunachal Pradesh and Mizoram these combined percentages of the Scheduled Castes and Scheduled Tribes are 79.09 per cent and 94.26 per cent respectively where the Scheduled Tribes constitute the major bulk of the population. This high population strength is also found in Orissa (38.20), Tripura (41.34), West Bengal (25.62), Bihar (22.86), Manipur (32,71), Meghalaya (80.86) and Nagaland (88.61). In Arunachal Pradesh, Meghalaya, Mizoram and Nagaland the tribal population represents an overwhelming majority whereas is the States of Orissa, Tripura, West Bengal, Bihar and Manipur the dominance of the Scheduled Caste population is well marked. This demographic situation in this region has its decisive role in shaping the socio-political and economic institutions. Despite this demographic situation there have been several lacunae in the formation of a satisfactory progress plan for this Scheduled Tribe and Scheduled Caste population and the desired goal of social and economic equality remains still far away. This discouraging feature happens to be an effect of disproportionate participation of this population in all spheres of developmental activities.

This region may be classified into three broad divisions: (i) comprising Orissa, Bihar and West Bengal (also the coastal region of West Bengal and Orissa; (ii) Plains of Tripura, Manipur and Assam; and (iii) Darjeeling district of West Bengal, Hill district of Assam, the hilly tracts of Manipur and Tripura, Arunachal Pradesh, Nagaland, Mizoram and Meghalaya.

In the first division agriculture is the main resource. Collieries are found in the eastern plains of West Bengal, extending to eastern and south-eastern Bihar and part of Orissa. Mining and quarrying are also found in this zone. Forest is another major resource. Fishing also plays an important role in the coastal region of Orissa and West Bengal.

Agriculture also forms a major source of livelihood in the second division. Side by side forests and tea gardens are found. Mining and quarrying play an important part in Assam.

In the third division, hilly tracts of north-eastern region, forestry and tea garden are the major sources of economy. Orchards also play a significant role. Minerals and such other natural resources are found in Darjeeling, Meghalaya, Mikir and Garo Hills and Manipur. Chinas clay, copper, dolomite, limestone, sillimanite, soapstone, coal, etc. are important minerals and other natural resources.

More than 150 tribal communities ranging from large (Santal, Oraon, Munda, Bhumij, Bondo, Juang, Khond, Nagas, Garo, Mach, Kuki, Ho, Savar, etc.) to small (Kora, Lodha, Kheria, Birhor, Chakma, Hojong, Mru, Abor, Mishmi Binjhia, Mahali, Chik-Baraik, Bedia, Asur, etc.) are found in this region. Some live in specific areas (Lepcha, Bhutia, Sherdukpen, Riang, etc.) and some large communities (Santal, Oraon, Munda, different branches of Naga, Kuki, Mech, Dimasa, etc.) are distributed in a number of states. They migrated from the place of their origin in search of livelihood. Some were taken to different industrial and plantation areas to work as labourers.

It has already been mentioned that the Scheduled Castes are mainly distributed in the States of Bihar, Orissa and West Bengal and to some extent in Tripura and Assam. As in the case of the Scheduled Tribes more than 150 Scheduled Caste communities are also found in this region. Some of these communities are large (Chamar or Much, Dom or Dhangad, Namasudra, Poundra, Rajbanshi, Bauri, Bagdi, Jhalo-Malo, Dhobi, etc.) and some are numerically less dominant communities. Most of the large communities are quite common to all of the aforesaid States.

It is expected that all these communities along with non-scheduled communities are utilising the resources of the region for their socio-economic betterment. If it be not so, the seminar may try to trace out gaps existing in the different spheres of economic activities. How far the small communities have been able to adjust themselves with the local condition may also be examined.

Inter-ethnic relationship pattern amongst the different groups of settlers and different classes of people may also be found in the context of resource utilization. Nature of conflict and extent of cooperation may be highlighted.

Traditionally, tribal communities of India, particularly those residing in Eastern India, had their own way of imparting training through bachelors' and maidens' dormitory system for carrying on the socio-cultural and economic activities in a cooperative manner. With the gradual spread of British Administration in India many of these traditional institutions became ineffective due to introduction of formal education. In addition, non-appreciation of the activities of these dormitories by the outsiders rendered these institutions totally disorganized and defunct.

The British Administration, in general, did not take much interest in introducing formal education in the tribal belts in a planned way. However, Christian missionaries backed by the British Administration did a tremendous job of spreading education in certain tribal pockets. But this spread of education was not uniform. Activities of these missionaries were selective in nature, as a result of which certain areas of the north-eastern region—Sundergarh of Orissa, Darjeeling of West Bengal, Chotanagpur area of Bihar, etc. were better exposed to many such educational programmes of modern type. The discriminating effect of such educational programmes was felt over a wide area. This left a vast majority of the tribals of this region into darkness of illiteracy.

After Independence, however, Government efforts have been gradually expanded to impart education uniformly among the tribals in all areas. In the successive plan periods investment for educational programmes among the tribals has been increased. Right from the First Plan period emphasis was given to the educational programme and, accordingly, large sums of money have been spent for different schemes like grant of free studentship, scholarships, free hostel facilities, midday meal, stipends for technical education, etc. Setting up of Ashram schools for boys and girls was one of these ventures. All these efforts notwithstanding inter-area and intra-area differences as well as differences at inter- and intra-community level are still observed in respect of the educational and literacy attainment.

It has been marked that the degree of literacy among the tribals (Lepcha, Bhotia, Nagas, Khasi, Garo, Mizo, Mech) of the north-east hilly zone in North-Eastern India is relatively high compared to the tribal communities of other zones.

As in the case of the Scheduled Tribes, similar trend is also noticed among the Scheduled Caste population. In West Bengal, Scheduled Caste communities can be differentiated on the basis of attainment of literacy among them. There are certain communities who progressed well in this regard; mention may be made about the Namasudra, Jalia-Kaibarta, Poundra, Sunri, etc. The same trend is also observed in other States.

In the light of the above observation it has become urgently necessary to probe into the causes of such differences in literacy attainment amongst different communities. Answer to such probing may perhaps be obtained from the racial differences and historical tradition of the population concerned. We may also try to find out whether there exists any relation between educational progress and ecological setup. Size of the respective population may also have a significant role in this differential attainment. It is also to be examined how far economy attributes to educational progress.

The main objective of the developmental programmes is to bring economic justice to all sectors of population. Despite planned programmes aimed at for the overall upliftment of the Scheduled Castes and Scheduled Tribes, the achievement so far recorded by these two sectors of population in the field of economy is rather poor.

If we want to understand their present wretched condition we should look back to the historical past and follow up the sequential incidents. This will unfold a long story of disorganization, deprivation and frustration. In case of the tribals we know that they had a self-sufficient economy, which provided them adequate livelihood. They were hunters, gatherers, collectors and fishermen and their resources were quite plentiful in the forest. But right from the British period different rules and regulations have been imposed in different forest areas, and the gradual abridgement of the rights of the tribals has had its adverse effect on their economy.

Most of the tribals had their own land, from which bulk of their population got economic support. With the gradual change in the Land Laws and Regulation, with the introduction of the zamindari system during British era, the tribals were dispossessed of their own land.

Further, wide establishment of industrial units uprooted a multitude of this population from their own land and forced them to life a live of uncertain economy.

Fate of the Scheduled Castes was also the same as that of the tribes. Particularly, dispossessed of their land they were similarly subjected to that old system of deprivation and oppression.

Because of thc unique position of the Scheduled Castes in the Hindu hierarchical system, they were also subjected to many stresses and strains through generations. Many of them had traditional caste-based occupations (cobblery, fishing, basketry, scavenging, etc.) and were conditioned to a fixed position which compelled them to remain static without any scope for mobility. The restricted economic scope pushed them into poverty and subjected them to the suffering of various social stigmas.

All this has been given due consideration in the post-Independence era and many plans and programmes for the overall improvement in the social-economic conditions of the Scheduled Castes and Tribes have been drawn up. Much concerted effort has been made in the country's overall planning to integrate them socially, economically and emotionally with the general Indian mass as quickly as possible.

In the initial Plan periods educational programmes were given more importance than economic on the presumption that with the spread of education these people will be able to establish themselves in the economic sphere and regain their lost status.

It was also realized that unless the Scheduled Tribes and Castes were provided with adequate land it would not be possible and practicable to translate various developmental measures quite meaningfully. Therefore, a number of legislative and administrative measures were adopted, amongst which mention may be made of the Land Revenue Laws of the States which imposed restrictions on the transfer of tribal land to non-tribals; Land Reform Legislation (particularly Tenancy Legislation and the Ceiling Law) provided for distribution of land to the landless giving preference to the Scheduled Castes and Scheduled Tribes most of whom belong to the landless class; to arrest indebtedness remedial measures were taken to scale down their past debts. To fight against the money-lenders in rural areas and to safeguard these people from Indian Shylocks, co-operative ventures were taken up. *Graingolas* were set up with the same intention. The Debt Redemption Act is the latest measure. But the truly courageous measure adopted was to abolish the inhuman system of bounded labour from the country. This measure primarily helped to emancipate the poor peasantry most of which belongs to the Scheduled Tribes and Castes.

Realizing the importance of economic dependence of the tribals on forests some concessional measures were adopted to safeguard the right of the people. With this aim the tribals were granted the rights to take timber for their domestic use, to collect minor forest products, graze cattle and cultivate unused forest land. Labour cooperative Societies were set up to protect the tribals from the exploitation of the contractors.

The Minimum Wages Act was passed to ensure economic justice to the Scheduled Caste and Tribe labourers. Reservation of jobs was provided to give adequate representation to them in the sphere of employment. The Untouchability (Offences) Act was intended to eradicate the discrimination the Scheduled Castes suffered due to pursuance of their traditional occupations. The spirit behind the Act was to make these down-trodden people conscious of their rights and privileges so that they may throw of the several social stigmas which were embedded in their caste-based occupations, and there by help them to take up other diversified occupational activities. With the diversification of occupations the chances of economic and social mobility were expected to be intensified.

To restrict the drain on the merge income of the tribals, the excise and prohibition policies of the State Governments were accepted.

All the aforesaid measures, enactments, rules and regulations are the outcome of the good intentions of the country after independence to uplift the Scheduled Castes and Tribes. It is a testimony of the courageous steps to rejuvinate a spirit of self-reliance in every sphere of their socio-economic activities. However, even though progress during the post-independence period has been impressive, several economic misdeeds perpetrated for ages could not be fully eradicated. There still remain, gaps between the target and the achievement, people still suffer from various economic disabilities, and most of them are still below the poverty line.

This invites fresh thinking on the economic planning to bring about quicker transformation in every sphere of the socio-economic life of the people. This requires a greater emphasis on agricultural inputs on minor irrigation, on animal husbandry, on horticulture, on cottage industries, etc.

With this view a new strategy of development for the tribals was adopted in the fifth Five Year Plan. A sub-Plan for the tribal areas was drawn up. The underlying idea was to have an Integrated Development Plan. It was felt necessary to bring about coordination in the different departments and ensure a rational inflow of funds from each sector to the tribal areas. The aim was to build up an infrastructure which may serve as the basis for the superstructure during the successive Plans. During the Fifth Five Year Plan a modest attempt has been made to set up large-sized multipurpose cooperative societies in selected I.T.D.P. areas. But the target could not be achieved due to several constraints. To overcome these, an approach has been formulated by the Government of India in the Sixth Five Years Plan.

The strategy adopted for the tribal development in the Fifth Plan covers about 65 per cent of the total tribal population in India. Thus, rest of the tribal population will remain unaffected. Therefore the Sixth Plan is to include the entire tribal population whether living within the I.T.D.P. areas or outside and to cover the areas by suitable developmental programmes. Different programmes are to be drawn up according to the needs and problems of the tribal communities in terms of the following categories: (a) Areas of tribal concentration, (b) Dispersed tribals in other areas and (c) Primitive tribal communities.

As in the case of literacy and educational achievement there remains a wide gap in the economic spheres of different areas and communities in different parts of the Eastern Indian region. Local resources were not properly utilized for uniform progress of these communities. Due to very low educational achievements amongst most of the Scheduled Caste and Scheduled Tribe communities "diversification of occupation" could not take place. Upward occupational mobility was achieved only by those few who could avail themselves of educational facilities. The limited economic development which has been achieved so far is further marked with disproportionate sharing of the benefits by Scheduled Castes and Tribes. Table 6 gives an idea about the workers of the Scheduled Castes and Tribes engaged in different occupations in different States and Union Territories of Eastern and North-eastern India.

It has been observed that those who are educationally advanced are also economically better off. The aggregate effect of individual performance has contributed to raise a community to a level higher than reached by others. It is now to be probed as to whether the differential performance of few persons belonging to a particular community in the field of economy and education has any relevance to historical tradition, leadership pattern, racial make-up, revivalism/puritanic movement, character structure, etc.

It is to be examined for the purpose of better utilization of resources, whether it would be possible to divide each State of the Eastern Region into different zones according to availability of resources, i.e. agriculture, forest industry, mining, plantation, etc. Simultaneously, communities living in the resource zones are to be identified with their occupational skills. Their capabilities and readiness to participate in those particular economic activities of those areas should be examined. The existing deficiencies are to be sorted out for making up the gap giving them useful education and training. This means education should be need-based and meaningful instead of stereotype, which is the existing trend.

Needs, aspirations and problems of the Scheduled Castes are quite different from those of the Scheduled Tribes. Development strategies are therefore to be adopted accordingly for tackling their problems by taking into consideration the uniqueness in the ecological, demographic, socio-economic and psychological characteristics of the population concerned.

Adequate attention has not been given to the formulation of plan programmes and a suitable implementation machinery has not yet come into existence for the development of the Scheduled Castes in accordance with their characteristic features. Also there is need for creating an independent machinery for the Scheduled Castes and Scheduled Tribes separately as was very rightly emphasized by Prof. L.P. Vidyarthi as Chairman of the Task Force on the Development of Tribal Areas and Member of the Steering Group on the Backward Classes during the formulation of the Fifth Five Year Plan.

It is a well-known fact that the tribal folk of India had an integrated well-balanced social system and functioning and used to lead a corporate life during the pre-independence era. But under the British Administration their corporate life received severe blow. With the direct and indirect support from the Administration the Mahajans, money-lenders, businessmen, zamindars, etc., started exploiting the people. This resulted in the breakdown of their socio-economic system and gave birth to tremendous racial hatred amongst them, culminating in flare-ups here and there. Instead of receiving sympathetic support and protection from the Administration they were subjected to further oppression and exploitation. This led to revolts in different tribal areas among different tribal groups at different times for restoration of their rights over land and resources. Important among these are the Santal Insurrection, Kol Insurrection, Chuar revolt, Birsa Movement, Tana Bhagat Movement, Hajang Peasant Movement, Naga and Mizo Movements, etc. These organized movements on the part of the tribal folk compelled the British Administration to keep these people and their territory partially secluded and undisturbed as far as possible. Thus the tribal folk were kept segregated from the main stream of Indian life and culture. The administrators thereby were very successful in creating a psychological barrier amongst the different sectors of its population.

After Independence the National Government made adequate provisions in the Constitution for the weaker sections of the population. According to the Directive Principles, all sorts of development programmes were executed for bringing this portion of the population and their area on a par with the rest of the country. However, despite all these efforts, integration of the tribal communities with the rest of the Indian mass could not be achieved. Some marked dissatisfaction in some tribal pockets is visible. Some of them are also in search of an identity.

This all indicates a shortcoming in the official approach.

It is quite known to the tribologists that most of the tribal societies had a socialist outlook and believed in community sharing. Institutions were also designed to meet cooperative ventures in every walk of their life and activities. India is also committed to Socialism. And because of the socialist characteristic of the tribal society it would have been quite easy to bring them under the democratic and socialistic fold. But the tribal brethren are still far away from the social mainstream.

TABLE 4.1

Distribution of Scheduled Caste and Scheduled Tribe Population in Eastern India

Sl. No.	Name of the State/Union Territories	Total Population		Scheduled Tribe Population			Scheduled Caste Population		
		No.	P.C	No.	P.C. to total S.T. Population of India.	P.C. total Population of State/Union Territories	No.	P. C. to total S.C. Population of India.	P. C. to total Population of State/ Union Territories
1	2	3	4	5	6	7	8	9	10
A.	*Union Territories*								
1.	Arunachal Pradesh	4,67,511	0.09	3,60,408	0.97	79.02	339	0.0004	0.07
2.	Mizoram	3,32,390	0.06	3,13,299	1.00	94.26	—	—	—
B.	*States*								
1.	Assam	1,46,25,152	2.67	16,06,648	4.05	10.99	9,12,639	1.14	6.10
2.	Bihar	5,63,53,369	10.28	49,32,767	12.98	8.75	79,50,652	9.94	14.11
3.	Manipur	10,72,753	0.20	3,34,466	0.88	31.18	16,376	0.02	1.53
4.	Meghalaya	10,11,699	0.18	8,14,230	2.14	80.48	3,887	0.005	0.38
5.	Nagaland	5,16,449	0.10	4,57,602	1.20	88.61	—	—	—
6.	Orissa	2,19,44,615	4.00	50,71,937	13.34	23.11	33,10,854	4.14	15.00
7.	Sikkim	2,09,843	0.04	—	—	—	9,502	—	—
8.	Tripura	15,56,342	0.28	4,50,544	1.19	28.95	1,92,860	0.24	12.39
9.	West Bengal	4,43,12,001	8.09	25,32,969	6.66	5.72	88,16,028	11.02	19.90
	Total	14,24,01,934	25.99	1,68,83,870	44.41	11.86	2,12,13,137	26.52	14.90
	Total (India)	54,79,49,809	—	3,80,15,162	—	6.94	7,99,95,896	—	14.60

TABLE 4.2

Distribution of Scheduled Caste Workers by their Occupations (Eastern and North-Eastern India)

Sl. No.	Name of the State/Union Territories	Total workers	Cultivators	Argicultural Labourers	Live-Stock Forestry Fishing	Mining and quarrying	Household Industry	Other than Household Industry	Construction	Trade & Commerce	Transport Storage & Communication	Other Services
1	2	3	4	5	6	7	8	9	10	11	12	13
A.	*States*											
1.	Assam	2,57,191	53.52	13.50	6.97	0.15	3.88	3.47	1.03	6.71	2.45	8.31
2.	Bihar	30,85,334	11.44	77.17	0.77	1.83	2.16	1.31	0.27	0.75	1.04	3.25
3.	Manipur	4,328	47.81	10.73	0.55	—	1.48	2.49	0.37	1.51	1.10	13.95
4.	Meghalaya	1,403	11.19	8.98	10.26	—	6.06	7.48	1.57	17.96	0.29	36.95
5.	Orissa	11,10,632	27.45	49.21	2.50	0.71	5.36	1.53	0.54	1.62	1.57	9.55
6.	Sikkim	4,802	68.07	6.28	0.31	0.12	3.33	8.07	1.43	1.19	2.99	8.19
7.	Tripura	54,154	47.72	30.24	4.55	—	1.53	1.96	0.65	4.07	1.80	7.48
8.	West Bengal	25,35,632	33.40	42.57	3.63	1.39	2.11	4.89	0.52	2.53	1.97	6.97
B.	*Union* Territories											
1.	Arunachal Pradesh	100.	17.10	30.00	—	—	—	—	—	—	—	53.00
2.	Mizoram	62	—	—	—	—	—	—	—	—	—	100.00

TABLE 4.3

Distribution of Scheduled Tribe Workers by their Occupations
(Eastern and North-Eastern India)

Sl. No.	*Name of the State/Union Territories*	*Cultivators*	*Argicultural Labourers*	*Live-Stock Forestry Hunting*	*Mining and quarrying*	*Household Industry*	*Other than Household Industry*	*Construction*	*Trade & Commeerce*	*Transport Storage & Communication*	*Other Services*
1	2	3	4	5	6	7	8	9	10	11	12
A.	*States*										
1.	Assam	83.31	7.13	0.60	0.02	0.53	0.27	0.24	0.61	0.50	4.79
2.	Bihar	61.90	28.10	1.14	1.49	0.68	1.81	0.46	0.22	0.84	2.61
3.	Manipur	89.60	0.35	0.11	ng.	0.68	0.10	0.33	0.41	0.19	8.23
4.	Meghalaya	78.40	9.60	2.51	0.15	0.65	0.72	0.66	1.47	0.65	5.19
5.	Nagaland	89.56	0.98	0.24		0.07	0.21	0.55	0.28	0.32	7.79
6.	Orissa	52.38	36.72	1.87	1.32	1.18	1.22	0.24	0.58	0.67	3.82
7.	Tripura	75.37	20.14	1.23		0.12	0.28	0.03	0.18	0.15	2.49
8.	West Bengal	31.18	48.95	10.88	1.11	1.01	1.59	0.31	0.71	0.82	3.44
B.	*Union Territories*										
1.	Arunachal Pradesh	94.79	1.49	0.15	ng.	0.10	0.03	0.04	0.27		3.13
2.	Mizoram	92.06	0.36	0.22	ng.	0.33	0.17	0.59	0.92	0.53	4.82

This all indicates a fresh approach. Examinations may be made about the relation between the socio-economic development and political consciousness. Size of population and political dominance, historical tradition and cultural heritage may have adequate influence on the socio-political situation of the present day.

A number of revivalistic/puritanistic movements were found among different Scheduled Caste communities. They were started to get rid of various social injustices and economic deprivation and were mainly aimed at regaining their lost status. Few such movements were responsible for upholding the causes of the Scheduled Castes. Mention may be made of the Vaisnavait Movement, Kabirpanthi Movement, Arya Samaj and Brahmo Samaj Movements, etc.

But despite these movements the position of the Scheduled Castes has not improved to the desired extent, though, generally they are in a little better position in the field of education and economy than the tribal folk. It would be worthwhile to find out the reasons.

Anthropological knowledge was first utilized during the British rule for facilitating effective Colonial Administration in India as was done in other Afro-Asian countries. If we look at the utilization of knowledge of Anthropology in the colonial Administration it would be found that the Royal Asiatic Society of Bengal founded in 1774 played a dynamic role in furnishing knowledge about Man, Nature and Culture of India. These pioneering activities of the Society stimulated the British administration and scholars to undertake surveys and investigations on the population in different parts of India.

Some British Administrators trained in anthropology were assigned to undertake specific studies in different parts of India. It was at that time that Dalton, Risley and O'Malley took up studies in East India. Similar work was assigned to Russel for Central India, Thurston for South India and Crooke for North India. As a result of their efforts ethnographic glossaries on different parts of India were brought out. In addition, Administrators like Campbell, Lathen, act., also undertook different types of ethnographical studies.

Some monographs on specific castes and tribes were also published. In this connection names of Hutton, Shakespear, Gordon, Mills, Parry, Grierson may be mentioned. Grierson made a monumental contribution conducting the "Linguistic Survey of India" and publishing his findings in several volumes. Side by side, some Christian Missionaries took up ethnographic and linguistic and folklore researches. They were Bodding. Hoffmann, Dehon, Man, and others. Their efforts resulted in presenting language Handbooks, Dictionaries, Grammars and books on different ethnic groups etc.

The basic intention of those studies was to acquaint the Administrators and the Government with the life and activities of the people of India so as to facilitate smooth functioning of the Colonial Administration.

From that time studies on tribes and castes were made systematically and that marked the beginning of anthropological studies in India. As a result several ethnographic monographs were prepared which helped not only the Colonial Administration but enriched the anthropological literature and created interest among different quarters for undertaking studies among the tribal folk of India. Works of Indian anthropologists like S.C. Roy, R.P. Chanda, D.N. Majumdar, G.S. Ghurye, V. Elwin, A. Iyer, C. Von Furer Haimendorf, A. Aiyappan, I. Karve, K.P. Chattopadhyay, T.C. Das and others were also helpful in understanding the culture and problems of the people concerned. These not only helped the British Administration but also in creating interest for further anthropological investigations amongst the academicians and researchers.

In 1921, the British Government established the Anthropological Survey of India to conduct research on the racial and cultural aspect of the Indian population.

The knowledge of this anthropological work was largely helpful for running the Colonial Administration but was least used for developmental programmes for the Scheduled Castes and Tribes.

However, after Independence, quite a numbe. o. tribal research and training institutes manned by social scientists were set up in different States by the Government in order to deal with the problems of the Scheduled Castes and Tribes and thereby help the present

Administration to look into the affairs of the people concerned and draw up plans and programmes in the right direction of their development. Studies so far undertaken by these institutes have received serious attention from the implementing agencies. Steps have also been taken by the Government from time to time to equip these institutes with different types of strategies adopted for the development of the weaker sections of the country's population.

Side by side, research projects were undertaken by different scholars the financial assistance for which came mainly form different funds of the Research Programme Committee of the Planning Commission and University Grants Commission. Later the Indian Council of Social Science Research was constituted for coordinating social science research in the country at different levels, so as to assist the Government. During this period different social scientists directed their attention to many intricate problems of Indian society and culture both rural and urban. Many such studies were applied and evaluative in nature, connected with development programmes and projects. A.C. Mayer's pioneering role in associating social scientists with community development studies is worth noting. The association of social scientists like Prof. D.N. Majumdar, Prof. M.N. Srinivas, Prof. S.C. Dube, Prof. L.P. Vidyarthi, Dr. Surajit Sinha, Prof. R.K. Mukherjee, Prof. B.K. Roy Burman, Prof. P.K. Bhowmick, Prof. T.B. Naik, Dr. Sachchidananda, etc., in many such research projects may be mentioned.

The activities of the Anthropological Survey of India have been largely expanded in different fields. Names of scientists like Dr. B.S. Guha, Prof. N.K. Bose, Dr. N. Dutta Majumdar, Dr. S.C. Sinha may be mentioned amongst others as Directors who took keen interest in the application of anthropology to the development administration.

And all these years though concerted efforts were made to carry out several developmental programmes, with the intention of overcoming the suffering and drawbacks to which the Scheduled Castes and Tribal population were subjected there still remains a gulf of difference between target and achievement.

There might be several causes for the many failures in implementing the developmental programmes. But it is high time the situation is evaluated and the line of future action readjusted. The responsibility of nation-building rests equally upon planners, implementing authorities and researchers.

We should keep in our mind that whatever development programmes are thought about for the people concerned there should have realistic and practical relevance to society at large. It is the human factor that plays the pivotal role in the utilization of inputs, be it material or non-material. Here lies the prime necessity to utilize and gear up the knowledge, experience and research efforts of Development Anthropology.

Our main objective today is to orient the action anthropological approach in its true sense of application in human development. It is presumed that sufficient care would be taken and efforts made to associate the social scientists at every phase of nation-building during the Sixth Plan period and onwards. Some methods and measures have to be evolved for expanding the scope for a meaningful application of Social Science knowledge in the development activities.

Social Formation in Tangsa of Arunachal Pradesh*

On an April afternoon in 1967, I was in the company of Nirmal Kumar Bose in his meeting with Vishnu Sahaya who as Governor of Assam was also responsible for the administration of NEFA, *i.e.*, Arunachal Pradesh of today. Among other things, the Governor had expressed his Administration's anxieties about the shape of things to come in NEFA, particularly the problem of creating a regional identity strong and sustained enough to cut through the numerous tribal, sub-tribal, village-level and even kinship-based ties of sentiments and loyalties. The frontier territory's socio-political alignments as well as resolution of internal lines of difference to forge a polity capable of subsuming the discrete tribal segments under it. Remained as moot questions for the Administration in those first two decades after independence. The politico-administrative conditions before 1947 were such that each tribal unite, large or small, maintained a sort of autonomous status in its dealings with the outside world. For a tribal segment, with its essentially kinship-

---

* Excerpts have been taken from a published paper of A.C. Bhagabati.

based social organization, there was very little scope or the need to expand the network of social relations involving other tribal segments in the surrounding habitat except for certain well-defined trade and barter transactions. However, over the years since Independence the impact of the many externally induced factors of change has been such as to alter the traditional model of inter-group relations substantially, besides bringing about new outlooks and attitudes as further factors of change[1].

1967 is mentioned as a sort of 'base year' in this narration, because my own field perception of the region began immediately after this meeting with the Governor. As part of Bose's field team, we toured through various parts of NEFA studying aspects of modernization with particular emphasis of the impact of education on the tribesmen[2]. This trip had also given us an opportunity of visiting the Tangsas at Chasnglang in Tirap district. In the course of the last few years, I had further opportunities of carrying out investigations among the same people in Nampong and Changlang areas of the district and thus acquaint myself with the character and tenor of social change and emergent cultural identity.

What follows is more in the nature of case reporting than any elaborate formulating of theory concerning social change and the dynamics of identity orientation. At the same time, the social processes described hare are not confined to the Tangsas alone. Much of what is happening among them are also to be discerned among other sections of the Arunachalese and other hill tribals in the north-east[3, 4]. I am concerned here with outlining how expensive identity is forged by a group of tribesmen in the context of rapid socio-economic change taking place among them. The argument offered is that consolidation of cultural identity and its subsequent assertion, even if in ethno-political terms, are almosts always concomitants of the modernization process.

The groups covered by the term Tangsa are concentrated in three administrative circles of Changlang sub-Division of Tirap District in the extreme north-east of Arunachal Pradesh. These three cricles are Changlang (also the name of the district headquarters township), Manmao and Nampong. There are also some Tangas, essentially recent migrants, in the neighbouring Miao Circle.

The Tangsa habitat covered by these three administrative cirlces lies between the plains of Assam in the north and Patkoi Range in the south and is watered by Tirap and Namchik rivers. These parts of Changlang District contain some 100 village settlements of the Tangsa people. The villages, with a few exceptions, are small. As per 1981 Census, the smallest have 10 to 15 inhabitants each while no village has more than 455 inhabitants. Only 10 villages can be called large having more than 300 persons each. The relatively small size of settlements compared to the situation obtaining among the neighbouring Nocte and Wancho tribesmen of Tirap District is the result of difficulties in *jhum* agriculture faced by the people. Shifting agriculture in this cis-Patkoi region has reached a stage when it is unable to sustain large-sized village settlements. Indeed, the largest village, Changlang, with a population of 455 persons is able to maintain this size because the villagers have gradually switched over to wet rice cultivation in the valley flats of Tirap river over the last 40 years.

It is somewhat difficult to state the size of the loose aggregate of units called the Tangsa. The 1971 Census mentions the total Tangsa population of 13,448 persons. But the computation of group size would vary according to the number of sub-tribal units included under or excluded from the label Tangsa. Thus, the computation for the 100 odd villages in 1981 also gives figure of around 13,000 persons covering various sub-tribes. As detailed later, one tribal unit, the Tutsa, is claiming an independent status as a distinct tribe of Arunachal Pradesh and perhaps in the 1981 Census it did not return itself as Tangsa. In any case, the Tangsas make up the third largest tribal category of Changlang District.

In terms of origin, the various units labelled today as Tangsa are tarns-Patkoi tribes who point to places in the highlands of Burma in the south as their ancestral homeland. In fact, oral historical traditions prevalent among various sections suggest migrations that must have taken place only within the last few centuries[5] Different groups have moved out at different times in search of *jhum* land or pushed out by feuds with other groups in the ancestral habitat.

In the east, the Tangsas have Singphos (in Bordumsa Circle) as their near neighbours. Different sections of the Tangsa appear, in the pre-British times, to have been under strong influence of the Singphos. The Singpho dialect was a sort of lingua-franca among them. However, the influence is now on the wane and Singpho is rarely, if ever, used in inter-tribal communication. The weakening of Singpho influence as well as loss of social contacts with trans-Patkoi tribes are both developments of the post-Independence period. As a matter of fact, even during the British period the various groups had come under increasing contact with people in the bordering regions of Assam plains in the north. Places like Makum Margherita and Ledo have long and regularly been visited by the tribals for occasional work (such as cane cutting) or for trade and commerce.

Let us now pass on the question of definition and identity. Who is a Tangsa? It should be made clear at this point that as a formal label, the term is akin to that of the *Adi* in Arunachal Pradesh or *Mizo* in Mizoram. Each of these names stand for a common elements of culture, language and social organization. In the same way, various tribal entities who have come to be designated as 'Tangsa' over the years do not in any manner represent one traditional societal or structural unit. The traditionally recognised societal units are what have come to be called 'sub-tribes'. Parul Dutta, writing in 1959, thus says, "The Tangsa are a large tribe comprising a number of sub-tribes" (1959: 1). But the traditional social situation in the hills was never one which offered any scope for the Tangsa to act as a sort of corporate functional entity. The smaller units or the so-called sub-tribes were on the other hand, meaningful social universes, each possessing most of the characteristic of the tribe, such as cultural and linguistic homogeneity, territorial contiguity, a common pattern of social organisation though not organized as single political units under any sort of centralized leadership of chiefs.

As a label for a sort of constellation of allied tribes, the term Tangsa appears to carry different meanings for different persons. Dutta states that 'Tangsa' means 'hill people', 'Tang' for hill and 'sa' for people. A literate informant of mine, well-versed in the tribal traditions, gave me an entirely different meaning of the term. According to him, 'Tang' stands for sacrifice and 'sa' for small. That is, groups which made ritual sacrifice of small things, such as pigs and cattle including buffalo. These tribal units which practised only animal sacrifice were therefore called 'Tangsa, even in the ancestral habitat in Burma, according to him. As opposed to the Tangsa, there are certain others tribes collectively referred to as the 'Pangsa' who too migrated from Burma, but much later than the Tangsa groups. Besides animal sacrifice, the Pangsa groups are reputed to have practised human sacrifice, a practice which they continued even in their new habitat. The last reported case of human sacrifice is said to have taken place in 1942. Effective intervention by William Walker, the British Political Officer at Sadiya, brought it to a halt and there has been no other case after that. 'Pang', according to my informant, means 'left behind' and 'sa', of course, stands for 'small' or 'the younger ones'. So 'Pangsa' refers to the group of tribes who were left behind in Burma and who followed the animal sacrificing Tangsas into their new habitat at much later dates. Since they came later, they were Pangsa, in other words, younger or the lesser ones.

It is pertinent to note here that the tribes of the Pangsa group are all subsumed under the Tangsa in common parlance including administrative recognition. Outsiders seldom have occasion to know that some sections of the tangsa are also known as Pangsa. In fact, all the five sub-tribes (Ron-Rang, Mosang, Khimsing, Lungri and Yogli) from whom Parul Dutta collected his field data for the monograph entitled *The Tangsas* (1959) belong to the Pangsa section. On the other hand, the cross-section of people I talked to in the field, including young boys and girls studying in the Higher Secondary School at Changlang, know that the Pangsa tribes are later immigrants who once practised human sacrifice. Thus I wrote in my field diary of 5 January 1982: "The Pangsa-Tangsa dichotomy is purely a matter of internal awareness of the involved tribal groups. Pangsa is certainly not a category for formal and external recognition".

My field perception was somewhat belied by a review of Dutta's book which appeared in *Arunachal News* in its April-May issue of 1983. The reviewer, Ms. Komoli Mosang takes Dutta mildly to task for falling to recognise the five groups he studied as Pangsa. To quote her: "Tangsa comprises many sub-tribes, like Tikhak, Lungchang, Moklum, Phong and many other sub-tribes which are commonly known as Rangpang or Pangsa. This includes all the sub-tribes including Morang, Kimsing, Sangwal, Yugli, Lungri, etc. So I feel it would have been more appropriate if the title had been 'The Pangsas' or 'The Rangpangs' as the study has been carried out on them only. The author has used the term probably on the basis of the fact that Tangsa is the accepted nomenclature" (p. 42)[6] In the remainder of the review, Ms., Mosang consistently uses the term Pangsa in place of Tangsa. I have mentioned this as an indication of another emerging orientation of identity even while the process of wider Tangsa identity crystallization is in progress.

Among the strictly Tangsa groups are placed the Moklom (or Moklum), Lungchang, Takhak, Have and the Ponthai by my informants. These groups are said to have migrated long ago from the other side of Patkoi Range. The Pangsa segment includes according to the list that I could prepare, Mosang, Morang, Kimsing, Ron-Rang, Yogli (or Yugli), Longri (or Lungri), Sanke and the Longphi. Besides, there are a few smaller groups such as the Yongkuk and the Sangwal, whose main concentrations are said to lie on the Burmese side. The Tangsa-Pangsa amalgam, broadly referred to as the Tangsa, is thus an assembly of some 15 named tribal units, each of which is also a dialect group.

It is difficult to make categorical statements in the sphere of emerging expansive tribal identity in the north-east. There is considerable fluidity in the situation. Yet to me it appears that the distinction between the Tangsa and the Pangsa is considerably blurred today and hence, the Yugli, the Longri and the Mosang are as readily called Tangsa as the Moklum, Lungchang or the Tikhak. Another group which in official classification is put under the Tangsa in Changlang Circle is the Tutsa. The Tutsas, are, however, claiming for recognition as an independent tribe. In terms of culture, language and social organization, the Tutsas show greater affinity to the neighbouring Noctes of Tirap District than any section of the Tangsas.

We have dwelt at some length on the question of defining and identifying the Tangsa to indicate the extent to which there is an age-old awareness of common origin and linkage among various groups, However, as already stressed, in the traditional context the effective societai unit was never the wider entry called the Tangsa (or the Pangsa for that matter), but corporate groups such as the Moklum or the Lungchang, call them tribe or sub-tribe. Each such group is divided into a number of exogamous sibs while the group itself is typically endogamous. Each group is also a distinct dialect group though there is often considerable affinity in the languages spoken by certain clusters of tribes. In the realm of culture, there are significant variations, of course within a framework of an overall similarity.

We may now briefly examine the impact of modern influences that have begun operating among the Tangsa tribes, mainly in the post-Independence period. Conscious attempts at forging a wider identity covering the different tribal segments appear to be closely linked up with the process of modernization.

As mentioned earlier, these tribal groups did not lead an isolated life in their hill habitat even before Independence. The groups living close to the Indo-Burmese border had trade and social contacts with tribes across the border while for others sojourns to the markets in the plains were common enough occurrence. Tea gardens with their motley populations have been familiar phenomena along the northern border of their habitat since 1850s. Groups of men used to visit Makum area in the plains for seasonal employment as cane cutters.

These were, however, contacts with the outside world of a very cursory and mainly material kind without any deep significance for the tribal societies. The plainsmen did not even bother to know the names of the tribes of the hill men when they met in the market or employed as seasonal labourers. They were just referred to as 'Naga', a thing which some tribals even now recount with a note of resentment.

In the three and a half decades since the creation (in 1954) of Changlang sub-division and administrative centre, there has been quite considerable investment in development in the area. For instance, from a stage in 1950 when there was only one inter-village school at Nampong to serve all sections of the Tangsa, the number rose to 48 primary schools, 2 middle schools, 2 secondary schools and one higher secondry school by January 1982. There is a clamour for a degree college for the Tangsa area on the ground that the two colleges in Arunachal Pradesh, located at Pasighat and Itanagar, respectively, are inconveniently distant for the local boys and girls to attend.

The most significant consequence of administration induced changes in the post-Independence years has been by way of bringing out individuals from practically every group outside the orbit of their respective village economies and immediate constraints of the village societies. Such individuals, as yet, make up only a small part of the total population, but they have come to wield influence far out of proportion to their number. For example, in the January 1980 election to the 30 member Arunachal Pradesh Legislative Assembly, two men of the Moklum group were elected from Noadihing-Nampong and Changlang constituencies. One among them, Shri Tengam Ngemu of Changlang, had become a minister in the 1980-84 cabinet of Shri Gegong Apang. Ngemu was elected as M.L.A. in the December 1984 election also from Changlang while the Noadihing-Nampong seat was won by a young woman candidate belonging to the Mosang section (Ms. Komoli Mosang, a master's degree holder).

A rough count undertaken in Changlang township itself in January 1982 revealed that there were 35 Tangsa of various tribal affiliations employed in different government departments. There were 20 others who had gone into business and commerce—from forest and P.W.D. contracts to petty shop-keeping.

In another rough count, also made in January 1982, it was possible to locate nearly all the Tangsas who held jobs of some importance. Besides a college lecturer and five circle officers, there were a dozen others holding gazetted and lower middle range government jobs in different parts of the State. There was none, till date, with professional qualifications; but 4 were studying medicine, 1 dentistry and 2 engineering. Another 4 were studying for master's degree and some 26-30 were in college at Pasighat and Shillong.

There is thus a small but rapidly expanding group of comparatively younger educated tribals from piratically all sections of the Tangsa. It is individuals from this group who are for the first time making an attempt to articulate the concept of the Tangsa as a wider identity symbol subsuming the various units under it.

The awareness of the people of older generation of cultural homogeneity of the diverse groups was never in the past a basis for unified action. As already mentioned, the corporate world of the sub-tribe was adequate enough as the framework of group identity. Being a Moklum or Lungchang or Tikhak was what mattered in every day life. In fact, such feelings persist fairly strongly. A Lungchang, for instance, will take pride in the fact that the 20-minute Tangsa programme broadcast from the All India Radio Station of Dibrugarh every morning is in Lungchang dialect. The feeling of inter-group rivalry and animosity also cropped up in many situations.

It was with a view to counter such feelings as well as promote unity among all sections that a formal association was started by the educated youths in 1977. It is called "Tangsa Social and Cultural Development Association". Modernization and reformation of Tangsa culture are also mentioned as one of its objectives.

The promotion of inter-group understanding and unity is sought to be concretely achieved through the celebration of an annual festival known as *moh, mol* or *kooh.* It is actually a village-level agricultural festival connected with the harvesting of *jhum* millet. But the organisers decided that this ought to be elevated to the level of a wider public festival, giving an opportunity to persons from all the Tangsa segments to come together. Though the right time for observing *mok* is in May-June, when the millet is ready for harvest, the public celebration is held in October every year. Since the organisers are mostly students, some studying outside Arunachal Pradesh, this is right season for them when they are at home in the Durga Puja Holidays. The festival is celebrated in different places of the Tangsa habitat in different years . Fund is collected through donations, mainly raised from businessmen of the area. The administration also gives a grant to meet the expenses. The day and night-long celebrations (for up to 4 days) consist of dancing, singing and community feasting. Participants (drummers, gong-players, dancers and singers) are drawn from all the segments of the Tangsa.

Besides organising this annual festival, the association also holds social service camps in backward and interior villages with a view to preach to the villagers the evils of opium habit and certain other tribal customs considered repugnant by the educated youth.

People of most of the groups, for instance, abandon the village site or agricultural fields if lightening strikes any part of these. Many groups cremate or bury their dead by the house site. Some practise infanticide when twins are born. The association seeks to dispel the superstitions connected with these practices so that the people gradually give up these customs. In all these there is a clear focus on the Tangsa as a wider group whose status and image are at issue.

Like the largely youth-led 'Social and Cultural Development Association' the Higher Secondary School Students' Union at Changlang has for many years played an important role in promoting the interest of the Tangsa as a group. The Union has often approached concerned government officials to ensure that local tribals got jobs and contracts. They also arbitrate in disputes involving villagers and seem to be strongly concerned with what they regard to be the Tangsa cause.

The educated youths increasingly tend to feel that compared to many other sections, such as the Adi and the Apatani, they are educationally and economically still rather backward. In order to move forward an secure opportunities for themselves in the context of Arunachal Pradesh, it is essential for them to project the Tangsa as a united and corporate front. After all, there is strength and bargaining power inherent in the size of a group. The young men are quite candid in understanding that their immediate aim is the advancement of Tangsa as a group. As one senior student of the Higher Secondary School put it: "The Tangsas are all brothers, only our elders did not try to bring the brothers together. They were busy smoking opium and going about their own separate ways. We now want all to be together. The Tatsas want to go their separate ways. Let them. They were never Tangsa; only the Government put them with us".

What, therefore, is taking place in this part of Arunachal Pradesh, is the revivification and consolidation of a traditional awareness of common immigrant origin and cultural homogeneity. As yet, the Tangsa youth does not appear to be particularly concerned with the regional social identity of Arunachal Pradesh as a whole. Advancement of sectional tribal (*i.e.,* Tangsa) identity has a priority over State-level identity. But this is not to deny its emergence of certain issues so required. In recent years, essentially student-led movements against the settlements of Tibetan refugees and Chakma tribals from Bangladesh in Miao and other parts of Arunachal Pradesh reflect a strong regional and not just tribe-specific interest articulation. Likewise, there are other issues, arising from time to time, when the identity-framework is in terms of being an Arunachalese. A regional, State level identity is, therefore, at this moment something that can be called 'episodic identity'. It surfaces, no doubt quite strongly, as and when a particular episode arises, *e.g.*, the All Arunachal Pradesh Students' Union led demands for demarcation of boundary with Assam, revocation of trading and contract licences of non-Arunachalese or explosion of foreign nationals from the State.

Lastly, it may be stated that the educated tribal youths in Arunachal Pradesh do not tend to opt or contract out of their respective cultural milieus as a consequence of modernization. The situation is quite different from a simple shift from tradition to modernity such as we normally envisage in a typical situation of acculturation. Instead, the youths here display a conscious commitment to their culture. Further, it is the youths who set the goal of wider identity orientation. They seem to be remarkably able to carry the older section with them since they themselves remain fully committed to the core values of their culture.

Economic Organization

The economic organisation of Indian tribes is not different from the primitive economic organization of other parts of the world. Basically, their economy is geared to the satisfaction of basic subsistence needs and hence they fall into the broad category of production-consumption economies. Contrasting this system with the more advanced one, Majumdar (1967) comments that with the accumulation of an economic surplus, human attention increasingly devoted not only to various material needs other than food, sex and shelter but also to the refinement of the manner in which these three primary, and other derived and secondary, needs are satisfied. These later types of economies are called the production-consumption-distribution type.

Another very remarkable characteristic of contemporary primitive economies is that they used to be run in the absence of currency and other modern economic phenomena before their contacts with the modern world. Primitive societies living in isolation are still managing without these monetary instruments.

Before taking up the economic organizations of Indian tribes it seems imperative to make a brief overview of various types of economies man evolved as a result of cultural adaptation in different situations. Adam Smith was the first scholar who tried to present a classification of economic organization. He talked of hunters, pastoralists and agriculturist and later the categories of handicrafts and industrial pursuits were added to make it more comprehensive. Earnest Gross, with the help of evolutionary perspective, put forward the following stages of development:

(i) Collectional economy

(ii) Cultural nomadic economy

(iii) Settled village economy

(iv) Town economy

(v) Metropolitan economy.

Similarly, Ehrenfels has put forward the four economic types among the early human societies of South Asia:

(i) Food gathers

(ii) Higher hunters

(iii) Plant cultivators

(iv) Nomadic herdsmen.

Most of the tribal people of India fall under the first and third of these categories.

Daryll Forde (1950) does not agree with the idea of economic stages because he does not believe that people live at economic states and finds no single exclusive economy but combinations of economies in the growth of cultures. Gordon Child holds more or less the similar opinion with regard to prehistoric economies. Ford agrees with Herskovit's (1952) five-fold division of economies:

(i) Collection

(ii) Hunting

(iii) Fishing

(iv) Cultivation

(v) Stock raising.

Also, both agree that a people need not abandon one economy to adopt another.

Thurnwald has presented a scheme of various types of economic life, some of which concerns us directly:

(1) Homogeneous communities of men as hunters and trappers, women as collectors. The Kadar, the Chenchu, the Kharia, the Korwa are some of the Indian tribes falling into this category.

(2) Homogeneous communities of hunters trappers and agriculturists. The Kamar, the Baiga and the Birhor are examples of this type from tribal India.

(3) Graded society of hunters, trappers, agriculturists and artisans. Most of the Indian tribes fall under this category.

(4) The herdsmen. The Toda and some sections of the great Bhil tribe furnish classic examples in India.

(5) Homogeneous hunters and herdsmen. This category is not represented among Indian tribes. The Todas do not hunt nor do they catch fish or birds.

(6) Ethnically stratified cattle breeders and traders. The Bhotiyas of the sub-Himalayan region of the Uttar Pradesh breed yaks, and jibus (cross between yak and cow) and are itinerant traders: they come down to the plains in winter ad go over the hills right up to Tibet in summer.

(7) Socially graded herdsmen with hunting, agricultural and artisan population.

These are some of the important classifications encompassing various facets of economic life as lived in different corners of the world. But it does not seem to be possible to study the economic organization of Indian tribes on the basis of any single classifications given above. Every tribe lives by a variety of economic activities.

A certain type of activity may, be playing a dominant role in the economic organization activities. A but some others are also there to supplement. However, the tribes of India may be divided into following broad categories on the basis of dominant economic activities in the respective economies:

(i) Food gatherer and hunter

(ii) Shifting cultivator

(iii) Cultivator

(iv) Pastoralist

(v) Artisan

(iv) Industrial labour.

Food Gatherers and Hunters

This is a fast vanishing category of tribes which persist in deep forests and mountain ranges. Due to fast expanding means of communication and consequently increasing culture contacts with the people possessing advanced technology, they are turning into cultivators. However, there are some tribes who still depend upon collection and hunting and are unaware of the techniques of cultivation.

This category includes those tribes who earn their livelihood through collection of edible roots, fruits and honey and hunt small animals for food. They also go for fishing if the avenues are there. Some such tribes also collect wax, gum, tusks, etc., for the purpose of barter or exchange. In this way they are able to fulfill their essential needs even in the absence of cultivation of foodgrains.

The dependence of gathering and hunting people on nature is so pronounced that they appear to be a part of the nature exhibiting excellent mode of cultural adaptability. Most of such tribes are found in southern India and prominent among them are the Kadar inhibiting the forests of Cochin, Malapatram, Paliyan, Pamiyan, Irula, and Kurumba of Tamil Nadu and the Chenchu dewlling in the Annamalai mountain ranges of Andhra Pradesh. Besides, the Birhor and the Kharia of Bihar, Kamar, Baiga and Abhujmara of Madhya Pradesh, Yenadi of Andhra Pradesh, Koya and Kontareddi of Tamil Nadu and Katkar of Maharashtra may also be included in this category.

The Onge, Jarwa, etc., of Andaman Islands also fall in this category. Though most of the above mentioned tribes are also engaged in some other subsidiary and economic pursuits, yet the dominant mode of economic organization still remains food gathering and hunting.

Most of the characteristics of primitive economic organization are present in the economics of food gathering and hunting tribes of India, foremost of which is the lack of resources, tools and implements. Mostly, they live by their physical prowess and competence amidst the awful lack of technological alternatives which is quite natural at this stage of technological development. The very notion of 'surplus' is absent in their economies because neither they are in a position to generate surplus nor they are equipped to preserve the surplus commodities of everyday life. Further-more, their nomadic existence also prohibits the development of techniques of preservation and conservation among them. Since their entire physical existence is spent in procuring food, there is hardly any scope of rapid development in any other sphere of life.

Shifting Cultivators

A conservative estimate suggests that above more than 90 per cent of the total population in India practise one type of agriculture or the other. Most of the Indian tribes who depend upon agriculture follow this pursuit in two ways. viz., primitive and traditional mode of slash and burn known as shifting cultivation and settled or plough cultivation with the help of various types of agricultural tools and implements. Since the problem of shifting cultivation among the Indian tribes has been dealt with in detail in a separate chapter on 'Shifting Cultivation' a brief account shall suffice in the present chapter.

Shifting cultivation is an age-old institution among the Indian tribes. This, in principle, means the cultivation of a plot of land for a temporary period and then leave it fallow. It consists of clearing the forest slopes, burning the fallen trees and bushes, and broadcasting the seed in the ash covered soil. The rest is left to nature. The sowing on the plot may be done for one or more seasons but not beyond this. After that, fertility of the soil is exhausted and then another plot of land is cleared and the agricultural operations are transferred to it.

In India this mode of cultivation existed in remote hill areas of north eastern region, Orissa, Madhya Pradesh, Bihar and to a lesser extent in several other parts of the country. Although it has been declared unlawful in most of the areas, it still exists on a lesser scale.

Shifting cultivation is known by different regional names in India. It is called *Jhum* among the tribes of Assam, Meghalaya, Tripura, Mizoram and Arunachal Pradesh; *Bewar* or *Dahay* in Madhya Pradesh; *Podu* in Andhra Pradesh; *Koman* or *Bringal* in north Orissa. The major tribes practising it are Lohta, Angami Naga, Khasi and Kuki of north eastern region, Asura of Bihar, Saora and Juang of Orissa, Baiga and Gond of Madhya Pradesh and Korw of Uttar Pradesh.

An interesting aspect of shifting cultivators is that they themselves inhabit permanent villages in a more or less settled way but keep on changing the plot of land for the purpose of procuring foodgrains.

Till recently, the shifting cultivators confined their agricultural pursuit to producing only foodgrains and cereals. Now some of them have started growing even cash crops clinging to their age-old mode of cultivation. The shifting cultivators of Assam, Meghalaya and Nagaland grow cotton as cash crop while maize, vegetables, etc., are grown for domestic consumption. The Juangs of Orissa produce oil seeds as cash crop and paddy for themselves.

Since this mode of cultivation is highly uneconomic due to extremely low yield, most on the shifting cultivators spend their days in poverty and misery. It has been pointed out that if shifting cultivation is not stopped it will tie down the tribes practising it to an undeveloped and low socio-economic level. However, it must be recognised that a change over from shifting to permanent plough cultivation cannot take place suddenly as the economic life of a people is woven inextricably with all the other aspects of their life.

Cultivators

Most of the Indian tribes have adopted the popular mode of cultivation, i.e., permanent plough cultivation like the rest of the peasantry of India. Such tribal cultivators have their own plots of land for agriculture and they employ various animals and agricultural implements in their agricultural pursuits. Adoption of this mode of agriculture has been either due to highly uneconomic and unproductive nature of shifting cultivation or due to culture contacts with the neighbouring peasantry.

The Mizos of Mizoram and the Apatanis of Apatani valley in Arunachal Pradesh are two such examples of shifting cultivators emerging as expert permanent cultivators. The Mizos grow various varieties of rice which is their staple food. The Apatanis are also expert cultivators of rice. Both men and women work together with dedication in the field and despite their lack of knowledge of modern agricultural implements and manures, get enough yield. They grow crops either on the meshy lands of lower plains or the terraces prepared on the mountains. Terrace cultivation which is another type of permanent plough cultivation provides a classic example of cultural and ecological adaptability of these people. The streams of upper forests are tapped in such a way as to provide each terrace sufficient quantity of water and, if need by extra water may be siphoned out. Though quite labour consuming, yet it exhibits the extreme dedication of the cultivator.

Among the tribals of India who have emerged as expert cultivators are the Santhal, Oraon and Ho of Bihar and Bengal, Tharu and Korwa of Uttar Pradesh, Gond, Bhil and Bhilala of Madhya Pradesh, Saora of Orissa and Badaga of Nilgiri Hills in Tamil Nadu.

The Tharus and Korwas of Uttar Pradesh have adopted settled cultivation to such as extent that they are aware of all the means of agriculture. Cowdung manure is used extensively, and dams are harnessed for irrigation and, above all, they grow Rabi and Kharif crops with the precision of the neighbouring peasantry.

It is also commonly observed that the tribes who have embraced Christianity are highly advanced in agriculture compared in other tribes. This may be due to the fact that missionaries working in these areas have not only preached the gospel of Christianity but have also equipped their followers to grasp the modern means of economic pursuits and take advantage of various development schemes floated by government and other developmental agencies. In this connection, the educational institutions run by the missionaries are playing important role in shaping the destiny of the concerned tribal people.

Pastoralists

Pastoral economy is another aspect of economic organization of the tribes of India. Most of the Indian tribes rear cattle for a variety of purposes but when a people breed and rear cattle for commercial purposes and make it their source of livelihood, they may be said to be living under pastoral economy. The Indian pastoralists usually lead a settled life and become wanderers and nomads only under the pressure of changing weather. The pastoral tribes who inhabit mountainous regions migrate to the plains alongwith their cattle during sever winters but go back to their permanent abode at the advent of summer season. Hence, they may be termed more or less as 'settled pastoralists'. Probably, this is a response to the urge of entering settled life from the food gathering-hunting nomadic life of bygone ages.

Among the Indian tribes the famous Toda, inhabiting Nilgiri Hills of Tamil Nadu, furnish a classic example of pastoral economy, their social and economic organization being built around their buffaloes. The Todas "obtain their living by drawing directly upon milk and milk products and by exchanging the same with neighbouring in people to acquire other necessities of life. The buffaloes are ubiquitous, figuring in all aspects of their life. They form the economic base of Toda culture. They or their milk, play the prominent part in the socio-religious and ritual life of the tribe. The daily life of the Toda men is mainly devoted to the maintenance and care of their buffaloes and dairies" (Majumdar).

The Gujjars of Himachal Pradesh are also prominent pastoralists and they rear cows, buffaloes and sheep for commercial purposes. The Bhotia tribe inhabiting Uttar Khand division of Uttar Pradesh are cattle breeders and traders at the same time. They breed yak and jibus (cross between yak and cow) and weave woollen pullovers, shawls and blankets and sell them in he cities of the plains. In this way, they are itinerant traders who come down to the plains in winter and traditionally go over the hills right upto Tibet in summer. But after the outbreak of war with China in 1962, their trade with Tibet had been ruined and now they depend mainly on the raring of sheep and goat for milk, meat, and wool. These animals are also used as beasts of burden. Under the increasing pressure of fast changing economic life they are also adopting agriculture as one of the means of livelihood.

Artisans

Artisans practising various handicrafts are found in all the tribal zones of India. But there are very few tribal communities who live by their handicrafts alone. Many tribal communities take it as their subsidiary occupation often pursued in leisure to supplement their income. The Maria Gonds distil spirits from forest produce. The Saoras devote themselves to mental working, weaving, cane working, pottery and so on. The Korwas and the Agarias are traditionally well-known iron smelters, producing tools for local use only, their techniques being very crude. The Ghasis make gut from the fibre tissues of animals. The Tharus make furniture, household utensils, baskets, musical instruments, weapons, rope and mats. The Irulas make bamboo mats and baskets, and ploughshares and wheels for local use only.

The Apatanis are expert makers of knives and swords and manufacture them for commercial purposes. The Kotas of Nilgiri Hills are efficient blacksmiths, carpenters and potters. The Mizos, Riyangs, Nagas and Apatanis of north eastern region and the Saoras of Orissa are expert weavers of cloth which they sell in the nearby markets. The Marias and Muria Gonds of Bastar are famous for their toys and icons made of clay and metal which are marketed by various handicraft emporia in the country. The Bhils and Bhilalas of Jhabua district weave beautiful *durris* and cushions out of old clothes and cotton fibres.

Industrial Labour

Industrial labour is a comparatively new phenomenon in the economic organization of some tribes of India. It encompasses very serious and significant implications. The problems of tribals as 'industrial labour' have been dealt with in a separate chapter on 'Industrialization' in tribal areas in view of the serious nature of this problem. Indian tribal people have come into contact with industrial life in two ways. Either they have migrated to industrial areas or industries have sprung up in the areas they inhibit. Large numbers of the Santhals, the Konds and the Gonds have migrated to Assam and taken up various jobs in tea plantations. The other manner of contact with industrial life is more important in view of its far reaching consequences. Certain tribal areas in middle India have been found rich in natural ores; coal, iron and steel, and other industries have sprung up in these areas. This has happened particularly in West Bengal, Bihar, Orissa and Madhya Pradesh. "Thus industrialization of these people's life has taken place, establishing a kind of tribal-urban continuum" (Majumdar).

The situation described above distinguishes two categories of tribes. The Santhal, Oraon, Munda, Kharia, Gond and some others may be lumped together in the first category. In view of growing economic hardships, they migrate to Assam and the adjoining areas to work as tea plantation workers, While some members of a family migrate to other cities and towns to work as unskilled labour. The other category includes the Santhals, Hos and others who are working in the mines and mills situated in their area. The steel complexes of Jamshadpur, Ranchi, Rourkela, Bhilai and Bailadila employ tribals in large numbers.

Industrialization of these areas has certainly presented millions of tribal people new and permanent source of livelihood, but the cost which the poor tribals had to pay is enormous and awful. Industrialization and urbanisation have damaged their social fabric substantially. Decay and disintegration in their traditional social institutions have set in. Industrial values have distorted their own value system. Liquor addiction, gambling and prostitution are eating the vitals of their social organization. They are the 'victims' of industrialization who have been pushed into an alien milieu without equipping them to face the hazards of a strange world.

Division of Labour

Compulsion of physiological factors like sex, infancy or old age and physical disability provide the only basis for specialisation in pre-urban societies. Majumdar opines that besides this basic recognition of physiological differences and their implications which are reflected in the division of labour in primitive societies, there have been extensions of this basic fact which have resulted in further compulsive factors decreeing a sexual division of labour. The inability to understand the variety of physiological processes connected with the healthy-life of a woman, life menstruation and childbirth, has given rise to strange norms. The pampered and well-treated Toda woman, for example, have been barred from touching the sacred buffalo or stepping into the dairy.

The association of women with infants has also imposed checks on them, preventing their full participation in the tasks of men. They have to take care of the infants and of cooking which naturally force them to stay longer at home. Among most of the Indian tribes, men never do the task specially assigned to women—the Toda tribe being a rare exception where men cook all such food in which milk and milk products are used, obviously on ritualistic ground. Women do undertake most of the task generally done by men. Women among Indian tribes gather food; engage in cultivation (sowing and harvesting); go fishing; make baskets, cloth and pottery and so on. But they never go for hunting big game, nor for felling in trees, nor do they become blacksmiths or carpenters.

The tribal women of hilly and mountainous regions are most hardworking, their menfolk being examples of laziness. The Khasa or Jounsari women of Jounsarbawar in Uttar Pradesh are glaring example of this situation. Here the women do all sorts of work from dawn to dusk, from collection of wood to carrying water from the mouth of steep slopes and from sowing and harvesting to taking care of the cattle, whereas the menfolk relax in tea stalls sipping tea, gossiping and smoking, discussing factional politics and scandals. The impact of industrialization, however, has affected both men and women. In such areas as affected by industrialization, men work in iron and steel factories, coal mines and tea gardens while women workers are engaged in mica and coal mines, in tea gardens, in quarries and so on. Engaging menial labourers is unknown in tribal India except among a couple of tribes like the Jounsari of Uttar Pradesh where the Kolta, the traditionally landless and ritually untouchable section of the tribe, are kept as slaves, bonded forever by the higher caste Rajput-Brahmin landlords. Thus except for a couple of such examples, division of labour between master and slave is un-known in tribal India.

Property, Ownership and Succession

The conception of property varies from one form of society to the other and hence modern conception of property cannot be applied to primitive societies. Among the tribes of India, all the commodities controlled and regulated by social values may be termed as property. Misra and Tiwari (1975) while elaborating this point in the Indian context express the view that even among the food gathering and hunting tribes, forests and means or implements of food gathering and hunting constitute property. Though the members of the society are entitled to use and consume forest produce and fauna in independent ways, yet their use is subject to certain social rules and values. Among the pastoral tribes, pastures, cattle, cattle-sheds, dwellings, clothes, objects obtained from animals, etc., are different forms of property. Similarly, land, agricultural implements, house clothing, etc., are forms of property among the agricultural tribes while sources of raw material, tools and implements, finished goods, clothing, house, etc., constitute property among the artisan tribes.

Among the Indian tribes both types of ownership, viz., collective as well as individual, are fairly known. In whichever form property may be recognised, its recognition entails the existence of some rules of inheritance. Inheritance acquires particularly importance when individuals possess property by themselves. In communal inheritance the group as a whole never ceases to exist suddenly as individual does, and is replenished through fresh recruitment from time to time. Though the emphasis nowadays is on individual ownership, there are instances like the Nagas who traditionally own the lands of the village collectively. Since the individual property is quite meagre, it is custom among tribes to burn the items of individual use alongwith the deceased.

The laws of inheritance may be patrilineal or matrilineal or some kind of a combination of both depending upon the social structure of a particular society. The daughters inherit the property among the matrilineal tribes, like the Khasi of Meghalaya, and the sons among the vast number of patrilineal tribes. In some cases the eldest daughter or son inherits the entire property. Among the Toda tribe of Nilgiri hills the eldest and the youngest son get an extra animal. The Badaga of the neighbouring region practise a different set of rules. Among these people the eldest son leaves home the moment he gets married. It is the youngest son who remains in the house with his parents and only he inherits the property of his father and becomes his lawful successor.

Market

Except with some food gathering and hunting tribes, the institution of market is seen to be present in one from or the other among almost all the tribes of India. However, regular markets are still a rarity among them. In most of the cases people assemble in an assigned place and on an appointed time and exchange their commodities with each other. Such markets are usually weekly or fortnightly. The markets held in tribal regions usually trade in commodities of local use like vegetables, cereals, meat, spices, salt, utensils, agricultural tools and implements, clothing cosmetics, etc.

Non-tribal traders are also seen to be interested in some of these markets which are visited by them in search of local produce at cheaper rates. Their transaction becomes easier when they lure the simple tribals with urban products and get away with the local produce at throw away prices.

The tribal markets usually run for a few hours and during the day time. Some markets are held once a year and they continue for days. In the Bastar region of Madhya Pradesh such markets are known as *Marai.* These are held usually after harvest and people visit these markets alongwith their families to buy necessary commodities for the year. Such markets present festive look where people sing and dance and engage in all sorts of merrymaking. They serve manifold purpose. Distant relatives meet each other, marriages are arranged, local polities is discussed and thus these annual markets carry a lot of social and cultural significance. The be more precise, the tribal markets not only fulfil certain needs of the buyers and sellers but also act as agents of culture change.

REFERENCES

1. Bhagabati, A.C., 1982, "Emergent tribal identity in North-East India". In *Tribal Development in India,* Edited by Buddhadeb Choudhury, New Delhi: Inter-India Publications.

2. Bose, N.K., 1966, *Report of the Commissioner for Scheduled Castes and Scheduled Tribes* (16th Report), New Delhi: Government of India.

3. Dutta, P., 1959, *The Tangsas,* Shillong: NEFA Research Department, Furer-Haimendorf, von C., 1980, *From Cattle to Cash,* New Delhi: Vikas.

4. Mosang, K., 1983, Book Review (*The Tangsas*), *Arunachal News,* Number 3, Volume 12.

5. Singh, R.K. Ranjit; A.C. Bhagabati, 1980, The Mosang of Manipur: A preliminary report on identity orientation. *The Bulletin of the Department of Anthropology, Dibrugarh University,* 9: 67-85.

FIVE

Socio-economic Status of Tribal Women

STATUS is considered as the ascribed position of an individual or the section of community at par with the necessities arising out of the ecological and traditional conditions. While Marxists and Beauvoir have emphasized the production activities or productive endeavour of a society in reckoning the status of women, it will be correct to say that in any society the status of women may be defined in terms of more than one criterion some of which can be enumerated as: Political participation, economic control, personal autonomy, interpersonal quality, legal adulthood and ideological position.

The study of tribal or primitive societies has been of special interest to anthropology for more than a century. And the status of women in tribal societies has not escaped attention. Here is an attempt is made to describe the status of tribal women in their social environment in Meghalaya.

Meghalaya was carved out of Assam and became the full-fledged state on January 21, 1972. The State is inhabited by the Khasis, Jaintias and Garos who follow and practice the matrilineal system. These tribal communities are the descendants of very ancient people having distinctive cultural traits and ethnic origin. The Khasis belong to the Austric race and their language is believed to be one of the very few dialects of the Mon-Khmer family of languages in India. The state has a population of 13.36 lakh of which 6.84 lakh are males and 6.52 lakh are females, in 1981.

Social Status

The Khasis and Jaintias share a common matrilineal tradition under which descent is reckoned from the female line and the children belong to the clan of the mother. The woman not only have the right to property but also have a right to choose their own life partners and to marry after widowhood the Birth of baby girl is a happy occasion in Meghalaya household. There is no discrimination against girls in terms of education and employment[1]. Bareh[2] (1976) stated that "Women and not man inherits the property and even sons receive nothing a except certain gifts which should be returned back tot he mother's house on their death".

Marriage System

The most remarkable feature of the Khasi marriage is that it is usual for the husband to live and stay with his wife in his mother-in-law's house and not for him to take his bride to his house, as in case of other communities[3].

"The social, cultural, political, religion and economic setup of the race is based on matrilineal system." According to this system, the children belong to the mother. Hence, no Khasi child can be illegitimate child, whether the mother bore the child from the husband with whom she has been formally married or not[4]. Divorce is very common among the Khasis. Men are usually blamed and condemned by the society if divorce takes place, while women are justified and sympathised.

Religion

Women are the founder of clan and religion. Therefore, the Khasi women are the rulers and priests in their own homes. The administrative and religious functions at home are handled by them. The Khasis, owing to the matrilineal custom, the mother is a person entrusted with important duties of performing family rites and ceremonies occupying the position of a family priestess. But the uncle of the family performs the religions rites outside the home[5].

Economy

Among the other sectors of the population, the scheduled tribe community is generally socio-economically more backward, Naturally, the women of the sector are also quite backward. But the

Khasi women are busy in different economic activities and giving a good economic support in the family.

Since women inherit both movable and immovable properties (house, land, wealth etc.), it is obvious to see that women do play a major role in agricultural production. For the whole year, women work equally hard as male counterparts in the agricultural operation. The nature of works, the women operate the collection of manure, ploughing the field, sowing the seeds, harvesting the crop, threshing, carrying the produces home and marketing. Another prominent role of Khasi women, is their immense involvement in trade and business activities. Their devotions, interests and skills cannot be ignored and can be seen in city markets and village markets. Women are also taking up contract and supply works with the government. Some of them are the suppliers of coal, bamboos, lime stones, timbers, broom sticks and other materials to other states and private agencies outside the state.

Khasi women have been found to be as economically enterprising as men. They have been involved in economic activities, in trading and commercial ventures. There are increasing number of women entrepreneurs engaged in private business found in today's modern society[6].

In Khasi hills, it would seem strange if a woman does not work, even in Shillong it is rare to come across a woman whose only occupation is that of a housewife. In villages, women work equally hard as men in the field, even carrying their babies on their backs. Even markets have as many women traders as man and they are astute in business matters[7].

Politics

The new political system of adult franchise that was introduced prior to our country's Independence is yet to get its influences on the women in Meghalaya. For that reason, the women in Meghalaya do not take interest in contesting the elections to different legislative and parliamentary bodies in the state. Of course, very few do enter the elections arena and as a result, there are negligible number of women representatives in the state and sometimes nil. Another possible factor for this non-involvement in election, is that the work load of Khasi women is very great. They have the various responsibilities like upbringing the children, looking after the clan, business, land and properties, agriculture, household chores, etc. These numerous traditional responsibilities are in fact, taken by women as priorities to be fulfilled rather than contesting the elections.

But in spite of non-participation in contesting election no one can deny the fact that their involvement in politics is also great, as women actively participated in different women's wing of different political parties and delivering public speeches especially during election seasons, their participation in political movement or agitation, contribution of their ideas and views in pamphlets and newspapers and moreover the most significant involvement is their participation in voting. It is noted that in some constituencies the percentage of women who come for voting is greater than men which clearly indicates their willingness, enthusiasm and their role in politics.

The following list shows the women members of different legislative bodies in Meghalaya:

1937—Ms Mavis Dunn Lyngdoh MLA-Minister of Assam. (Perhaps the first Indian woman to be a minister).

1945—Ms. Bonniely Khongmen MLA, Assam.

1952—Ms. Bonniely Khongmen MP, Assam.

There were only 3 women MDCs (Members of District Council) in the Khasi Hills District Council during the period of 1952–88 and their names are giving below:—

1. Ms Brosila Lamin,
2. Ms Estris Syiem,
3. Ms Maysalin War.

There is only one lady MLA in Meghalaya Legislative Assembly. Ms. M. War won the MLA election in 1988.

Women in Decision-Making

I. As a rule in a matrilineal society, the children belong to the mother. The father has to come and dwell in his wife's house and also shares and enjoys her property and wealth. This situation provides enough scope for the female members of the family to take decision in different domains of their daily life.

II. Women play a vital role in making decision whether in business, trade or anything related to her property. A woman who inherits the land/house/wealth has in mind in idea what to do with it, because maternal uncles may have a different ideas and her husband may have another plan. The uncles/husband cannot impose their decisions on her rather they have to convince her. If she does not agree with them or with one of them, she takes her own decision. In certain cases, if her ideas are similar to one of her uncles, she may abide by that decision. But if she thinks that husband is reliable, she may take a decision to support him against her uncles. So, in this way woman decides what to do and what not to do. Mawlong[8] observes that "though the males take the leading role in the deliberations yet the females too have equal voice and no decision can be taken if the females resent."

III. Again, woman as the mother of the house, takes her own decisions regarding division of property. In her land, she alongwith her unmarried uncles, husband and children may cultivate, sow and harvest the crop. The whole lot of production will be taken in trucks to the markets with the assistance of her husband or uncles, but the earning goes to her. These process continues for years and in course of 5 or 10 years time, the mother will again take a decision to distribute her wealth among her daughters or she may construct a houses for her daughters etc.

Jobs

There is no discrimination against girls in terms of education and employment. In the State Secretariat alone women are 83% of the total employees. The women occupy some top managerial posts in the state. They are capable of taking up any type of works from domestic chores to ploughing, teaching, doctors, engineers, agriculture, administrative jobs and others. The present opposition of the women Gazetted Officers in Meghalaya are given below:

1. In the Meghalaya Civil Services, there were 20 women, acting as Deputy Commissioners, Additional Deputy Commissioners, Deputy Secretaries, Directors, Sub-

Divisional Officers, Block Development Officers, Extra Assistant Commissioners etc. (Women constitute 20%)

2. There are 11 (32%) women Under Secretaries in the State.
3. Out of 55 Superintendent posts 17 (31%) posts are occupied by women.
4. There are 45 women and 36 men as Lecturers in different government colleges.
5. 13 women out of 17 Gazetted post are working in Social Welfare Department.
6. Out of 21 Stenographers (Grade I) post, women occupy 12.
7. In university out of 30 Khasi teachers, 13 are women. At present there is one Khasi woman as Dean of Education, 3 readers and 9 lecturers.
8. In the Health and Family Welfare Department, there were two ladies DHS(s), one DDHS, 7 top ranking lady officers and 71 gazetted officers.

Education

Literacy for tribal aims at giving them better knowledge of tribal development is particular and national development in general, thereby enabling them to rise their standard of living and simultaneously giving them enough expertise in agriculture, industry and commercial sector so as to make them produce more and earn more in their respective capacities. In Meghalaya the educational status among the female is better than the males.

The results of the Primary School Leaving Certificate and scholarship examination 1984 and 1985, and the Middle School Leaving Certificate and Scholarship Examination 1983, published by the Meghalaya Board of School Education, showed that the number of Khasi girls passed in these examinations are more than the number of boys. In the case of Jaintia Hills District, the number of girls appeared in the examination showed two fold increase. The total number of girls passed in 1983 was 319 against 189 boys. Again, the 1984 result showed that 440 girls passed the examination while the number of boys passed was 222 only. The result of the

Primary School Leaving Certificate and Scholarship Examination 1986, showed that the number of girls passed was 2968 while the number of boys was 2243. The Middle School Leaving Certificate and Scholarship Examination 1986, also showed the same trend where the number of girls passing out was higher than the boys. The B.A. (Honours) result 1988 published by the North-Eastern Hill University, showed that out of 68 Khasi students who passed the exam. 41 are girls and 27 are boys. This trend is also continued at the university level. In the North-Eastern Hill University the ratio of Khasi boys to Khasi girls is 1:3. Also there are 33 women as research scholars and 11 men only. The Khasi girls constitute 68% of the total students population who study outside the state in different professional lines. This shows that if girls are properly motivated, provide them with educational facilities and opportunities, encourage them and give them responsibilities, there is no reason why girls can not do well. If the Indian girls from Maghalaya can achieve why not our girls from other parts of our country. Therefore, it all demands on the parental treatment, behaviour and their attitudes towards girls.

Conclusion

If change has to be brought in the Indian society, the social values that affect the growth and development of women ought to be modified and that too should be based on humanitarian considerations. Again, if change has to occur, there must be a change in the attitudes and hearts of both men and women.

In the context of Indian society, "boys are always considered as assets while girls as liabilities". But in other societies both sons and daughters are assets of the family. These are all in deed, man made values. "Our children (both sons and daughters) are the light of tomorrow, the security of parents, and the hope of the nation." So parents much provide them a fair deal, equal treatment and equal opportunities in all respects of their life.

Interview with the DPI, 1988

Excepted Meghalaya, and some parts of Kerala, the Indian society in general still adhere to patriarchal system and practice and women are lacking sense of security and face adjustment problems. Parents therefore, if they could, should provide some securities in the form of wealth and properties, so that women may feel secure. Her security should not merely depend on her husband. Parents should be able to provide her security. Women in Meghalaya feel very secure, their securities much depend on their properties to her parents, brothers, sisters or uncles. She continues to stay in their own house with her children and work.

Among the Khasis, the curriculum for women has existed for centuries and perhaps from time immemorial. The curriculum that favours women is already there in the culture, practices, beliefs and in our way of life. The syllabi at the college education stage in respect of Khasi literature, includes the main tenets of the Khasi customs and culture. Hence, the position and status of women are very much reflected in their favour. (Mawlong 1984). But in other societies, curriculum for women ought to be introduced in schools and colleges and even in the universities.

Lastly, education should be provided to all children. But providing education alone is not enough, children should be given equal educational facilities, opportunities and encouragement. Parents and teachers have a great role in motivating both sons and daughters, boys and girls to achieve higher things in life. If Khasi girls are achievement oriented why not other Indian girls. McClelland[9] stated that "the future development of any country will depend upon the present level of achievement motivation of the youths. This is so, because if the youths of a country are highly motivated, they, after fifteen years, will occupy high positions as decision makers in the country and lead the country to progress". Therefore, if girls are given some educational facilities as boys and properly motivated, undoubtedly the percentage of stagnation, dropouts and wastage will definitely decrease and consequently the women will surely come in different academic fields to be at par with the men.

In conclusion, for projecting the desired status of women in Indian society, care should be taken to generate a spirit of mutual understanding, mutual helpfulness and mutual cooperation and not confrontation with the other sex. Though competition and confrontation are the facts of life which exists in the society, but at the moment such confrontation may lead to undesirable tensions, discord, unhappiness and frustration leading to immense social problems.

REFERENCES

1. 'Shillong ideal location for SAARC meet'. *The Sentinel*, Vol. IV. No. 22 dt. 5 May, 1986.
2. Bareh, H., 1967. *History & Culture of Khasi People*, Nobe Nudran Pvt. Lt., Calcutta.
3. Gordon, PTR., 1975. *The Khasis*, Cosmos Publication, Delhi.
4. Lyngdoh, R.S., 1972. 'The Khasis', *North Eastern Affairs*, April-June 1972, Vol. I, No. I, p. 22, Ri Khasi Press, Shillong.
5. Dr. Lyngdoh, II, 1941. 'The Role of Women in Church' *Christian Journal* (Pateng of Kristan, Vol. 5, No. 9, September 1942), published by the Assembly of the Presbyterian Church. Ri Khasi Press Shillong.
6. Syiem, 1988. 'Women in Khasi Society', Paper presented at the Seminar on Status of Women in Tribal Cultures of Meghalaa, 13 & 14 July, 1988, organised by the Centre for Literacy & Cultural Studies, NEHU, Shillong.
7. Gee, E.P., 1957. 'The Land of Women' *The Sunday Stateman*, Calcutta, March, 31, 1957.
8. Mowlong, M., 1984. 'A Note on the Status of Women', Speech through the A.I.R. Shillong.
9. McClelland, 1964. *The Achieving Society*, N.Y. The Free Press.

SIX

Social Interaction Among the Tribes

WHILE dealing with the social organisation of the three tribes living in Deophar, Marku and Banjhi villages respectively the focus will be on common characteristics and also on the differences in the social life of the three tribes. The social organisation of the three tribes will be compared in terms of family and marriage, lineage and clan, and village and inter-village organisations as a basis of socio-cultural integration.

Family as a Basis of Socio-cultural Integration

Among all the three tribal communities, the nuclear family is the basic unit of socio-cultural integration. The family consists of the husband, wife and unmarried children. The married couple set up separate households after marriage, while a married daughter goes to stay with her husband's family. She visits her parents occasionally an in case of divorce she returns to them. Joint family with married sons are rare. Patrilocal residence is the general rule among all the three tribes. The father is the head of the family and his authority is the supreme. However, he does not act arbitrarily. The husband and wife co-operate with each other in the economic sphere. The wife helps the husband during agricultural operations and also plays an important role in meeting the daily expenses as well as taking charge of the kitchen and the children.

The family structure among the Maler of Deopahar reveals that nuclear family consisting of husband, wife and unmarried children is the most common type and 61.5% of the household records nuclear family. Among the Mal Pahariya of Marku the nuclear family is the dominant type constituting 72.7% of the total number of household whereas the percentage of nuclear family among the Santhal is only 37%. The percentage of other types of families (See Table 6.1), taken together constitute 63% but percentage of the each type of family is less than the percentage of the nuclear family.

The next is the nuclear family having one or more dependent such as widowed father or mother, unmarried brothers or sisters or both or deceased brother's widow or unmarried sons or daughters and so on. Such households neither represent nuclear family nor joint family and thus may be termed as intermediate family. It may be termed as extended family but it will be difficult to distinguish between nuclear family with dependants and join family consisting of married brothers and their wives and unmarried children or husband, wife with married sons, their wives and their unmarried children. Such families are called intermediate families because if both the parents were alive and were staying with their married sons, wife and their unmarried children, it would fall under joint family of vertical type, but in absence of any one of the parents it is nuclear family with dependent. Similarly after the marriage of a brother and a sister the intermediate family consisting of married couple and their children along with unmarried brothers and sisters of the head of the household, the family will either break into two nuclear families or combine as a joint family of horizontal type. Hence the family at present is of intermediate type, meaning thereby that it is neither nuclear nor a joint family.

The intermediate families among the Maler record 12.9% while among the Santhal 28% of household fall under this type whereas among the Mal Pahariya there is none under this type. Among the Maler 7.7% of the intermediate families constitute of married couples, their unmarried children with widow mother and unmarried sisters, while in other cases it comprised of a married couples, their unmarried children and unmarried sisters. Among the Santhal 15% of the total households which fall under this type constitute of married couples, their unmarried children and widowed father and in one case deceased brother's daughter stayed with the family. The remaining 13% of the households falling under intermediate type constitute of married couples, their unmarried children and head of the household's unmarried brothers and sisters.

The vertical joint family consisting of married couples alongwith unmarried and married sons and latter's wife and children records 7.7% among the Maler and 11% among the Santhal. Only one percent horizontal joint family was recorded among the Santhal but none among the Maler and the Mal Pahariya. Horizontal joint family is rarely found among all the three tribes.

Besides these, there are some such type of families which constitute of a widow or widower with unmarried children. Such families show the absence of the other partner due to death or divorce or in other words the nuclear family which was in existence is now broken by the death or divorce of a husband or wife and hence is called broken nuclear family. Among the Maler 5.1% of the total number of households represent broken nuclear family as against 9.1% among the Mal Pahariya and 10% among the Santhal. The broken nuclear family among the Maler is comprised of a widow and her unmarried son, while among the Mal Pahariya it constitutes of a widower and his unmarried son. Among the Santhal 9% families constitute of a window and her unmarried children while in one case it was a widower with her unmarried children.

Apart from these there are two more types of families such as uni-member family and incomplete nuclear family. Among the Maler 5.1% are uni-member family which has one male member each who have been separated by the divorce of their wives, whereas only one uni-member family has been reported among the Santhal which constitutes of a widow. But no such type was recorded among the Mal Pahariya.

There are some such families which may be categorised under incomplete nuclear family due to the absence of children. In other words the incomplete nuclear family is simply a conjugal unit made up of a husband and wife without any child—or a potential nuclear family. The Maler record 7.7% of the total household under incomplete nuclear family against 9.1% among the Mal Pahariya and 7% among the Santhal.

The last type of family is the other type of family which is not a general feature among any one of the three tribes. Under this type 9.1% of the Mal Pahariya families fall which constitute of married couples, their unmarried children, alongwith wife's father and his unmarried daughter. Similarly 5% of the Santhal families are under this category of *'others'*, out of which one family consists of a married couple, their unmarried children alongwith wife's mother and wife's unmarried sister, while the other does not have wife's unmarried sister but wife's mother is living with it. Among the other three families, one consists of a married couple and their married daughters and latters children, while the other one consists of a married couple, their unmarried children with father's widow sister and her children and the last one constitutes of the married couple their unmarried children along with head of the household's married sister, her husband and her daughter.

TABLE 6.1

Types of Family Among the Three Tribes

Types of family	*Tribes*					
	Maler		*Mal Pahariya*		*Santhal*	
	No.	*per cent*	*No.*	*per cent*	*No.*	*per cent*
Nuclear family	24	61.5	8	72.7	37	37
Intermediate family	5	12.9	...	...	28	28
Joint family	3	7.7	...	...	12	12
Broken nuclear family	2	5.1	1	9.1	10	10
Uni-member family	2	5.1	...	...	1	1
Incomplete family	3	7.7	1	9.1	7	7
Others	...	...	1	9.1	5	5
Total	39	100	11	100	100	100

Lineage or Clan as a Basis of Socio-cultural Integration

All the three tribes are patrilineal but the main difference between them is found in their system of descent. For example, the social organisation of the Maler shows that lineage plays the most important role in their society. The lineage known as *Bhaiyader* or *Gotia* is traced back patrilineally to a common ancestor who is identified by the Maler. The lineage among the Maler is an exogamous unit. During marriage particular care is taken so that the couple should not be of the same lineage as such a relation is regarded incestuous. The Maler do not marry within their close relations upto three generations from father's and mother's side. Though clan is conspicuous by its absence, among the Maler, the Mal Pahariya and the Santhal have a number of clans which are exogamous. Clan exogamy is strictly followed by the Santhal but the Mal Pahariya do not adhere to this law with such strictness. The clan is known as *Paris* among the Santhal and *Padhap* among the Mal Pahariya.

Among the Maler of Deopahar eleven lineages are recorded in the village. The genealogical tables provide sufficient example of marriages showing lineage exogamy. There has been only one case of marriage in the same lineage. Katgu Pahariya's sister married Meinya Mesa who is the son of Katgu's father's father's sister. It is true that the marriage did not take place in the mother's direct lineage yet such marriage is prohibited and the Maler held that Meinya Mesa and his wife were in love with each other and Meinya Mesa had to pay a heavy amount of bride price.

The Mal Pahariya have 12 clans as do the Santhal. The different clans called *Padhap* are as follows:—

(1) *Ahri* (2) *Dehri* (3) *Girhi* (4) *Majhians* (5) *Babuano* (6) *Naiya* (7) *Sing* (8) *Pujhar* (9) *Kunwar* (10) *Kurail* (11) *Sikdar*. The name of one of the clans has been forgotten by them. But Marku village having eleven families has only two clans in all. These are *Ahri* and *Girhi* clans. Chamra and Radha Mal Pahariya held that the members of *Ahri* clan settled first in the village and were followed by *Girhi*. The total percentages of families belonging to *Girhi* and *Ahri* clans come to 54.6% and 45.4% respectively.

The clans among the Mal Pahariya are regarded to be exogamous and it is the rule not to marry in the same clan. Marriage within the same clan leads to excommunication of the couple but it is conspicuous to note that in reality, clan exogamy is not followed strictly. Chamra Mal Pahariya and his brothers belong to *Ahri* clan but they have married in the same *Ahri* clan. Among the members of the *Girhi* clan too, it was found that some have married within the clan.

It is true that some of the Mal Pahariya marry in the same clan but the sense of social restriction is there and they think that they did wrong. Several explanations are put forward to account for that. They held that as the Mal Pahariya are not found in the neighbouring area (as the main concentration of the tribe is in Dumka and Pakur Damin), they sometimes marry in the same clan. Defending himself Chamra Mal Pahariya said that though he married in the same clan, he and his wife belonged to different villages and different sub-clans. He classified *Ahri* into *Chota Ahri* and *Bara Ahri* in terms of worship of *Chor Danu* in the *Bhitta* land where the *Chota Ahri* sacrifices a pig but *Bara Ahri* has to sacrifice a hen. So marriage between such sub-clans was practised. The statement given by Chamra Mal Pahariya in favour of clan endogamy is refuted by other villagers who held that there was no such distinction between *Bara Ahri* and *Chota Ahri* and there were no sub-clans among them. However, all of them stressed that the couple should not be of the same village and same lineage.

In the Mal Pahariya village there are thus examples of inter-clan and inter-clan marriages. Radha, Shoma, Dukhan of *Girhi* clan married in the *Ahri* clan, Chota Deba of *Girhi* clan married in *Majhians* clan, while the rest married in the same clan.

The functional classification of the clan among the Mal Pahariya is similar to that of the Santhal. *Ahri* clan of the Mal Pahariya has its resemblance with *Marandi* of the Santhal and that of *Pujhar* with *Murmu* and *Kunwar* with *Besra.*

In this way the Mal Pahariya of Marku could trace the similarity between the existence of clan among the Santhal and the Mal Pahariya themselves.

The Santhal have 12 different clans. The names of the different clans found among the Santhal are given below with English equivalent[1] in bracket.

(i) *Hansdak* (the original goose or duch).

(ii) *Marandi* (the name of a weed, commonly found in the rice field).

(iii) *Soren* is the one who killed a sun bird.

(iv) *Hembrom* (the one who suggests hortin for deer).

(v) *Tuddu* (the one who killed an owl, which also certainly suggests the sound made by drum).

(vi) *Kishu* (a generic name for king fisher).

(vii) *Baskey* (who made a bundle of stall rice).

(viii) *Besra* (one who carried an umbrella over his head).

(ix) *Choren* (the one who killed a rough-necked ignana).

(x) *Pauriya* (who killed a dove).

(xi) Bedea[2] is the lost clan given by P.O. Bodding.

(xii) *Murmu* (the one who restores than to tribal status).

The Santhal suggest occupational basis for the clan classification.[3] According to them the *Murmu* became the priest of the tribe, the *Soren* were the warriors associated with Sipahi or sepoy, the *Marandi* were rich traders, the *Tuddu* were drummers and the *Kishu* were Rajas and so on. The Santhal of Banjhi classify their clans in terms of occupational difference which reflects the influence of the neighbouring Hindus. On the above occupational basis the Mal Pahariya correlate their different clans with the of that Santhal.[4]

The *Hansdak,* the *Marandi,* the *Soren,* the *Tuddu,* the *Hembrom,* the *Baskey,* the *Murmu* clans go to suggest the totemistic basis of the clan classification. But this totemistic basis[5] of clan classification is absent among the Mal Pahariya who envisage the importance of clan organisation in terms of occupation.

The clan, known as *Paris* extends the range of relationship from family to clan level. These clans descend through the father and after the marriage of the girls they are taken into the clan of their husbands. The ownership and inheritance of land is conceived in terms of clan. The Santhal will never allow the transfer of land from one clan to the other. The offices of the headman (*Manjhi)* and *Gorait* are hereditary and are vested exclusively in one clan (the clan of the headman or Gorait).

In Banjhi the Santhal families belong to ten different clans and their clan-wise distribution has been given in the following Table 6.2.

TABLE 6.2

Clan-wise Distribution of the Santhal Families of Banjhi Village

Sl. No.	*Name of the clan*	*No. of houses*	*Percentage*
1.	Kisku	9	9
2.	Kansdak	13	13
3.	Marandi	12	12
4.	Murmu	31	31
5.	Hembrom	7	7
6.	Soren	9	9
7.	Tuddu	9	9
8.	Baskey	5	5
9.	Besra	4	4
10.	Choren	1	1
11.	Pauriya		...
12.	Bedea	...	...
	Total	100	100

The members of a particular clan are not allowed to marry within the same clan. If they do so, they are ex-communicated, and in their own words *Bitlaha*[6] takes place. *Bitlaha* or social ostracism is the most severe type of punishment known to the Santhal, and is imposed for a violation of the rule of clan exogamy and tribal endogamy (Datta-Mujumdar 1956:47). But the *Bitlaha* has lost its rigidity among the Santhal and now a days the persons marrying in the same clan are out-casted. No one will take a meal at their place or will help in the agricultural operations. With the consent of the headman (*Manjhi), Paramanik* (Asstt. headman) and *Jog Manjhi,* they are settled outside the village and the end of the *Kulhi* (street).

They are not invited to the birth, marriage and death ceremonies. However, no such case of ex-communication was found at Banjhi.

Village as a Basis of Socio-cultural Integration

Besides family, lineage or clan as bases of socio-cultural integration, the next larger unit of socio-cultural integration is the village. As the ecological conditions of the three tribes are different, they have different socio-ecological situations which reflect different levels of socio-cultural integration.

As regards the Maler, the *Manjhiye* is the head of the Maler village and the post is hereditary and vested exclusively in one lineage. The *manjhiye* is the traditional head of the village panchayat, which works for the welfare of the entire village and also for the maintenance of law and order in the village. *Manjhiye* also collects land revenue and other elderly members of the village cooperate with him. Besides these the *Manjhiye* (headman) has the religious or sacred functions as well. In the *Pilai* festival, the headman takes his bath and observe the *Pilai* ceremony, alongwith other villagers. In the first instance, the worship is done at village level and then on family level by the each head of the family.

The villagers regard the headman and the *Gorait* (assistant to the headman) as superior to them and abide by the orders, of the *Manjhiye* (headman) communicated by the *Gorait.*

Political activity brings the whole village together making the village the smallest political unit of a region.

During the *Pilai* festival the Maler worship *Chale Gosain* and *Charka Gosain* on the village level. During this *Pilai* festival the Maler also sacrifice cow and buffalo. The entire village jointly collects subscription and purchases a cow and buffalo for the sacrifice. Cow is sacrificed almost every year but the sacrifice of buffalo depends upon the yield of the crop in the respective year. If the yield is bumper, this festival is observed on a large scale. In this regard we find that the Maler have a well-knit village.

Like the Maler and the Santhal the Mal Pahariya are co-operative and help their fellow-villagers in need and seek the general welfare of the community. At the time of agricultural operations one helps the other, by lending cattle and offering free labour. The people of other clans are also regarded as kins, and boys and girls of the same village treat each other as brothers and sisters. Owing to this consideration, marriage within the village does not take place.

With the birth of any child there is pollution for the family and the parents are not allowed to go outside and they abstain from moving to any other place. After taking purificatory bath on the fifth day, the mother of the newly born baby puts vermilion mark on the husking lever grinding stone, winnowing fans and streams etc. She also goes to every house of the village and marks three or five times with vermilion on the grinding stone. She cannot cook food till *Narta* ceremony is observed, however she is allowed to fetch water from the stream and the well. The feast is given to the villages and from this day the mothers' pollution ceases and she is allowed to cook food.

On the occasion of marriage too they have a give to feast when all the villagers and other kins are invited and entertained. In case of death in a Mal Pahariyas family, we find that they observe *Bhoj* ceremony and a big communal feast is given to the villagers and other relatives. It is held that the large the invitees, greater is the glory of the deceased. So in the social and economic life as well, one notes an integration on village level among the Mal Pahariya.

In the political sphere the villages panchayat exercises the right which concerns the Mal Pahariya community as such. It decides intra and inter family disputes. Charma Mal Pahariya looks after the disputes of Marku village. For the collection of rent, Mesa Manjhiye, the headman of the Maler village, acts as the headman of Mal Pahariya village too. Sometimes he also decides some of their serious disputes in consultation with the Mal Pahariya headman.

In the sphere of religion, the Mal Pahariya worship their *Ganwa Deoti* in the month of *Magha* (January-February) and *Bhadra* (August-September) while taking the first crop from *Bhitta* and *Kurwa* after the harvest. The villagers join together and offer a brown goat and *Pochai* (maize or *Bajra* beer). This worship is done by Chamra Mal Pahariya, headman of the village and it is believed that with the propitiation of this deity the yield will be bumper and it will protect the villager from epidemic and disease and will not let any harm come to them. We see that in the field of religious, social and economic life of the Mal Pahariya the integration at a village level is quite significant but in the political life of the Mal Pahariya the village as such does not function as a unit, as among the Maler and the Santhal.

Among the Santhal the village level of integration is much stronger than that of the Maler. The economic activity of the Santhal is characterized by strong co-operative activity such as repairing of the houses is done by the villagers and one helps the other. In the *Sankrat Sendra* during *Magha* (January-February), the entire village goes on a ceremonial hunt.

In social life too, we find that marriage not only binds the two individuals, two families and two clans, but in a marriage the two concerned villages come together. It is again the headman and especially the *Jog Manjhi* who is concerned with arranging and concluding the marriage in a village.

In other ceremonies connected with the life cycle of a Santhal, the whole village participates. After the birth of a child, when *Nim dak Mandi* (name giving ceremony) is observed, the whole village joins in the feast. When a person dies in the villages, all the villagers join in the funeral procession and bury the dead. Again on the occasion of *Bhandan*[7] ceremony, when sacrifices are offered to the dead ancestors, participation at the village level takes place. In the feast other kinsmen of the bereaved family are invited along-with the fellow villagers.

Politically the village community is the smallest unit. The village is governed by the Panchayat or a council of the village elders. A number of political officers go to make a judical organ of the Panchayat i.e. (i) Headman (*Manjhi*) of the village (ii) *Paramanik* or Assistant headman (iii) *Nayki,* village priest who worships the village deities on annual festivals, (iv) *Jog-Manjhi,* who looks after the morals of the youth. These are the most important officials of Banjhi village panchayat. The posts of the above officials are hereditary but they may be changed if they are incompetent to do their duties.

The main function of the village Panchayat is to take care of the village community and solve different problems which affect the community as a whole. When a problem arises, a meeting of the entire village is held to discuss the matter and take a decision.

Apart from the economic, social, and political life, the religious life of the Santhal also show an integration of the whole community at village lever. In the religious sphere we find that there are different *Bongas* or supernatural, beings worshipped at different places, e.g. the chief of them are *Maran Buru Moraeko-Turuiko, Jaher-Era,*

Gosai Era, Pargana Bonga who resides at *Manjhithan* inside the village near the house of the headman where the headman makes regular offerings, while the rest reside at *Jaherthan* where a *Nayki* observes the ritual. The annual festival of *Baha* and *Sohrai* are also observed at the village level.

Inter-village Organisation as a Basis for Socio-cultural Integration

The inter-village level of integration among the three tribes respectively are also evidently noticed. The *Pilai* festival[8] is an important occasion when the Maler, in association with their relatives of different villages, join in the worship of different deities and their dead ancestors and also in merry-making, (i.e. in singing and dancing). The relatives of every Maler family are invited to join the festival which provides opportunity for merry-making, dancing and enjoyment. The younger boys and girls have opportunities to select their partners. The headmen of the neighbouring villages never fix the same date for the celebration of the *Pallai* festival as the villagers visit one another and join in their respective celebration which continue even for a month. In the political field the *Sardar* above the *Manjhiye* (head man) functions on an inter-village level. A *Sardar* has a number of villages under his jurisdiction. His post is hereditary and he has two main functions. Firstly, he is the head of all the villages which are under him and his court is the highest court of appeal for the Maler. Secondly, he is responsible for the collection of revenue of villages under his jurisdiction. He forces the headman of the different villages to deposit the land revenue in time.

Among the Mal Pahariya we also find socio-economic or socio-cultural integration at an inter-village level. The Mal Pahariya villages are very few in number and are located at a considerable distance from each other, but Chamra Mal Pahariya of Marku village, as a *sardar* of inter-village political organisation brings them closer. However, integration among the Mal Pahariya at inter-village level is not so remarkable as in the case of Maler and the Santhal. Further, the observance of *Narta* (birth rite) and *Bhoj* (annual death rite) is a matter of family concern in which the Mal Pahariya of different villages of the region participate still on a large scale even now-a-days.

The inter-village relationship among the Santhal are reflected specially at the time of annual hunt and during performance of the political activities. Politically, the village panchayat is part of a larger political unit, consisting of a number of villages. The head of this larger political units is called the *Parganait,* elected by the headman of the constituent villages. Inter-village disputes if not settled by the village councils concerned, are settled in the court of *Parganait.* There are about 100 villages under the *Praganait* of Banjhi Bangalow. The *parganait* system of the Santhal, in many ways, is similar to Maler's *Sardari* system and *Parha*[9] system of the Oraon and the Munda of Chotanagpur.

Besides the *Pargana,* the other large unit is the Hunt Council or *Lobir.*[10] In the *Lobir* all the Santhal have equal status. *Lobir* is the highest court of appeal and its judgement is final. The decision of ex-communication of a person from Santhal society can be taken and executed only in *Lobir.*

In religious sphere *Sohrai* (*Bandhna*) similar to Maler's *Pilai,* and *Baha* are the two important festivals of the Santhal which bring the neighbouring villages together. *Sohrai* is the harvest festival and it continues from five days. *Sankrat* celebrated on the last day of the *Pausa* (December-January) is associated with annual hunt and ancestral worship. It is celebrated by the entire village and a large number of invitees from other villages join in dancing, singing and merry-making which takes place around the sacred grove (*Jaherthan*) and village streets (*Kulhi*).

Baha festival is observed in the month of *Magha* or *Phalguna* (January-February or February-March). It is similar to *Holi Parab* celebrated by the Hindus. It is observed in the spring season and is marked by the offering of first fruit of *Mahua* and other wild flower namely *Sarjom Baha.* It also provides opportunities for participation in dancing and singing by the neighbouring villagers and reflects an example of inter-village level of integration. The two festivals also provide opportunities to the boys and girls to select their mates.

Caste Hierarchy

The discussion on various levels of socio-cultural integration of the three tribes does not show any evidence of caste like stratification within their own society but each tribe is assuming a position for itself and is also setting the position of others in the regional social structure. As such all the three tribes reflect and acknowledge the influence of Hinduism and it was found that the caste hierarchy has a place among them. There seems to be a sort of compromise between the tribal social structure and the Hindu social structure of the region, though there is no caste stratification within any of the three tribes. But each of the tribes is striving to have some place in the Hindu caste hierarchy.

The caste hierarchy is well reflected in the responses recorded about the respective social status of the three tribes. The opinion of one about the other differs in different contexts. In one context a tribe may be regarded of higher status while in the other context the same tribe is regarded a enjoy lower status. This factor may be analysed from the available data recorded in the following Table 6.3.

It is evident from the above table that the Mal Pahariya held superior social position in the hierarchy whereas the Maler have the lowest position and the Santhal occupy an intermediate position. Though the above table shows only subjective feeling of superiority and inferiority among them still the social hierarchy has set for them a relative social distance from one another. The Mal Pahariya regard the Maler and the Santhal of low social status and they do not accept meals prepared by them. Many arguments are put forth to justify this caste-like hierarchy.

(a) Ritual Status

The most important reason is that the Maler and the Santhal are beef-eaters but the Mal Pahariya abhor it and instead they show reverence to the cow. Whenever their (Mal Pahariya's) cow dies with a rope round its neck, the family has to observe *Bhoj* (ritualistic feast) in the name of the dead cow. The Mal Pahariya also do not take water from that well or stream where any cow has died. Further the Mal Pahariya also do not touch the dead cow and the dead body is removed by the Maler mostly, who eat its flesh when the cow is died due to the wound caused by wild animals. The Santhal in the absence of Maler also help in the disposal of the dead cow from Mal Pahariya's village.

The Mal Pahariya are of the opinion that they follow more strict ritualistic rules whenever a birth or death takes place in a family. They further observed that they do not accept meals cooked by a woman in her menstrual period till she takes bath and is free from it. The Maler and the Santhal and even the Hindus of this area are not so orthodox and they accept meals prepared by a woman during her menstrual period. At the time of delivery the Mal Pahariya segregate the pregnant woman into a separate hut where she stays for five days till she take purificatory bath. Moreover, they never accept meals prepared by her till *Narta* ceremony is observed, which generally takes place after three months. But the Maler and the Santhal do not follow strict rules as a result of which the Mal Pahariya regard them to be of low caste and abstain from taking meals at their places.

The Maler and the Santhal in general are of the opinion that the Mal Pahariya never accept meal at their places as they regard themselves superior to the other two tribes.

Now, we pass on to the relation between the Maler and the Santhal. According to the Mal Pahariya, the Santhal occupy the next position, because they do not accept mean cooked by the Maler. While on the other hand, the Maler have no objection in accepting food from both the Santhal and the Mal Pahariya. Thus they regard Santhal to be superior to the Maler, in so far as the rules of commensality is concerned.

The Santhal on the other hand also regard the Maler as low because of their beef-eating. On enquiry as to when both the Santhal and the Maler eat beef, why only, the Maler were regarded to be low the Santhal informants gave a convincing reply and said that the Maler eat flesh of the dead cows and oxen, but the Santhal do not and owing to this they regard the Maler to be inferior to them. The Santhal further said that among the Maler both husband and wife take meals together, but the Santhal and the Mal Pahariya do not, therefore they consider the Maler to be ritually inferior to them.

(b) Economic Status

Now, following the economic implication of the hierarchy, we find that the Mal Pahariya occupy the lowest position. All the Maler and the Santhal are of the opinion that the position of their tribe in

TABLE 6.3

Social Status of the Three Tribes in the eyes of one another

Name of the respondents	*No. of respon-dents*	*Name of the tribe about which referred*	*Social position of other tribes according to respondents*							
			Superior person	*percent*	*Inferior person*	*percent*	*Equal person*	*percent*	*No reply person*	*percent*
Maler	49	Mal	7							
		Pahariya	32	65.3	17	34.7	...	...	...	...
		Santhal	25	51	24	49	...	...	...	...
Mal Pahariyas	13	Maler	...	...	13	100	...	...	...	...
		Santhal	...	...	13	100	...	...	...	...
Santhal	90	Maler	...	...	89	98.9	...	...	1	1.1
		Mal Pahariya	73	81.1		7.8	5	5.5	5	5.5

the eyes of the Mal Pahariya is superior. On the other hand the Mal Pahariya opine that the position of their tribe in the eyes of the Maler and the Santhal is inferior, i.e. the Mal Pahariya held that according to the Maler and the Santhal they are the poorest.

So far as the economic condition is concerned the Santhal are referred to be better-off than the Maler and so the Santhal are said to be occupying the highest position in this respect. The Santhal also claim that the Maler are economically poorer than the Santhal, but former (the Maler) are economically superior to the Mal Pahariya.

(c) Stereotypic Status

All the three tribes contemptuously assign a particular position to the other taking their different dominant traits into consideration and they also assign there own position in comparison to others.

The Maler and the Santhal regard the Mal Pahariya to be low because they steal grains and other things. The Maler and the Santhal call them (the Mal Pahariya) as '*Kalwer*' in Malto and '*Komro*' in Santhali, meaning thereby thief. In view of this the Mal Pahariya occupy a very inferior position in the eyes of the Maler and the Santhal. The Maler refer to the Mal Pahariya as '*Mader Kalwer*' (Mader stands of Mal Pahariya and *Kalwer* for thief. Similarly the Santhal refer them as *Komro Bero Mar* meaning thereby the notorious Mal Pahariya thief (*Komro* means thief and *Mar* stands for Mal Pahariya).

But in the moral context the Maler and the Mal Pahariya regard the Santhal to be inferior because they are immoral as among them pre-marital and extra-marital sexual relations are common. The Santhal capture any girl in the market and take her away by force but there is none to object to it among them.

On the other hand the Santhal and the Mal Pahariya are of the opinion that the Maler are inferior to them because they are very dirty. The Santhal contemptuously call the Maler as *Munde.* By *Munde* the Santhal mean a low class people who eats with his wife and accepts meals cooked by people belonging to different caste and communities and are also of very dirty habits. Similarly the Mal Pahariya call them (Maler) as *Chet,* a corruption of Hindi *Chit* meaning supine. The Maler contemptuously refer to the Santhal as

Neru Mochken in Malto and *Jomro Jojom* in Santhali meaning thereby snake eaters. The Maler emphatically opined that the Santhal eat snake, frog, and flesh of every animal excepting dog and horse.

The analysis of the above situation shows that the three tribes have a flexible hierarchy. The position is inter-changeable with the changing context. In the social and rituals side we find that the Mal Pahariya occupy the highest position followed by the Santhal, and the Maler who hold the lowest position. In the economic level the Santhal are taken to be well off and the Mal Pahariya are the poorest of the three.

When we come to the question of stealing habit and the extent of criminality among them, it is gathered that the Maler and the Santhal think that the Mal Pahariya are thieves. Owing to it the Mal Pahariya, who occupy the highest position in the hierarchy now fall to the lowest position. Likewise when the question of morality comes that Santhal occupy the lowest position whereas when cleanliness is taken into consideration the Maler again occupy the lowest position. So we find that the hierarcy is not rigid, it is flexible.

The discussions centred round the social life of three tribes show that the three tribes living in the three different ecological settings have three different levels of socio-cultural integration and also that the three tribes occupy different positions in the Hindu Caste hierarchy and the Mal Pahariya being ritually superior among the three tribes maintain social distance from the Maler and the Santhal in so far as the rules of commensality is concerned.

Inter-personal Relationship among the Three Tribes

In addition to their socio-religious interactions at the level of villages, individuals among them do interact with one another. A few individuals among the three tribes have intimate friendship with one another.

The nature and extent of such friendly relations, however, are limited because of geographical distance, ethnic, linguistic and cultural differences. Friendship is expressed as '*Pera*' among the three tribes. *Pera* is a common term for a friend used by the three tribes. The number of such *Pera* in communities other than their own has been given in the following Table 6.4.

TABLE 6.4
Inter-tribal Friendship

Name of the respondents	*Percentage of those having friends*			*Percentage of those having no friends*	*Total percentage*
	Maler	*Mal Pahariya*	*Santhal*		
Maler	...	6.1	51	42.9	100
Mal Pahariya	61.5	...	38.5*	38.5	100
Santhal	8.9**	8.9		91	100

* 38.5 per cent of the Mal Pahariya stated that they have both the Maler and the Santhal as friends.

** 8.9 per cent of the Santhal reported that they have both the Maler and the Mal Pahariya as friends.

The Opinion of Maler and Santhal about Mal Pahariya Friends

From the Table 6.4 it is evident that the Maler and the Santhal have fewer friends among the Mal Pahariya, whereas the Mal Pahariya claim more number of friends among the Maler and the Santhal. This question can be easily understood in context with the following description.

Firstly, we have noted that both the Maler and the Santhal regard the Mal Pahariya as ritually superior. Owing to this they do not accept them (Mal Pahariyas) as friends, because the latter do not accept food cooked by them. During investigation only one Maler individual (Katgu Pahariya) reported that one Durga Botra (a Mal Pahariya) formerly living near his house at Deopahar took meal at his residence on some occasions. But the others claim that the Mal Pahariya do not take meals prepared by the Maler. Once the author had the occasion to join the Maler and a Mal Pahariya while they were distilling *Mahua* liquor in the forest near a stream. Distillation was being done by Durga Botra, a Mal Pahariyas while Meinya Mesa, Rupa, Mesa Manjhiye etc. were also there. It was observed that Durga Botra distributed the liquor to the Maler who were present there. The headman of Deopahar, Mesa Manjhiye, and Rupa Pahariya (*Mukhiya* of Paharpur Panchayat) a resident of Deopahar were referring Durga as '*Mita*' (friend). Again at the time of offering worship in the month of *Magha* (January-February) in the house of Chamra Mal Pahariya the author heard Mesa Manjhiye addressing Chamra's wife as '*Bahu*' as the Hindus call their younger brother's wife and daughter-in-law.

Secondly, owing to the poor economic condition of the Mal Pahariya, the Maler and the Santhal do not regard the Mal Pahariya as their friends and do not claim friends among them. Though the ecological conditions of Mal Pahariya and the Maler are not very dissimilar and visits between the Maler and the Mal Pahariya are frequent yet the Maler do not claim the Mal Pahariya as their friends. The Mal Pahariya have very small plots of land which are not sufficient for their livelihood. Hence, the Mal Pahariya are not in a position to maintain reciprocal give and take relationship and are unable to return the gifts received from their friends belonging to the Maler and the Santhal communities.

Thirdly, as the Mal Pahariya are regarded as notorious thieves, both the Maler and the Santhal do not want to be on friendly terms with them as they think that if they are intimate with them, they may manage to cut *Sendh* i.e. break into the walls and may take away the grains and utensils. It is also held that the Mal Pahariya steal goats and crop from the fields.

The Opinion of Mal Pahariya about Santhal and Maler Friends

On the other hand, the Mal Pahariya being in a very poor economic condition have to depend on the Maler for bamboo and on the Santhal for rice and paddy. Owing on the dependence, they count many Maler and the Santhal individuals as their friends. Among the Mal Pahariya 61.5% claimed that they had Maler friends, whereas 38.5% of them reported that they had also Santhal friends.

Again as the Mal Pahariya are hard and notorious drunkards and habitual distillers of *Mahua* liquor both the Maler and the Santhal, while crossing through Marku, purchase wine at the rate of 50 Paise per bottle. The author has personally noticed many such dealings in wine of the Mal Pahariya with the Maler and the Santhal. The Santhal women while returning from the forest with Sal leaves at times, also purchase wine from the Mal Pahariya and share them jointly.

The Maler and the Santhal Friends

Relation between the Maler and the Santhal are more cordial because the different ecological settings limit their resources and put them on the mutual dependence of one another and give rise to a particular pattern of economic and social relationship. The '*Pera*'or friends are entertained with drink and feast, whenever one pays visit to the other. Among the Maler 51.% have Santhal friends, who invite them on every joyous occasion and entertain them with feast and drink, and also offer them some seers of grains for their families. In return the Maler also give grains and offer wine and palm juice etc. It is true that the Santhal regard them to be inferior and maintain a distance, yet the Maler and the Santhal are friends. Whenever, any Maler visits their Santhal friends they give a few seers of paddy or pulse or maize and, in return, the Maler also give maize to their Santhal friends. The relationship is quite cordial and reciprocal as regards the Maler and the Santhal friends are concerned.

The Maler and the Santhal both agree that they maintain the give and take relationship, but the Mal Pahariya do not. The main reason put forward by the Maler is that the Santhal are rich and economically their position is higher than the Maler. In the reciprocal offering of grains and feast to their friends the Santhal are liberal. Hence the friendly relationship between the Maler and the Santhal lasts longer in this regard. The Santhal state that the Maler maintain the friendly relation often, and offer grains, bamboo etc. to their friends. At the time of construction and repair of the house the Santhal take bamboo from their Maler friends free of cost, and during harvest and other such occasion they entertain the Maler with feast and drink. *Paramanik* of Banjhi and Somai Baskey of the same village had friendly relation with Katgu Pahariya of Deopahar and they took bamboo from Katgu Pahariya free of cost, whereas Katgu occasionally enjoyed their company while drinking and eating.

The Santhal of Banjhi show that a small percentage (8.9%) of the informants have friends among the Maler. The main reason is that the Maler villages are situated on the hill covered with dense forest separated from Santhal villages by the forests and hills. The movement of the Santhal on the hill is restricted and owing to this only 8.9% of the informants have their friends at Deopahar, situated 3 miles away on hills from Banjhi.

In addition to Banjhi there are other Santhal villages within a distance of one and half miles from Deopahar, viz., Paharpur in the east and Tetulia in the west. The Maler have friends in these two villages as well and so the percentage of the Maler informants having friends among the Santhal is greater than santhal having friends among the Maler.

Birth Rite

Invariably the expectant woman among the three tribes is attended by some old and experienced women of the village. Among the Maler, however, in absence of any such woman, the husband attends to his wife and the umbilical cord *Kude* is also cut by him in all cases with a knife or sharp piece of bamboo. The placenta (*Makoda*) is buried by the father near the house, whereas the umbilical cord (*Kude*), when it falls after drying in about a week's time, is carried by the father in an earthen pot. Oil and a leaf with ashes are put in a pot and it is hung on a three, preferably the *Karam* tree. But among the Mal Pahariya and the Santhal the husband is not allowed to enter the house let alone attending the wife.

Birth pollution is observed by all the three tribes and the period varies from 3 to 7 days varying from tribe to tribe and the sex of the newly born child. The Maler clean the house with cow dung after a period of 5 or 7 days from the day of the birth of a child and the members of family take bath to free themselves from pollution. During this period avoidance of relationship is maintained and it is a taboo for the mother of the newly born child to cook food or touch the grains. Such a taboo is observed by the father of the child as well. He is also not expected to shave his beared or cut his hair. The couvade observed by the father is a remarkable feature of the Maler. At the time of purificatory ceremony he also observes a brief ritual by placing a *Karam* branch on the ground in front of the house offering some rice and sacrificing a chicken whose blood is dropped on the rice. The child is taken round the *Karam* branch and is made to bow down twice to touch the rice in which blood was dropped. Later on the branch is stuck on the roof. This ceremony marks the end of period of pollution during which the head of the family is debarred from attending any ritual or religious ceremonies outside the village and is not allowed to partake of the sacrificial meat. These taboos are strictly followed by the Maler. In fact the author observed that Mesa Manjhiye, who was on this pollution period, did not attend *Pilai* festival at Pakuriya village.

Among the Mal Pahariya also the mother, father and the newly born child are considered to be unclean for five days. The expectant mother enters a temporary shed called *Kuriya* which is prepared by her husband and she has to remain there for five days after the delivery. The husband has also to remain outside his own house and is not allowed to touch water of the house nor is he allowed to enter *Kuriya.* It is a taboo for him to go to jungle for bringing logs and wood or to climb a tree or roof or get engaged in agricultural operation. On the 5th day purificatory bath is taken by the father, mother and the child. The nails are pared and the hair of the father and child are cut and they undergo a ritual bath which purifies them only partially. The woman is allowed to fetch water from the stream but she cannot touch grains or cook food till the *Narta* ceremony is performed. This is observed after two to six months from the birth of the child depending on the capability of the family to procure provision for feast to be given on this occasion to the kinsfolk, villagers and friends. On the *Narta* day the members of the family take ceremonial bath in the stream and put vermilion mark on its bank. The child's mother goes from house to house putting vermilion marks on winnowing fan, pestle, grinding stone, husking lever, hearth etc. This process is known as *Kuladali.* In the night the child's mother prepares food and serves it to all who are present there. The child's father takes the first morsel and then the others start eating.

Among the Santhal the period of pollution is three days in case of birth of a girl and five days in case of a boy after which a purificatory bath is taken by the family members. The purificatory bath and the ceremony attached to it are called *Janam chattihar.* The male members shave their head and beard which is not confined only among the members of the family but also extends to the village headman, the priest and the other villagers. The last to be shaved is the child. After the shaving of the head and beard, the men and women go to the neighbouring pond to take bath. The midwife ties a thread soaked in turmeric around the child's waist. Then the child along with the villagers assembled there are purified with rice-flour and water. Later the name is given to the child by the parents and it is announced before the villagers. The name of the newly born child corresponds to the name of one of the dead relatives. The eldest son is given the name of paternal grandfather, the next of the maternal grand father and the third of the brother of the paternal grand-father and so on. Similarly the daughters are named after the deceased grand-mother and grand father's sister etc. The ceremony ends with a purificatory feast and drink called *Neem-Dak-Mandi.* The *Arwa* rice is boiled with *Neem* leaves is distributed to the villagers.

Puberty Rite

There is no special religious rite connected with the puberty of the girls among the Maler and the Mal Pahariya. In both of these communities during the menstrual period the girl is not allowed to cook food, touch grain or enter the cattle shed because of the pollution. The Maler consider this period as dangerous because the girl is more susceptible to evil influences of the spirits. The Mal Pahariya observe the period of pollution more strictly than the Maler and the Santhal. The Maler observe a simple *Tokwaro* ceremony at the time of first menstruation of the girl which is at the age of 12-13. The nearest kin of the girl purchases a piece of cloth called *Tokwaro* from the market and gives it to the girl to cover her breast. No religious ceremony or worship is performed on this occasion.

When the menses stop, bathing and washing of clothes purifies the girl and than she is allowed to perform the household duties.

Among the Santhal the situation is different. The boys and girls on attaining the age of puberty, must perform *Chacho Chattihar*[11] in order to be admitted into the society as a full-fledged member. It allows them to attend the communal worship of the deities and to eat the sacrificial meat. The ceremony is performed by serving rice-beer to the assembled villagers in the house which is followed by dancing and singing. This ceremony must be performed before the marriage or death of a person because it is considered that without it the impurities of the youth will not be washed away and without this initiation the youth will not be allowed to participate in the village affairs. However, this ceremony is confined to the Santhal only and the Maler and the Mal Pahariya are not invited to it.

Marriage Rite

The marriage season among all the three tribes beings after the *Moti Jharna* fair, which is held near a waterfall of the same name near Maharajpur Railway Station on the occasion of *Shivaratri,* a festival of the Hindus signifying the day of married of Lord Shiva with Goddess Parvati. It generally falls in the month of *Phalguna* (February-March).

The marriage negotiations are conducted through the match-makers known by different names among the different tribes like *Sitodar* among the Maler, *Sithu* among the Mal Pahariya and *Bartul* or *Raebarik* among the Santhal.

Among the Maler the *Sitodar* gives a *Punno Mala* (garland of glass beads), one *Tokwaro* and a rupee to the girl as the contract money and she gets betrothed to the boy. Before the acceptance of the contract money the girl's consent is sought, and the question of bride-price (*Baṇdi-Taka*) and date of marriage are fixed by the two *Sitodars* according to the lunar calendar usually falling after the market days. The *Sithu* among the Mal Pahariya makes the selection of the match with the consent of both bride and bride groom. And then the groom's party as in the case of the Maler gives a *Punno Mala* (garland of glass beads) to the bride. Similarly the *Bartul* or *Raebarik* among the Santhal meets the *Jog Manjhi* and selects the bride in consultation with her father and other relatives.

In case the marriage is not performed in the same year the Mal Pahariya and the Santhal have to give a gift of cloth to the bride known as *Saljogani* cloth among the Mal Pahariya and *Khandi* and '*Painchi Parhan*' among the Santhal. The Mal Pahariya present *Saljogani* cloth on the eve of Dussehra or Durga Puja (which generally falls in October) and the Santhal present *Khandi* on the occasion of *Sohr ai* or *Bandhana* and *Painchi Parhan* in the month of *Asadha* or *Sravana* (June-July or July-August). There is no such obligation among the Maler.

Payment of bride price—called *Bandi Taka* among the Maler, *Pon* among the Mal Pahariya and *Gonong* among the Santhal—is a common feature of all the three tribes.

Apart from these, there are other similarities in the marriage rituals of the Mal Pahariya and the Santhal, which are in many ways different from that of the Maler. The Maler do not observe *Marwa* ceremony as it is observed among the Mal Pahariya and the Santhal. But *Senduradan* (application of vermilion) is the essential and the final rites among all the three tribes. In order to have a detail picture of the marriage rites of the three tribes we shall now describe these for each tribe separately.

Among the Maler the groom's party carries a *Bandi Kissu* (marriage pig for the bride's village) along with maize flour, pulse, spices, oil, mat and new clothes, consisting of *Tokwaro* and Sari for the bride. Before starting they get a feast at the groom's place. The marriage party or *Bariat* is ceremonially obstructed while entering the bride's village till a customary payment or *Dasturi* of Rs. 2 is made. The groom and his near relatives are received by the bride's parents and their relatives are offered *Chuti* (hand made cigar). The young boys and girls dance in two separate groups (bride's and bride groom's) throughout the night. The groom's legs are wished and smeared with oil after which both the groom and the bride join their own respective dancing groups. Next morning the groom's party makes over the promised bride price and other gifts to the father of the bride. In the meanwhile bride's mother's brother kills the *Bandi Kissu* by piercing an arrow head just above the ribs. The meat is distributed with a rupee from *Bandi Taka* among the closely related kins such as father's brothers, mother's brothers, and village officials like *Manjhiye, Paramanik* and *Gorait.* A piece of meat is also distributed among those villagers who participate in bride's dancing group. This is followed by a feast consisting of cooked maize and pulse brought by groom's party. The feet of both the bride and the groom are washed, body smeared with mustard oil and scented oil is put on their heads. They sit on a mat facing each other so that they are in direction of south and north. The groom applies vermillion on the forehead of the bride which she repeats on the groom's forehead. After this the groom feeds the bride boiled maize (*Jagu*) and pig's meat twice and the bride follows the suit. Later the *Sitodars* of both sides join the hands of the groom and the bride following which the groom forcibly takes the bride away from the house while the bride's relatives and friends throw coloured water on them. On having crossed the village border they are provided with an umbrella by the groom's party under which the proceed to the groom's village. On arrival there the feet of the bride and the groom are washed and smeared with mustard oil. The wet clothes of the bride and the groom are changed and food is served to them.

The Mal Pahariya observe *Mandowa*[12] (marriage shed) which occurs one day before the actual marriage. The central pillar consists of a *Mahua* (Bassia Latifolia) branch and a freshly cut banana tree. The other poles are of *Sakhua* (Shorea Robusta) tree. A *Kalsi* (pitcher) full of water with mango leaves is kept near the *Mahua* pillar. On the *Mandowa* day the *Dehri* (priest) sacrifices a pair of chicken near the central pole. The bride and the groom are anointed with oil and turmeric, at their respective villages, which is first applied by the headman of the respective village and the rest of the village follows the suit. In marku village, the headman being a Maler did not anoint with oil and turmeric but threw it on the ground and the rest of the villagers anointed it. A feast is thrown on this day to relatives and friends. On the arrival of the *barat* (marriage party), they are welcomed by sprinkling of water through mango leaves from *Mandowa Kalsi* by the bride's party. This ritual is called *Parichan.* This is accompanied with the dance and songs from each party ceremonially abusing one another. Later the bride and the groom are made to sit near their respective parents in the *Mandowa* at bride's hair and the bride does so on the groom's forehead. This rite is called *senduradan* (gift of vermillion) which is received by the shout of *Haribol* (remember God). The bride and the groom are given parched rice as breakfast in separate bowls which is followed by *Chuma wan* or *Jatuk* ceremony (showering of ritualistic rice) symbolising the blessings of the parents and other elders. After this they return to the groom's village. Sometimes the Mal Pahariya groom wear wedding crown (*Mauri*) during the marriage. After seven days the groom and the bride return to bride's place marking an end to restriction on visiting each other. This is called *Sathara.*

The Santhal, like the Mal Pahariyas, observe *Marwa* ceremony in both the houses of the groom and the bride before the actual marriage. At groom's house it is performed four days before marriage and in bride's house three days. The *Jog Manjhi* fixes the central pillar of *Mahua* tree and the villagers fix the four outer pillars. Two small earthen pitchers, called *Kandwas Thilli,* containing water and mango leaves are placed near the central pole by the *Jog Manjhi*

After the erection of the *Marwa* a feast is thrown to the villagers. The *Jog Manjhi* selects three girls to assist him during the marriage who anoint the villagers and the groom or the bride, as the case may be, with oil and turmeric. The next day drinking of the remaining *Pochai* (millet or maize or rice beer) continues. It is known as *Marwa Baski.* A day before the scheduled departure of the *Barat* party *Da Bapla*[13] (water marriage) is performed which, according to Sona Murmu, headman of Banjhi, is very similar to the Hindu *Mathkor* ceremony observed a day before or on the same day as *Marwa* ceremony.

On reaching the bride's village, the *Barat* party performs dance and goes round the village where from every household the groom is given *Gur* (jaggery) and water. This ceremony is known as *Gurjom* ceremony. When they reach near the bride's house they are received with a dance from bride's side. The groom is bathed in the *Kulhi* (street) by the bride's party and a cloth is given to him from the bride's side. The *Raebarik* or the *Bartul* takes the bride's clothes brought by the groom's parent in a basket (*Dalia*) to bride's house where she is bathed by the groom's party and her friends help her in wearing the clothes. The bride is brought in the *Kulhi,* where the groom sprinkles water thrice with mango leaves. The bride seated on a flat basket is raised to the level of the groom who applies vermilion on the forehead and puts her into his won *Doli* (Palanquin) carried by men. The couple is brought inside the house where they eat together. After the application of the vermilion (*Senduradan*) a feast is held and the groom's party returns to its village with bride after due salutations. Some friends and relatives of the bride also accompany her upto groom's village.

Death Rite

The final rite centres round the burial or cremation of the dead body. The Maler bury the dead in a ground seat apart for the purpose and away from the village, the Santhal bury them in their own fields whereas the Mal Pahariya cremate the dead at the burning ghat.

In Deopahar, the Maler carry the dead body to *Masani* (burial ground) on the cot used by the deceased. A grave is dug and leaves and branches of the trees are put inside it then the dead body is placed in the grave alongwith its personal belonging like plates, sickle (*Tatru*), bow and arrow etc. The grave is field with earth and on top of it a big stone, a broken cot and thorny twigs are placed to protect it from wild animals. The near relatives offer food in the name of the deceased and other spirits and a pitcher full of water is left near the grave. Some water is also sprinkled over it.

After the burial the first *Bhoj* (feast) is given within five days near a stream outside the village where the sacrifice is made in the name of the spirits to appease the dead. Only the male can participate in the feast without which the family and the village are regarded as polluted.[14]

Annual feast (*Pilai* or *Bhoj*) is observed on a particular day by the entire village, each family inviting its near relatives and celebrating the ancestor worship by feasting and drinking, dancing and singing. Sometimes subscription is raised and a common sacrifice of *Kara* (buffalo) is offered to the ancestors which is known as *Kara Puje* or *Managerwe*. On this occasion drinks, clothes, pots etc. Are also offered to the ancestors at the burial ground. When buffalo is not sacrificed and only drinks and feasts are offered to the ancestors the ceremony is called *Palai* or *Bhoj*. After the first annual feast the widow or widower is allowed to remarry.

In Marku village the Mal Pahariya carry the dead on his cot and the relatives put turmeric paste and mustard oil on the dead body. The women in their period and those who have not yet performed the *Narta* ceremony (birth rite) are not allowed to do so. The corpse is taken to the burning ghat where some boiled rice is taken by the relatives of the deceased and a pyre is built on which the body is placed. The husband or the eldest or the youngest son lights the pyre from both ends. The head of the person who lights the pyre is shaved and the relatives and villagers shave their beards and pare their nails. After bathing they return to the village and anoint their body with turmeric and mustard oil and also eat *Sattu* (fried maize or beans flour) and salt at the deceased's house. This ceremony is called *Kunthawaday*. If this ceremony is not performed the bereaved family will have to give up the use of turmeric and salt for five days and throw a purificatory feast to be free from pollution.

Bhoj or final send off is given to the deceased on the 10th day or a month or a year after the death. Sometimes it is put off for years due to poor economic condition. On the *Bhoj* day the relatives of the deceased are invited from Champa Pahar, Gawai Bhitta and other villages. On this day they all go to *Masani* (burning ghat) with three pieces of cloth soaked in turmeric, *Pochai* and about quarter kilogram of cooked rice. In earthen pots are carried fried paddy and mustard oil. A symbolic house is made with these cloths—one is used to make a roof, the other placed below it and the third is to cover the effigy of the dead prepared out of rice. The fried paddy (*Lawa*) is offered in the name of the dead to the effigy. Then it is lifted with the help of threads soaked in mustard oil and put in an earthen pot. The person who had lit the pyre gets his head, moustaches and beard shaved near the stream, takes bath and throws the pot containing fried paddy in the stream and the party returns to the house where a goat is sacrificed and a chicken is offered near the hearth of the house in the name of the dead. *Pochai* is also offered to him. The meat and rice are cooked and the feast follows with wine and *Pochai.* The bigger is the party the greater is the respect for the dead. As such the Mal Pahariya often go in for heavy debt to express greater respects for the dead resulting into land alienation.

The burial ceremony of the Santhal differs from that of the Maler in as much as the hair and nails of the dead are cut and are kept on a *Mahua* or *Sakhua* leaf before laying the body in the grave. This is known as *Janbaha. Janbaha* is not performed in case of death due to pox or cholera. The relatives also put some money and utensils in the grave and before covering it the head of the family puts some fire on the mouth of the corpse signifying that the Santhal used to burn the dead body. Due to lack of logs and firwood in the plains they bury the dead. The cash money found under the pillow of the dead is spent in drinking wine and *Pochai* by those who carry the body to the grave. On return from the grave an offer of a chicken is make in the name of the deceased and nearest kins share it. Then they take their bath and the house is cleaned.

In order to get free from pollution *Garate* ritual is performed when boiled rice with pulse (*Khichari*) and chicken are offered to the dead near the stream. *Garate* is also known as *Nai-Gora* (paring of nails). The hair and nails of the dead are immersed in the stream. Some take it to river Damodar for its immersion. Till this ritual is performed the family cannot touch the seed, worship the deity or perform marriage.

Bhandan, a feast in which the sacrifices are offered to the ancestoral spirits, is the last rite connected with death. This ceremony is attended by a large number of persons including villagers and relatives. A cow or a calf is sacrificed in the name of the dead ancestor and the invites are entertained with its meat, *Pochai,* wine, etc. These days the poor economic condition and prohibition of calf's slaughter have contributed in decreasing such sacrifices yet some of the Santhal still sacrifice cow in the name of the dead ancestor at late night. The mourning period ends with this ceremony.

Inspite of the differences in the mode of the disposal of the dead there are certain similarities among the three tribes. All the three worship their dead ancestor, make offering to him, observe a period of pollution and throw a feast or *Bhoj* to the community in the name of the dead ancestor.

The interaction in social life of the three tribes depends on the nature and extent of their participation in one another's birth, marriage and death ceremonies. In subsequent paragraphs efforts have been made to identify the degree of social participation among the three tribes which are reflected in the rites of birth, marriage and death.

Among the Maler the birth rite is observed at the family level unlike the Mal Pahariya and the Santhal. It is observed strictly at the family level to free the family from pollution, and as the pollution is not extended to the kinsmen and village they do not invite their kinsmen, and fellow villagers. Also they do not invite their friends from other communities like the Mal Pahariya and the Santhal. In course of investigation only 4.1% of the Maler said that the Mal Pahariya attended the birth rite while only 2% of them (the Maler) acknowledged the presence of a few Santhal friends in the birth rite of their children. However, all the Mal Pahariya except one, and all the Santhal who were interviewed denied their presence at Maler's birth rite.

The Mal Pahariya on the other hand said that they invite their kinsmen, villagers and friends from other communities in the ritual connected with birth. In the *Narta* ceremony the Mal Pahariya arrange a feast in which they invite their kinsmen, fellow villagers and their friends from the Maler and the Santhal. While observing *Kuladali,* the mother of the newly born baby visits every household and puts vermilion mark on various household materials and with this the restriction on her movement is over. All the Mal Pahariya informants of Marku village and those from Champa Pahar and Jhirkdinga who came to attend the *Narta* ceremony at Buddu Mal Pahariya's place reported that they invite their kinsmen, villagers and friends. The Mal Pahariya of Marku village also stated that their Maler and Santhal friends from neighbouring villages Deopahar, Tetulia and Paharpur were invited. At Buddu Mal Pahariya's place, Mesa Manjhiye, Rupa, Dewano Gangu, Kago Gangu and Surja attended the *Narta* ceremony. All the Mal Pahariya said that the Maler headman alongwith some of his friends attended *Narta* ceremony at their place while 32.6% of the Maler informants said that they attended the *Narta* ceremony at Marku village.

About the participation of the Santhal in *Narta* ceremony 23.1% of the Mal Pahariya said that their Santhal friend had also joined in their celebration. Chamra Mal Pahariya invited Jetha Santhal and Pandu Santhal of Tetulia to attend the *Narta* ceremony and they attended this ceremony at Chamra's place but none of the Santhal from Banjhi reported that they had attended *Narta* ceremony. Hence such a case of Santhal being invited is rare and it was an exceptional case that they participated.

The Santhal like Mal Pahariya also invite their kinsmen, village officials and the other villagers in the rites connected with *Janam Chattihar* and *Nim-Dak-Mandi,* who have to observe shaving ceremony[15]. It is believed that village as a whole including kinsmen become polluted and this ritual marks the purification of the kinsmen and the village as a whole and only after this the village deity can be worshipped. No friends from other communities are invited by the Santhal and the Santhal informants reported that the Maler and the Mal Pahariya do not come to their village on this occasion. The Maler and the Mal Pahariya informants also confirmed this.

Among the Maler and the Mal Pahariya there is no initiation ceremony. The membership to the tribes is a birth-right. In the *Tokwaro* ceremony of the Maler there is no participation even by the entire village rather only two nearest kins are involved in it.

Among the Santhal the whole village participates in the initiation ceremony but others are not invited.

Unlike the birth rite, the participation of the three tribes in one another's marriage ceremony is more. Apart from inviting their kinsmen and fellow villagers the three tribes invite their friends from other communities also.

The Maler invite their kinsmen related to him through his wife and mother as well as his sisters and father's sisters married in some other villages. Usually the invitation is extended while they meet in the common market and if they fail to do so they go to their respective kins to invite them.

The nearest kinsmen have mutual obligations to observe. In the marriage of a boy the nearest kins help the father of the boy with cash and kind so that he can purchase a *Bandi Kissu* (marriage pig for the birde's people) and some amount may also be given as a *Bandi Taka* (bride price) to the bride's father Maize and other grains are also given by the kins for sending them to the bride's house and also for preparing rice beer and other drinks for a large scale consumption. The nearest kin, sometimes, stay with the family for a few days and they are entertained with food and drinks.

In the marriage of a girl, the nearest kins are invited and from the amount received as *Bandi Taka* (bride price), they get a share and the share from *Bandi Kissu* is also given to them. So we find that this type of mutual obligation among the Maler leads to kinsmen's participation in the marriage. When the bride and the bridegroom do not pull on well and when a divorce is decided, the nearest kinsmen who take share from bride price and *Bandi Kissu* return the gifts immediately to pay of the bride price.

The Maler also invite the members of their own community from other villages.[16] A formal invitation is extended to them through the *Gorait.*

The Maler from distant villages come on invitation (and at times without it also) and they actively participate in the dance. The marriage is treated as an important occasion when the unmarried boys and girls come to meet one another and select their mates. The gathering of the Maler in any village during marriage is a matter of great joy and they refer it is a *Mela* or a fair.

In addition to the active participation of the kinsmen and other villagers, as reported by all informants in case of the marriage of the girl, the headman and other village officials get a share from the *Bandi Kissu* and *Bandi Taka.* Moreover, at the time of marriage of a boy or a girl the headman and other village officials are invited and consulted in various matters and at different occasions. On the occasion of a boy's marriage the headman alongwith other village officials and elders of the village. Go to the bride's village in *Bariat.*

On the eve of marriage all the villagers join together in making the village tidy and neat and also in participating in the dance for three nights. The fellow villagers are also entertained with food and drink.

The Maler usually do not invite the members of the other tribal communities viz., the Mal Pahariya and the Santhal but sometimes a few members from these two tribes attend the marriage of the Maler. The Mal Pahariya beat drums on the occasion of marriage in a Maler's family. It was reported that at the time of marriage of Meinya Mesa and Gango (Mesu's son) of Deopaher three Mal Pahariya named Chutio, Kandana and Ratan Mal Pahariya beat drums. Such a participation of the Mal Pahariya on the occasion of marriage of a Maler is unanimously accepted by all the villagers of Deophar. About the payment to the Mal Pahariya it was said that there was no fixed rate, it depends on the capacity of the person concerned. Meinya Mesa gave 10 seers of maize to all the three. All the Maler do not afford to employ the Mal Pahariya as drummers during the marriage as mostly the fellow villagers, and few young boys from neighbouring villages participate in dancing with drums like *Mandar* and *Duggu,* for which they do not have to pay anything. In the capacity of a guest, a Mal Pahariya is rarely invited. Only one informant admitted that he invited his Mal Pahariya friend in the marriage.

Similar was the response about the Santhal friends as most of the Maler informants said that they did not invite the Santhal on the occasion of a marriage. The Santhal, however, come to see the marriage dance and if some of their friends come, a gift of half a seer of maize is given with some *Lahari* (*Arhar*) pulse. Only one information admitted in favour of the institution of a Santhal at his place during the marriage. It was also recorded that as the Maler bring musical instruments from the Santhal of Paharpur and Tetulia villages on payment of Rs. 2 to Rs. 4, the Santhal come to know about the marriage among the Maler. Some of them also come to participate or watch the dance. Among the Maler 46.9% admitted that the Mal Pahariya had come to see the marriage and 36.7% of them replied that the Santhal also watched the dance party. In admittance to this fact 76.9% of the Mal Pahariya and 3.3% of the Santhal replied that they attended the Maler's marriage at Deopahar.

Tha Mal Pahariya also invite their kinsmen, other villagers and their friends from other communities. Marriage among the Mal Pahariya is a matter of great joy and the occasion is celebrated by inviting the near relatives or kinsmen related through wife, mother, father and sister. The near relatives who come to attend the marriage bring some gifts of wine and grains and they also offer some gifts a bride and bride groom. The nearest kins are entertained with feast during their stay in the village and especially on the *Mandowa* and marriage days. They also invite their fellow villagers on these occasions and they are also entertained with feast and drink. All the Mal Pahariya of Marku regard it as their duty to participate as actively as the kins. The villagers are regarded as kins and the marriage between the boy and the girl of the same village is prohibited among the Mal Pahariya. The Mal Pahariya from neighbouring villages are also invited at Marku village. The population of the Mal Pahariya in the neighbouring area is meagre and thus they maintain a face to face relationship among themselves. In the marriage of Chamra Mal Pahariya's sister, for example, his relatives and friends from all the neighbouring Mal Pahariya villages viz. Champa, Sihli, Gawaibhitta, Jhirkdinga and Pagal were invited and they came to attend the marriage.

The Mal Pahariya of Marku village have a number of friends in the Maler and the Santhal villages. But the Mal Pahariya (who are socially superior) are economically poor and are not in a position to invite all their Maler and Santhal friends. Among the Maler friends the Maler headman is friend of all because he is also a virtual headman of Marku village and so he is always invited. The Maler headman is always accompanied by other members of his village and the Mal Pahariya host offer them food and drink. Before the marriage of a girl of a boy the Maler headman offers oil and turmeric on the ground and then whole village anoints the bride or the groom with the paste of oil and turmeric. After the marriage of the girl the Maler headman gets fifty Paise from the groom's party as it is believed that with the taking away of the bride the whole village is polluted and it affects the prestige of the headman. All the Mal Pahariya said that the Maler participate in their marriage on invitation, while 51% of the Maler informants said that they had attended the marriage ceremony at Mal Pahariya's village.

The Mal Pahariya also invite their Santhal friends but as the Santhal villages are slightly far away from the Mal Pahariya village, the Santhal do not participate in the marriages of the Mal Pahariya. Only Chamra Mal Pahariya said that he invited Pando Santhal and the late Sufal Manjhi of Tetulia in the marriage of his sister. Among the Mal Pahariya 7.7% of them said that the Santhal were invited to attend the marriage while 23.1% said that the Santhal came to attend the marriage through the they were not invited. Thus it is evident that the participation of the Santhal in Mal Pahariya's marriage is comparatively less than to the Maler's participation in Mal Pahariya's and Santhal's marriages.

The Santhal also invite their kinsmen, fellow villagers and their friends from other communities in marriage ceremony. When and marriage is settled the Santhal of Banjhi send invitation to their kinsmen to attend the marriage ceremony (*Bapla*). The invitation is extended with a betel and *Lagan* which is represented by a sal leaf tied with thread soaked in turmeric. The number of rounds made by the thread in the *Lagan* indicates the number of days after which the actual marriage will be performed. So the near and dear once come and participate in the marriage. The kinsmen bring gifts of rice-beer and grains.

The marriage of the Santhal is marked with joy not only for the bride or bridegroom and their families but also for other kins and the entire village. The head of the household arranges the marriage with the consent of *Jog-Manjhi* and headman. The entire village is invited and the villagers extend their help and participate on different occasions, such as *Marwa* and *Da Bapla* in which the village officials like *Jog Manjhi* has certain rituals to perform while the villagers join in the feast and drink on the occasion of *Marwa* and *Marwa Baski* and offer *Gur* (jaggery) to the bridegroom when the *Barat* goes round the village. All the villagers also join in singing and dancing and enjoy collectively, on all important occasions like *Marwa. Marwa Baski, Da Bapla, Parichan, Senduradan* etc.

The Santhal of Banjhi usually do not invite the Maler and the Mal Pahariya but the Maler and the Mal Pahariya come to observe the *Senduradan,* an important marriage rite of the Santhal. Among the Santhal 28.9% of them said that the Maler participated in the marriage at Banjhi, while only 18.9% said the same thing about the Mal Pahariya. The Santhal also said that on such occasion when the Maler come to attend they are offered drink and meals while grains are given to the Mal Pahariya because they do not accept cooked food from the Santhal. Further 51% of the Maler of Deopahar and 76.9% Mal Pahariya of Marku admitted that they attended the marriage rites of the Santhal at the neighbouring Santhal villages.

The Maler and the Mal Pahariya go to the plain frequently and observe the marriage of the Santhal, though they are not formally invited. In the marriage of the present *Jog Manjhi's* sister of Banjhi, the author has seen Chamr Mal Pahariya, Kandana, Kanhai and Chutio of Marku village and Mesaa Manjhiye, Tika Jawra, Rupa Pahariya and few other Maler of Deopahar. As it was a market day there was a huge crowd to observe the *Sanduradan* ceremony.

Apart from these it was also gathered that the Mal Pahariya also beat drums in the marriages of the Santhal. Chutio, Kandana and Ratnan Mal Pahariya have bead drums in the marriage of Sona Murmu's daughter at Banjhi. Sona Murmu gave them Rs. 8 in all and 10 seers of rice each. At Pando Santhal's house in Tetulia village Chamra Mal Pahariya and others have beat drums in the marriages of all the five sons of Pando, so they got one goat and ten seers of rice each. Thus we find that the participation of the Mal Pahariya as drummers in the marriages of the Maler and the Santhal is quite remarkable.

The social relations of the three tribes in the death rituals show that comparatively their participation is more than at the birth rite. On the death of any relative of the Maler they invite their kinsmen and fellow-villagers. Immediately after the death of any person, the near kins and relatives living in the villages rush to the house of the bereaved family alongwith other villagers and village officials.

No formal invitation is extended to the kinsmen, fellow-villagers those friends and relatives who are living in other villages. The villagers and near kins join the funeral procession and also cover the grave by putting some handful of earth in the grave. With the death of a person the village gets polluted and worship of the village deity is prohibited till first *Bhoj* is observed. But in annual death rite known as *Pilai* festival, the nearest kins from the village and other fellow villagers and the friends and relatives from distant villages are also invited to attend the function and also in the feast. In *Pilai* festival entire village participates in mourning the death of their ancestors as in dancing and singing.

Regarding the invitation to the Mal Pahariya and the Santhal, the Maler said that no formal invitation is extended to them but they come from neighbouring villages to see the rituals and dances during the *Pilai* festival. Among the Maler 81.6% said that the Mal Pahariya from Marku came to see the *Pilai* festival, while 54% of them said that the Santhal also came from the neighbouring villages of Tetulia, Paharpur and Banjhi. The offerings made by the Maler, such as clothes, pots and other articles at the burial ground were taken away by the Mal Pahariya and the Santhal of the neighbouring villages. All the Mal Pahariya admitted that they brought the pots and clothes offered by the Maler to their dead relatives from the burial ground.

Unlike the Maler, the invitation to the kinsmen, fellow-villagers and other relation and friends is not extended when a person dies in a Mal Pahariya family. However, the *Gorait* of the village informs the nearest kin living in other villages viz. Gawaibhitta and Champa Pahar who come to the house of deceased to show sympathy and mourn the death of their relative. The villagers also assemble there of their own and they join the funeral procession up to the burning ghat. But the nearest kins put mustard oil and turmeric on the dead body and become polluted for five days. They do not take meat, fish, turmeric, salt during the period-till purification feast is not given—and shave the beard and cut their hair along with the primary mourners. A brief feast is arranged on the return from the burning ghat in which the fellow villagers and the nearest kin attend. On such occasion no invitation is extended to the Maler and the Santhal. But the Maler headman is invited at the time of *Bhoj* ceremony.

Though the Maler in general are not invited some of them from Deopahar accompany the Maler headman during *Bhoj* ceremony and all of them are entertained with food and drink. But only 15.4% of the Mal Pahariya said that they invited the Santhal from Tetulia and Paharpur and entertained them with food and drink but none from Banjhi were invited.

Though the Maler and the Santhal are not generally invited but they come to attend the *Bhoj* ceremony. All the Mal Pahariya said that the Maler attended the *Bhoj* ceremony at Marku village while only 23.1% of them said that the Santhal had also attended the ceremony. Among the Maler 40.8% admitted that they had attended the *Bhoj* ceremony of the Mal Pahariya while only one per cent of the Santhal attended the same.

The Santhal invite their kinsmen, other villagers, as well as their friends belonging to other communities. but not the Maler and the Mal Pahariya on various rituals connected with death.

The news of the death of any relative or villager spreads in no time in the village and the nearest kins assemble immediately at the house of the bereaved family. The nearest kins from neighbouring villages also come if the news reaches them in time. All the relatives and friends take the dead body to the burial ground. They join in a *Garate* and they are also shaved by the *Napit* (barber). The kinsmen put some offerings of money and utensils act. The headman, *Paramanik, Gorait* etc. are the important village officials who also join in the rituals. In the last rite connected with death (i.e. *Bhandan*) the nearest relatives and other kinsmen are also invited from distant villages either through a messengers or personally when they meet in the local market. An invitation is extended to the fellow villagers along with other village officials in which feast and drink are arranged on a large scale by the bereaved family. The fellow villagers participate more actively in dancing and singing which continues for day and night. *Bhandam* shows a greater degree of participation of the nearest kins and other relatives as compared to *Garate*.

Generally the Maler and the Mal Pahariya are not invited during the *Garate* and the *Bhandan* ceremony. But the Santhal said that the Maler come during the *Bhandan* ceremony at their village and they are offered *Pochai* and food. About the Mal Pahariya, the

Santhal said that they do not come in *Bhandan* ceremony because the Santhal sacrifice a cow or a calf and the Mal Pahariya being non beef eater do not join. Among the Maler 51% of them said that they had attended the *Bhandan* ceremony at Santhal's village while none of the Mal Pahariya admitted that they had ever attended the *Bhandan* ceremony in any of the Santhal village. Thus it is true that the formal participation of the other two tribes in the death rite of the Santhal is not so significant but actual attendance of the Maler is quite considerable.

Process of Conflict

All the three tribes belong to the different villages and have different sets of customs which they observe at the family, village and on community levels. While there are several occasions of participation among themselves, there arise certain points of conflict as well. In case of birth, one does not find any clash but in marriage conflict may be noted in some sphere. We know that all the three tribes practise tribal endogamy and regard intertribal marriage as an offence which leads to inter-tribal disputes. The Mal Pahariya and the Santhal strictly adhere to this law. Whenever a Mal Pahariya or a Santhal marries a member of another tribe, he is out-casted. A few cases of marriage of the Mal Pahariya and the Santhal in the Maler tribe have been cited by them. The Mal Pahariya of Marku village said that a Maler of Naugachi Pahar married a Mal Pahariya girl of Champa Pahar; another at Champ Pahar, the Manjhiya's brother (who was a Maler) married a Mal Pahariya girl, at Jhirkdinga also a Maler married a Mal Pahariya girl. In all these three cases, the Mal Pahariya girls were out casted.

The Santhal of Banjhis said that Dudgu's niece married a Maler boy of Mandro, who was a servant at Dudgu's place, while another case was at Durga tola where a Maler boy married a Santhal girl. The families in which the Maler have married have been excommunicated and nobody invites them on any ceremonial or festival occasion.

Marriage between Santhal and Mal Pahariya was not reported. Among the Maler, it is said that there is no rigidity in the observance of tribal endogamy, though they also said that one should preferably marry within his own tribe. But they approve of inter-tribal marriage and the following case is cited in favour of the above statement. When Madu Bobe's father was alive he had a large amount of paddy land which was cultivated by Boso Santhal and his family of Banjhi. Boso had a good looking girl who was very efficient in paddy cultivation, so Madu Bobe's father, who was unmarried, wanted to marry Boso's daughter, but he could not marry the girl.

The villagers said that they will not object if a Maler brings wife from the Mal Pahariya and the Santhal, but the Mal Pahariya and the Santhal in turn will refuse to give a girl to a Maler. They on the other hand will have no objection if their girl is in love with a Mal Pahariya or a Santhal and marries him. But in Both the cases the Mal Pahariya and the Santhal will out-caste the couple.

The Mal Pahariya and the Santhal say that they are in conflict with the Maler because they do not follow tribal endogamy rigidly and they do not punish the couple and the family to which they belong. In this respect the conflict between the Mal Pahariya and the Santhal is not noticed.

The conflict in the death rite is not so apparent and her the Maler and the Santhal show no significant difference of opinion in matters of observing certain rites and beliefs. As the Mal Pahariya are non-beef eaters they do not approve of the sacrifice of a cow or a calf in the *Bhandan* ceremony of the Santhal and apart from not participating in the rites, they ridicule them. This has not led to any serious fight but the dispute though latent, is present in the minds of the Mal Pahariya. The Maler are indifferent in this respect. The Santhal also have no conflict with the Mal Pahariya.

Process of Competition

The *rites-de-passage* connected with the ritualistic observance of birth, marriage and death does not show any sort of competition among the three tribes. If the three tribes have any thing in common and if their interest clashes with that of others there may be some sort of competition. But we do not find such evidence of competition in any of the rites associated with birth, marriage or death.

The social organisation of the three tribes living in different ecological conditions show different levels of socio-cultural integration. The Maler living in the hilly and forested areas are more integrated at the family level and to some extent at the lineage level, whereas the Santhal living on the plains and accessible areas show greater degree of clan, village, inter-village and community level of socio-cultural integration. But the Mal Pahariya who are having an intermediate ecological setting are more integrated at clan (though not remarkable), village and inter-village level.

Referring to clan organisation, it may be viewed that the Mal Pahariya do not follow clan exogamy rigidly but in case of marriages within the same clan care is taken so that the couple may not be of the same lineage. Thus their position in this respect is also intermediate. Further the clan organisation among the Mal Pahariya has similar occupational basis as found among the Santhal. As they are known as the Hinduised section of the *Pahariya* (hill people) their lineage exogamy reflects their association with the Maler. However, with the contact of the Santhal and the neighbouring Hindus they have borrowed the clan classification but clan exogamy is not followed strictly.

Similarly the family type of the Maler and the Mal Pahariya shows existence of nuclear type while among the Santhal other types of family are also found in significant number. It is because their economic resources are much better to support a large family than the Maler and the Mal Pahariya. Thus there is a great deal of heterogeneity among the Santhal.

As far as the interactional aspect is concerned there is less active participation in the different social ceremonies and functions than in the economic activities. On the social side we find that the participation of the Maler and the Santhal in one another's birth ceremony is almost nil whereas the participation of the Maler in *Narta* ceremony of the Mal Pahariya is important but is of the least significance to the Santhal. On the other hand the Mal Pahariya do not participate in the birth ceremony of the Maler and the Santhal.

The participation of the three tribes in the marriage ceremony of one another is more than the birth ceremony. Though there is less active participation, they go to observe the marriage rites and participate to some extent in its performance. The Mal Pahariya's participation as drummers in some marriages of the Maler and the Santhal shows that they are more activity associated with the Maler and the Santhal of the neighbouring villages. Heer, of course, we find a level of participation which is different from the level of participation recorded in case of economic interdependence. In economic sphere the three tribes participate most actively and are interdependent but the social relations connected with different rituals like birth, marriage and death are at a very low level.

In spite of the fact that the level of participation in different ritual and social customs is low the three tribes show many common features in the performance of various rituals. The purificatory feast is arranged by all the three tribes (except the Maler) in case of a birth in the family. Similarly in case of death in family all the three tribes arrange a purificatory feast to the villagers and they also observe annual death rites in which offerings are made to the deceased.

In marriages there is a great deal of similarity between them. The *Senduradan,* a most important rite connected with marriage is a common feature in all the three tribes .The payment of bride price is another common feature. Similarly we again find that all the three tribes employ in intermediary to select a mate for a boy.

The construction of marriage shed (*Mandowa* or·*Marwa*) is a common feature for the Mal Pahariya and the Santhal. This is not found in case of the Maler. While water marriage (Da-Bapla) is a remarkable feature of the Santal only.

The role of the barber during birth and death rites is another common feature of the Mal Pahariya and the Santhal. Thus it is evidently noticed that the Mal Pahariya and the Santhal are gradually moving toward the fold of Hindu caste system. The illustration of the process are many such as acceptance of more Hinduised rituals like *Mandowa, Sanduradan,* anointment of oil and turmeric, and role of barber. In support of this process it may be pointed out that all the three tribes are also trying to associate themselves with the neighbouring Hindus. In this regard they also ascertain their position and the position of the other two tribes in the regional social structure and in the Hindu caste hierarchy. This process is gaining ground among the three tribes which bring them more closer to one another.

REFERENCES

1. The English equivalent is not clearly explained by the Santhal except a few like *Hansdak, Hembrom, Tuddu* etc. For detail *see* W.J. Culshaw's *Tribal Heritage*, Chapter VI, p. 67, London, 1949.

2. Bodding, P.C., *A Santal Dictionary*, Oslo 1932-36, Vol. IV, p. 596.

3. (a) Rowat, F., *Santals—Census of India 1931*, Vol. I, India Part III, Ethnographical, 1935, pp. 107-108.

   (b) Hearn, W.N., *Santals—Census of India, 1931*, Vol. I, Part III, Ethnographical, 1935, p. 168.

   (c) Mukherji C. C., *Santals, Census of India 1931*, Vol. I, India Part III, Ethnographical, 1935, pp. 111-112.

4. Among the Santhal as well as the Mal Pahariya, no trace of occupational specialisation among the various clans was noticed and according to them all enjoy the same social status. However, the *Besra* among the Santhal and *Sing* among the Mal Pahariya are regarded as inferior to other clan members and hence the members belonging to other clans express their unwillingness to have marital relations with them.

5. For details of to temistic basis of clan classification *see:—*

   (a) Culshaw, W.J., *Tribal Heritage: A study of the Santals*, London, 1949.

   (b) O'Malley, L.S.S., *Bihar District Gazetteer*, Santhal Parganas, Patna, 1938, p. 130.

6. For details *see:*

   (a) O'Malley, L.S.S., *Bihar District Gazetteer*, Santhal Parganas, Patna 1938, p. 136.

   (b) Datta-Majumdar, N., *The Santal–A study in Culture Change*, Delhi, 1956, pp. 47, 95, 105-6, 112.

   (c) Sachchidananda, Bitlaha Ceremony of Santhal's, *Eastern Anthropologist*, Vol. 9, No. 4 pp. 42-48, Sept.–Nov., 1955.

7. *Bhandan* is the annual death rite observed by the bereaved family. Only after the performance of this ritual, the marriage and other important activities can be resumed by them.

8. Vidyarthi, L. P. *The Maler, A study in nature, man and spirit complex of a hill tribe*, 1963, p. 63.

9. Roy, S.C. (a) *The Oraons of Chotanagpur*, Calcutta 1915 pp. 419-29.
   (b) *The Munda and their Country*, Calcutta, 1912.
10. Datta-Majumdar N., *The Santhal—A Study in Culture Change*, Delhi, 1956 p. 47.
11. For details see P. O. Bodding's *Traditions and Institutions of the Santals*, Oslo, 1942, pp. 25-28.
12. Similar ceremony is also performed by the Hindus which is known as *Marwa* marriage shed.
13. For details consult P.O. Bodding, *op. cit.*, pp. 439-44 and Culshaw W. J., *Tribal Heritage—A Study of the Santals*, London, 1949, pp. 140-141.
14. On the death of a son of Kesho Pahariya a day before the last day of *Magha* (January-February), the month during which *Mugali Nado* (a village deity) is worshipped created a problem as this worship could not be postponed beyond *Magha.* Earlier due to a child birth in the family of the headman, Mesa Manjhiye, this worship could not be performed. As such Kesho Pahariya was forced by the headman and the villagers to observe *Bhoj* on the very day his son died so that the worship could be performed next day to avert supernatural calamity that might befall the village. Since the worship of village deity was involved purification by way of *Bhoj* was necessary. Otherwise death pollutes the particularly family. Other families may perform may perform worship of their family deities.
15. Datta-Mujumder, N., *The Santals—A Study in Culture Change*, Delhi, 1956, p. 87.
16. In course of investigation it was observed that at Deotikri village in Taljhari block the Maler from Digra, Deodandi, Darwas Pusurbhitta villages came to participate in the marriage dance.

SEVEN

The Concept of Structure: Tribe, Caste and Nation

THERE are two assumptions, which the reader may challenge. The first of these is the identification of 'structure' with ultimate consistency, and the second is the admittedly crude estimate of political motivation, which is an easy target for superficial criticism, although it is less easy to impugn its pragmatic usefulness.

Structure, in the way that we have used the term, is of course an abstraction, a set of generalizations abstracted from regularities of behaviour or from statements about whey ought to be regularities of behaviour. It is possible to use such a structure as a model, and to 'set it working while assuming that other factors are 'equal' and do not affect the working of the model. This is, so to speak, to work upwards towards further and more remote abstraction. I have not done this: I have looked downwards and related structure to the realities of behaviour—in other words I have considered as many variables as possible.

Rules which may not be inconsistent with one another at the level of 'static' structure, may in practice (in a dynamic analysis) conflict with one another. In a static analysis there is no inconsistency in the two rules that a man must be generous to his own sons and to his sister's sons. In practice, when we take into account the fact that wealth varies from man to man and that some men may not be wealthy enough to meet both obligations, the rules may conflict with one another. This is not a contradiction at the level of static 'structure': it is a conflict apparent not in a static but in a dynamic analysis.

Structural analysis at the dynamic level consists in showing how, in spite of conflict, the static structure presented still remains an illuminating description of social life. There are various ways of doing this; the rule is dramatized and reinforced by the punishment of deviants: conflict in smaller groups may bring into action—perhaps even into existence—larger groups; and there are various secondary rules designed to cope with conflict and prevent it from changing or destroying the structure.

'Contradiction', as distinct from 'conflict', is primarily an heuristic device used to diagnose the presence in a social situation (or social 'field') of more than one structure. This means that a contradiction cannot be recognized immediately upon its perception. Nor can it be recognized at the level of static analysis, because there it is by definition ruled out. Conflict appears at the level of dynamic analysis: and it can only be recognized as a contradiction by the absence of self-regulating factors, such as those mentioned above. Thus a man allies himself to group B and in doing so defects from group A. If the result is to bring into action a larger group of which both A and B are part, *and yet which is in some sense neutral between them,* and if this larger group settles the conflict, then we are not here dealing with contradiction. The case can be stated with the same result in terms of rules and institutions. If a man follows rule A and deviates from rule B. And if there is a third rule or institution designed to settle such situations on the grounds that *in this particular situation* one or the other rule is appropriate, then this is not contradiction. The phrases in italics are of particular importance. If the group which comes into action is not neutral between A and B but is in fact one of the sanctions of B (or A, as the case may be), and if it is effective, then there is a contradiction between the two allegiances and not merely a conflict. Similarly if the third rule or institution is simply an assertion of one or the other rules as being invariably and automatically the right one, then this is contradiction. An example is provided by the first case given in this book. This is a contradiction between the Kond rule of landholding and the Administration's rule. There is no body or institution neutral between these two for settling the conflict: the following of one rule is automatically the negation of the other.

The assumption of 'consistency' as a part of the definition of structure is a means of enabling us to use the idea of structure for the study of social change. The first step is the identification of a logical consistency between the rules of behaviour: this I have called a 'static' analysis. The second step is to identify those institutions which seal of conflict and which tend to keep behaviour in conformity with the logical model: this I have called a dynamic analysis. The third step is to move from a 'conservative' towards a 'radical' approach in the study of society[1] and to study conflicts which are not contained or sealed off within one structure. I cannot emphasize too strongly that without the 'fixed points' which are provided by a static structural analysis, we have no means of describing the change that is taking place. In the last resort the description of all movement—even walking across the room—must identify two or more points if the direction of movement is to be conveyed, and more than the bare fact of motion is to be noticed.

While the concept of a static structure is necessary for a description of social change, it also has its dangers and its inadequacies. It is to meet some of these that I have used the concept of sub-structures, and the concept of a 'field'.

It is all too easy to assume that in some way one structure can fill all fields of social activity in any given society and that one may speak of *the* social structure. Indeed any analysis begins with this assumption because it is heuristically necessary. The corresponding error in studying social change would be to assume that the different structures follow one another serially and as whole, each in turn filling the whole field of social activity. Because there are places where caste no longer functions politically, it is not to be assumed that caste is just as dead in every other social field. If it were true, there would be no need to invoke more than one structure in any total social field, and there would be no contradiction, no bridge-actions, and the task of analysis would be much simpler.

While one needs whole structures in order to establish the direction of change, one cannot analyse the process of change without dealing with sub-structures, because the immediate contradiction is between these sub-structures rather than between total structures. For example the tribal system of kinship is not in contradiction with the caste system. I have pointed out their similarities, and, indeed, the caste system walls off one set of kinship relations from another. Similarly Kond rites and beliefs are not, on the whole, in contradiction with the Oriya rites and beliefs. There is rather a mutual accommodation, and these are two ritual sub-structures which do not conflict with or contradict one another. The contradiction between the two structures was localized in their political and economic sub-structures: this was the point of impact between them. It is for this reason that in the political field the Kond tribal structure has all but passed out of existence, while at the same time it remains in full existence as a kinship structure and important as a ritual structure. This would to some extent be true of the caste system, where problems of change are brought to notice by the incongruence of ritual behaviour and political behaviour between high and low castes. Social change, then, must be conceived of not as the replacement of one *total* structural by another, but by changes in sub-structure within one or another field. The change and contradiction, in other words, is not between total structures or systems, but between sub-structures within one social field.

The gives rise to difficulties. At the level of static analysis it is enough to point out the logical consistency between different rules of behaviour. In a dynamic analysis, which is concerned with self-sealing mechanisms and mechanisms of adjustment, the writer must show not merely that one rule entails the other, but also that at the operational level these rules sanction one another. This is the point of continuing of use the word 'structure' in a dynamic analysis; the Earth cult of the Konds sanctioned political behaviour and vice versa. Why, then, if structure has the systematic character which I have assumed, does not the destruction of one sub-structure (e.g. the political) lead to the destruction of the other sub-structures? It does, of course, lead to the destruction of the total structure, since this has been defined as the relationships between the different sub-structures. This phenomenon—differential rates of change—has been most noticeable in the ritual field, and to ritual is ascribed some kind of cultural 'inertia'.

The different sub-structures seem to have some kind of autonomy independent of the total structure. This is not a perfect autonomy; I am not throwing away the fundamental heuristic postulate that all aspect of social life are connected with one another. If the point of impact has been—as it usually is—in the politico-economic field and in this field sub-structure A gives way to sub-structure B, than the other sub-structure in the total structures. A in the end either wither away or become modified so as to make them consistent with the total structure B, or indeed they may already be largely consistent with it.

But the time-lag involved in this process brings in its train more difficulties. I have spoken of only two structures, using the signs A and B. But in the analysis I have dealt with three—the tribal structure, the caste system, and the Administration—and I could have brought in at least one more in greater detail, namely the modern representative democracy which is in many important respects in contradiction with the system of Administration. My interest has been in the political field and in the three (or four) political sub-structures. The process of change in the political field is once again not to be conceived of as in series, but the different systems overlap with one another. I have shown how all four are relevant to an understanding of political activity to-day. But at this point my difficulty is in the fate of the other sub-structures: kinship and ritual. I have postulated as 'fixed points' the various total structures, conceived of as static. But from the point of view of the Konds (or of the Oriyas) these fixed points cannot be thought of as stages in a course of development or evolution, through which they must pass. This is true from several points of view. Firstly there is no evidence that the Oriyas ever went through a 'tribal' stage. Secondly, although there was a time when the Konds came near to the Oriya political model, their total social structure never was the same as that of the Oriyas. To-day, when their political activity is centring on the Administration and the political democracy, their kinship system is still consistent (for instance in scale and in rules of exogamy) with the tribal political system which now is all but defunct. If and when the Kond kinship system changes to the small-scale system which seems—in India at least—to fit with an expanding capitalist society, it will have 'by-passed' the caste system. The kinship sub-structure will, so to speak, have missed out a stage through which the political sub-structure passed.

It may be that in lighting upon Kond hills society in the last hundred years, I have encountered a situation of unusual complexity.

It may be that the Oriya colonization, the Mariah Wars, the subsequent infiltration of Oriya mercantile classes, the growth of the Administration, and finally Indian independence and the coming of a system of representative democracy have induced an unusually large degree of 'anomie' and created an unusually extensive field of political choice and an unusually severe degree of conflict and contradiction. In these circumstances the analysis of political behaviour as part of a single consistent structure—as a sub-structure in a total structure—is certainly impossible. Yet I do not think I could have brought even this slight degree of order to the enormous heterogeneity of social activity without the concept of structure, as a system of logically consistent regularities of behaviour. The search for consistencies clears away, so to speak, much of the primary disorder, and lets us see where in fact the contradictions, lie, where are the points of impact, and what is the direction of change. What it does not do is provide abstractions which are useful in understanding the process of social change. This does not take place at the level of total structure but within one field between sub-structures and ultimately at the level of individual choice.

The Political Field

Political relationship are concerned with the distribution of resources and power. 'Distribution' includes not only those situations in which men co-operate with one another to achieve control over territory, or to protect their territory against outsiders, but also a wider field in which people do not co-operate but instead complete against one another for the control of resources. In other words a 'relationship' does not mean only harmony and co-operation regularly practised, but it can also mean relationships of institutionalized (i.e. regular) and competition.

In presenting the relationship in which the Baderi Konds are engaged I have tried to move from the simpler to the more complex. The 'Kond political structure' as a 'structure'—the that is, as a set of generalizations—complete in itself and it can be satisfactorily analysed without reference to the relationships which Konds in fact have with their own Pans as dependents, or with the Oriyas and the Administration, as their masters. The analysis demonstrates interconnections between various roles and relationships, and shows that there are no contradictions within the system so presented. A

Kond in Baderi village has relationships with other Konds in his community as an agnatic relative (he does not marry their daughters or their sisters and he has a common ancestry with them through male links); as a member of the same Earth congregation (if they pollute the Earth he is put into ritual danger, and vice versa); and as a member of the same political community (he fights of defend them, they fight to defend him, and there is no fighting between them). These roles are consistent with one another: they do not necessarily involve the actor in contradictory and inconsistent attitudes or actions towards other people of his community or towards people outside his community: and one role tends to reinforce another, as when a breach of the rule of exogamy pollutes the Earth, or as when political status is denied to those who are not agnates. These three institutions—warfare, agnation, and the cult of the Earth—define the group (the clan or the allied clans) and do not set up relationships between clans which might blur the loyalty of the members towards their own political community. Such an analysis identifies groups by the fact that several institutions are associated with one another in defining behaviour within the group and towards outsiders. We are satisfied with the analysis because we have identified political, ritual, and kinship functions for the group, and have shown that these are consistent with one another (i.e. they contribute towards the 'unity' of the group) and that this kind of relationship does not pass out beyond the group, and so blur the exactness of the structure.

A structure of social relations is *in the end* a statement of the absence of contradiction between different ways of behaving. But in order to present such a system it is necessary to hold 'other things equal', to postulate ideal conditions for the maintenance of the relationships which make up the structure. On necessary pre-condition of the tribal political structure was an appropriate ratio between population and land within each community. The system would work in the coherent way in which we presented it, if conditions were appropriate. But because the population grows too big for the land, or becomes too small to protect its territory, or for other reasons, there arise conflicts. Behaviour in fact does not conform to the abstract perfection which we have described. As son as we see the structure in action, we have ceased to hold some 'other things' equal, and we have to present not a static structure but a dynamic system which is not isolated but is affected in its working by 'outside' factors.

We continue to use the idea of structures, but we no longer present a static chart of groups and their inter-relationships. We try to identify the process which make groups and inter-relationships become similar to the chart, but which in fact never succeed in reaching its finality and perfection. Several words have been used to describe this process. The relatively mild disequilibrium set up by death and growth, countered by succession and inheritance, has been termed 'social circulation'.[1] The actors are conceived of as passing through various positions in a structure. More serious disequilibria, as when there is an imbalance of land and population followed by migration, fission, and subsequent accretion, have been called 'repetitive equilibrium'. The word 'repetitive' means that we see instance after instance of the same *type of* relationship: the group which migrates either joins another groups or sets up on its own in exactly the same *kind* of relationship which it previously had. Such a system is 'fluid but unchanging'. In order to take in the dynamics of the system we have had to introduce 'outside' factors—in this case birth and death rate, the amount of land under cultivation, and so forth. Without these we have no means of explaining why all relationships are not of all kind found on the static chart of structure which guides the analysis. These 'outside' factors clearly deserve to be called by that adjective, for they cannot be connected into the structure in the same way as, for instance in the Kond structure, the Earth cult is connected with agnatic kinship. They are not part of the system, but they affect it from outside.

To stand the structure one is to achieve it by demonstrating the consistency of its different parts, by showing that the ritual, economic, and political relationships of, for instance, the Pans towards the Konds, all coincide and reinforce one another. This too, just as the tribal system, can be viewed in action, and the factors which set it in motion are the same—for instance, too many people to be supported by the resources which the group commands—and the process by which a return to equilibrium is achieved are the same: migration and the assumption in the new home of ties exactly Similar to those which were held in the old location. (There are, of course, other factors—quarrels, pressure from outside, and so forth—

which set the structure in motion and I have chosen to consider only one particular set of them.)

The Kond-Pan relationship is not in the same system as the Kond-Kond relationship. Both can be described as complete structures in themselves without reference to the other, so long as we confine the description to the static chart of groups and their inter-relationships. At that level these are two separate structures. The role of clan member and the role of master of clients are neither consistent nor inconsistent with one another: they are merely separate: it is possible to be both and a full enjoyment of one role does nothing to detract from or add to the full enjoyment of the other. In a *static structural analysis* these roles neither reinforce nor contradict one another: for instance the Earth cult is neither consistent nor inconsistent with the relationship between a Kond master and his Pan client, nor do the rituals of sub-servience between the master and client have anything to do with the master's relationship with other Konds. But as soon as we begin to describe *structures in action,* than it may be necessary to bring in one set of relationships in order to complete our description of the working of the other set of relationships. When there is a ritual crisis in a Kond house, the Kond makes use of his Pan clients to help him in his tasks. Some of these tasks consist of entertaining other Konds who are related either as agnates or through uterine or affinal ties, and the Kond may only be able to fulfil his obligations towards other Konds with the help of his Pan clients. By making use of his relationships to the Pan, the Kond is able to further his purposes in the system of Kond-Kond relationships. Again Ponga's rivalry with Liringe in the Kond system of relationships affected the role which Ponga played in the dispute with the Baderi Pans. We may chose to regard the rivalry between the two Konds as an outside factor affecting the course of the dispute and the return to equilibrium in the system of Kond-Pan relationships. Just as the growth of population is an outside factor. In reality, as the examples show, the two types of relationship may affect one another, and it much be counted a weakness of a 'one-structure' analysis that it cannot take account of this fact, except by treating the relevant relationship as something intruding from outside the system.

In his third role the Kond is brought into political relationships with Oriyas. This structure too may be presented as something complete in itself: and political, ritual, and economic ties can be interconnected so as to show their consistency. But in this case the gap between the structure and reality is much wider than in the other two cases. The only way of presenting this as a structure is to pretend that the Konds were reduced to a position of dependence similar to that of their own Pans. In fact they were not. We may present the system as an equilibrium point towards which relationships tended, but in fact the 'self-sealing' mechanisms, so apparent in the tribal system, are here scarcely discernible. The Oriya system of political relationships is not only different from the tribal system, but is contradictory. This contradiction may be seen at the level of conflict between groups, in which the Konds tried—initially at least—to extrude, even to exterminate, the Oriyas. Oriyas could not be fitted into the Kond political structure because they would not become relatives. The Oriyas tried to bring Konds into the Oriya political structure, which can incorporate persons who are not only unrelated but even are of different cultures. They did not in fact succeed in doing so because they were too few in number to subjugate the Konds. The contradiction can also be seen in roles, in that allegiance to the Oriya Sirdar may conflict with loyalty to the clan: clanship ties demand that Kond outsiders should be admitted to the clan territory only if they take on agnatic responsibilities: but the Sirdar demands that allegiance should be to him, and admits people who do not take on clanship ties.

The role of clan member may be in direct contradiction to the role of retainer to an Oriya chief, when both these roles claim to give an exclusive right to the same piece of territory. There can be no self-sealing mechanisms in the Kond-Oriya political system, because there is no such system. There are two systems in contradiction, and an analysis of Kond-Oriya political relationships as a single integrated structure must await the elision of one or the other systems, at least in so far as they are political.

We need to shift our analysis away from the interconnections of a structural analysis and the demonstration of one whole coherent system towards the analysis of an area of social action in which these different systems impinge, towards the exploration of a social field. The effort should not be to hold other things equal, and invite the reader to grant a gentleman's agreement to disregard 'outside' factors, on the ground that they manifestly belong to a different system, but to concentrate on those outside' factors. I have given first a static structural description: I have then transformed this into a dynamic analysis, showing how the structure (if I may reify in order to be brief) copes with disturbance set up by 'outside' factors; and in the third part of the analysis I have tried to show that some of these 'outside' factors are themselves part of other systems of relationships, and that in order to describe adequately any field of social relationships we need to describe not only the structures which are found in that field, but also what might by called the 'bridge-actions' between those structures. Liringa's action in making use of the Manda–Goneswaro relationship to further his ends in his own village is an example of a 'bridge-action'. It is not part of the village structure: it is one of those 'outsider' factors which keeps the structure in motion. Nor is it part of the caste and Administrative structure in which Manda and Goneswaro are interacting. It is a bridge between these systems. We cannot understand the motives of the actors, nor judge the outcome of any dispute or conflict, nor assess its importance, unless we concentrate on these bridge-actions.

The Individual and Choice

As the analysis has passed into more complicated stages, I have focused attention more and more on individual actors. In the individual actor, more often than in a group, the different systems meet, if I may put it that way. It has, of course, long been recognized that no individual has but a single role to play: and man who is a father in one family may at the same time be a son in another family: farmer may also be a ritual expert; and so forth. By and large structural analysis consists of pointing out that these roles do not contradict one another, or, if they conflict, that there is some means of settling such conflicts without altering the type of social relations which are characteristic of the system. In the Kondmals there are several political systems. There is one system governing relationships about land between Kinds. There is a different system governing relations between Konds and Pans and distributing not the land, but the produce of the land, between them. There is a third system, similar in intention to the Kond-Pan system, governing the relationships over land between the Konds and the Oriyas. I am not here concerned with the fact that there may be different structures concerning ritual and kinship and politics, and the these may not add up into one grand system, but rather with the fact that there are at least three distinct political systems, and that every Kond has a role in all three of these, as well as the roles he may play in kinship and ritual. The three political systems all have the same 'aimcontent', and the individual cannot operate in all there at once but must choose between them.

A *static* structural analysis does not have anything to do with choice: it presents either the norm in the moral sense—what a man ought to do; of the norm in the statistical sense—what most men do; and it does not take account of the fact that some men do not do what is expected of them. But within the *dynamic* analysis of a single structure there must be elements of choice: the Damanikia people can join either Balimendi or Gondrimendi. These are the kind of problems which 'social structure' cannot meet, and which must be considered by 'social organization' or some similar concept. Choice at this level is one of the things which it is agreed to 'hold equal' so that a structural or systematic analysis can be made. When we consider a man as a locus of several roles which occur in different systems, all of which claim to do the same job, we must take into account choice. In the examples I have given, I have stressed the element of choice by comparing the way different people acted, and by showing that they could have acted differently if they had wished to do so. Ponga and Nrusingh seemed to have an unspoken agreement not to involve their relationship as seller and buyer of turmeric in the tax dispute. Manda could have acted in several ways in his dispute with the Sirdar, but he preferred to stress his role as a *proja,* as a subject of the Sairdar, and to leave it to others to point out that he also had rights as a citizen of India, and that as a members of the Baderi community and the Balimendi clan he could call on the united support of a large group of Konds. Sociologically speaking he was free to choose between these different roles and to select that which he thought might be the most effective.[2] The choice is not unlimited: the actors are, so to speak, creatures of their social environment: neither side, for instance, could gain its end by force: but within set limits of possible action the actors were, sociologically speaking, free to choose what they would do, according to their abilities to gauge the course which would best achieve the ends they had in view.

In some cases this element of choice is not going to affect the continuance of a social system. Whether the Damanikia people joined Balimendi or Gondrimendi, the result is the same from the point of view of the continuance of the system. The choice is within the system and not between systems. They were not choosing between different types of relationship, but between the persons with whom they would have a relationship which was already set for them. But where the choice lies between different types of relationship, the continuance of a social system may be affected. The more often Nrusingh chooses to behave as a man of affluence towards Goneswaro, the more does he erode his role as a *proja.* The more people like Manda in similar situations stand upon their rights a law, the more is their role as a *proja* diminished. In the example I have frequently quoted, the more people choose to join a territorial group by buying land and not by joining the clan which owns the land, the more is the political role of clan membership diminished. People can, so to speak, when there are several systems of political relationships between which to choose, opt out of one system and into another. This is the process by which the clan lost its political function to the *mutha.* Where systems contradict one another, it is choice which allows the more 'efficient' system to drive out the others.

But the analysis of change simply by identifying and describing the structure towards which, and the structure out of which, a particular society is moving is jejune and unsatisfactory. It seems too far removed from reality. It is an advance to be able to indicate that the society one studies is not to be considered as one single political structure. But the hypothesis of a past structure and a future structure, although they help as to understand the broad picture of what is going on, does not do justice to the complexity of the present or the subtlety with which choice can be made between the different systems. Nor can the allocation of a particular action to a future structure or to a past structure help us to see *how far* the society has moved from one structure to another. This can be done only by examining a series of disputes and conflicts, which have a diagnostic value for the study of social change.

Conflict and Social Change

Besides focusing attention on the single actor, I have also been much concerned with conflict, dispute, and competition. Competition underlies the whole analysis, for my whole conception of an actor is as a person (or group) trying to gain his ends against other people who would prevent him or would gain the same and for themselves. Sometimes this competition takes place within the one system of social relations, and although, the outcome of it may be a victory for one side or the other, the result of the conflict is not a change in the *type* of social relationships. At other times the actor may play upon the roles which he has in different systems of social relationships, so as to win for himself the support of more effective allies. These 'bridge-actions', which occur in situations of conflict, may be divided into two kinds: those which are symptomatic of social change and are the process through which change takes place, and those which are not. In a case Ponga treated himself to a few mild aspersions on Liringa's ineptness in handling the Baderi Pans. This is a bridge-action through which Ponga scored a point over Liringa in their rivalry for leadership in the village. None of these actions are symptomatic of social change: the actors remain aligned in their groups, and the use which Ponga was able to make of the Pans and the fact that they became his unwitting allies, did not mean that a new group consisting of Ponga and the Pans was emerging as a structural unit in the village society.

But in the same case the Pans were able to draw on outside alignments in order to modify their position in the village. They make part of their living outside the village economy: they are identified with the 'Harijans' of Bisipara. The Baderi Pans did not make overt or spectacular use of these ties, and did not seek to dramatize their alignment with these outside groups and their consequent independence of the Konds. But these new alignments are none the less real, and it is likely that in the future the Baderi Pans will use these alignments to make themselves more independent in Baderi village, in just the same way as the Bisipara Pans are in their village. The use of these alignments is a bride-action, and it is one which leads to social change. The Pans are able to opt out of the Baderi Kond-Pan group, and to join the wider group of Harijans. The traditional caste-relationship of Baderi village, and the new relationships in the modern political system, in which the Harijan group operates, are in contradiction to one another. In this case a bridge-action detaches the Pan from one group and makes him a recruit in another: the Bridge-action means the decay on one system and the growth of another.

A bridge-action may result in change when the appeal is from one system of social relations to another which contradicts it. Besides the example of the contradiction between the role of a village Pan and the role of a Harijan, I have also given the example of the role of a clan-member against the role of a *mutha*-member. These are two examples of a single process. This does not mean, however, that wherever there are bridge-actions between systems which are in conflict, there must inevitably follow the decline of one system and the growth of another. It depends (and her I cannot avoid reification) upon the relative strength of the two systems. In an another case a man from Rupamendi attempted to use his role as a citizen of India and as a tax-payer, whose name appeared on the Record of Rights, to own and cultivate land in Baderi. His Bridge-action was an appeal to a system of land-holding which was in conflict with the traditional land-holding system of the Konds. The latter lays it down that no-one who is not a member of the village community ought to hold land in the village. The Government system implicitly says that community-membership is irrelevant to the holding of land. But the bridge-action failed. The Rupamendi man was forced to give up his land. The integrity of the Baderi community remained unbroken. This case shows that bridge-actions led to structural change only when they are usually successful, and when the actor by directing his allegiance elsewhere gains his end.

It is often said that a dispute is a means of stating the rules of the structure and bringing home to the disputants the continued strength of those rules and so holding the society together. A breach of the rule, followed by corrective action, serves to strengthen the system. Disputes and conflicts are seen to have the same effect as ritual—stating publicity the right relationships within a given system. A dispute may have this effect: but it also may be a means of testing the efficacy from the individual's or the group's point of view of a particular system of social relations. The outcome of the dispute may not be to re-affirm the structure, but to make public the inefficacy of that particular structure as a means of gaining one's ends, and to demonstrate that some other form of social alignment is the more effective. This kind of dispute is, so to speak, a proclamation of social change.

In theory there is no difficulty in gauging change by this method. We have to examine a series of disputes which are connected in that they concern the same object—let us say control over land. History does not tell as how the dispute between Balimendi and Gondrimendi started, but let us suppose that a man from Manipara village began to break new land in the jungle to the north-east of his village. After he had begun the work he was impeded—or perhaps the field or the crops on it were seized—by a man from Tendriguda, the nearest village in the Gondrimendi clan. Each of the contestants could draw upon an ever-widening circle of people united to them as agnates: first their fellow-villagers, then their clans, and then the clans in alliance. Now suppose that the war between these groups continued for some time and reached a stalemate (and was not settled, as in fact it was, by the alliance of the migrant group from Damanikia with the Balimendi clan). Then it might occur to one side or the other that there were other social ties on which to draw. They might invite an Oriya chief, the head, for instance, of a large and powerful village like Bisipara, to intervene on their side, and he might win the war for them. If that happens, then the dispute is a public statement that an alliance with an Oriya chief is—in this case at least—an effective means of gaining land. Such incidents might become more and more common until it is widely known that the most effective alignment for validating a claim to land is that with the Oriya chief, and in the end the disputants might no longer bother to call on the clans in alliance, who for reasons of distance might be less effective allies than an Oriya chief who lived in the vicinity. Through a series of such cases the growing ineffectiveness of one alignment and the increasing efficacy of others are demonstrated.

In order to gauge social change we have in theory only to examine a series of such cases and show how men increasingly disregarded one alignment and increasingly invoked another *type* of alignment in order to gain a particular end. In practice it is very difficult to do this, because we do not have the material. Historical records in areas like the Kondmals are seldom full enough in the details of the social alignments of the various actors to let us present a case like this. I certainly have not been able to do so, except for the most obvious of alignments: for instance, it is clear from the records that war as once on effective means of validating a claim to land, that one's allies in such a war were the members of a clan, and that to-day this method is completely ineffective and that a man no longer needs the help of his whole clan in order to validate a claim to territory. Consequently there are to-day many people who belong to no territorial clan at all—like the people of Arapaju in Besringia, or the people of Bandibari in Balimendi, and the members of a territorial clan do not rely completely on one another's political support, so much as upon ties of other kinds.

But even this is too extreme. It is exaggeration in saying that the clan has lost its political functions. We are talking of what *may* be a future state of social relations, but what is not so to-day. The clan members no longer band together in the dramatic political activity of war: but clan ties may still be relevant politically. The clan still exists, through the system of internal recruitment, as a corporate unit having kinship functions, and some ritual functions. It retains some overt political functions in the clan membership gives a right in the earth, and this may be relevant to migration.

It may also be possible, through a bridge-action, for an actor to make use of clan membership, especially by recalling explicitly or implicitly the former warlike functions of the clan. This is the import of Liringa's remark, 'We will show you and Nrusingh what it means to be Sirdar of Balimendi'. He implies that the Konds of Balimendi are the members of one clan: they cannot be bullied and cheated as can people in heterogeneous *mutha* like Besringia: they will stand together against the Sirdar, Liringa does not specify the means that they can employ, but it would be possible, for instance, for them to write a petition against the Sirdar and have it signed by the whole clan. He asserts—and probably truly—that in Balimendi loyalty to the clan takes precedence over loyalty to the Sirdar.[3]

I have called these bridge-actions in situations of competition 'diagnostic'. But it must be remembered that these are not prognoses so much as *post mortem* examinations. We can only identify change retrospectively. Continuing the metaphor and looking at the situation from the point of view of the tribal system of land-tenure, the bridge-action of the Rupamendi man who used his status as a citizen of India to acquire land in Baderi, is a malignant symptom. But we have no means of telling from this action alone whether the body-politic will survive and cure itself, or whether it will die. After the event we can be wise. In fact Baderi got rid of the outsider. Similarly it is only after the event that we can say that fission in the clans has led to a decline in clan-membership and the emergence of the *mutha.* In other words, we need to have seen a large number of patents die of the disease, before we can say, no diagnosing the first symptom, that the disease is likely to prove fatal.

Political Motivation

The individual's motive in giving or continuing to give his allegiance to a political group is that in this way he expects to gain his ends and retain or achieve command over men and resources. In this way we postulate a 'political' man. 'Political man' is as much a sitting target as 'economic man' has been. There are close analogies between these two concepts, although I would not wish the same value ideas of utilitarian philosophy to be attached to 'political' man. It will be instructive to see how close my 'political man' comes to the assumptions of late nineteenth-century economists about the housewife who maximizes her utility undeterred by social obligations and other external factors. Must we assume a 'free market' and perfect competition in politics, as once was assumed in economics? Would it help our enquiry to do so? Have we in fact done so? Can our whole analysis be brought to the ground by showing that motivation is not the simple thing postulated in the first sentence of this paragraph?

Viewed in this way the factors which make for imperfect competition in politics, to continue the metaphor for the moment, are loyalties, to various groups, which cause a man, knowingly or unwittingly, to sacrifice his own self-interest. It would be foolish to deny that men are swayed by loyalties of this kind, and there are often considerable social pressures urging a man towards self-sacrifice, and publicizing any act of this kind. Secondly there is the factor of ignorance: even if a man is resolutely self-interested, he may be incapable of assessing the best means of gaining his end. If therefore my analysis is based on the assumption of the political equivalent of 'perfect competition' and perfect knowledge of the 'political market', then clearly it is wrong. But in fact I have assumed nothing of the sort: I have assumed only the existence of the political equivalent of the entrepreneurs—of some individuals who are out to maximize their political utility, and who know how to set about doing it.

The dichotomy of 'self-interest' on the one side and 'group loyalty' on the other side poses a false problem—at least in so far as it concerns the Kondmals material. The opposition of these two concepts seems to give several suggestive openings, but in my opinion most of them are blind alleys. For instance, at first sight the number of men whose acts are self-interested against those who are still bridled by the traditional loyalties seems to give a measure (ignoring the enormous difficulties of measurement) of integration, of the persistence of the structure, or of the stability of the society.

But is a mistake, I think, to oppose self-interest to group loyalty. Rather loyalty to one group is opposed to loyalty to another, and self-interest is equally present or absent in both. Those observers who see one system as right and good and who see change as bad[4] distort the situation by labelling a man's loyalty to the first system as 'group loyalty' or 'selflessness' or 'public spirit' and reserve the term 'self-interest' for the act of taking on new loyalties. Those who make the opposite estimate of the value of the two systems may reverse the procedure.[5] But from a position which is natural one must assume that self-interest is equally present or equally absent in both. In short the opposition of group loyalty to self-interest is useful only in tracing the downfall of one particular structure or system: I have not found it useful in studying social changes from one structure to another, for in this situation 'integration' is not a characteristic of a whole society, but a measure of the pervasiveness of one structure in that society.

Our description of political motivation is not a comprehensive assessment of human nature. It is only a brief way of saying that those who transfer their allegiance from one group to another, or who choose to follow one rule rather than another, except that by doing this they will achieve some end, which they would not have done otherwise. It is a statement about 'political entrepreneurs', not about everyone.

The Dominant Caste

The caste system of India has lent itself more frequently to evaluation than to analysis. It is either condemned as a affront to human dignity, or it is praised as a remarkably mature and intelligent solution to the problems of living in a plural society. An emotive description is seldom an exact description, and those who find the caste system to their taste have exaggerated the harmony with which the system works, by stressing the degree of interdependence between the different castes. Interdependence means that everyone depends on everyone else: it means reciprocity. From this it is easy to slip into ideas of equality: because men are equally dependent upon one another, they are assumed to be equal in other ways. Equality of rank is so manifestly false when applied to a caste system that the final step in the argument is seldom taken, and the exposition rests upon a presentation of mutual interdependence, and the hint that, because one caste could bring the system to a standstill by refusing to play its part, castes do in fact use this sanction to maintain their rights against the rest. In fact, of course, the system is held together not so much by ties of reciprocity, but by the concentration of force in one of its parts. The system works the way it does because the coercive sanctions are all in the hands of a dominant castes. There is a tie of reciprocity: but it is not a sanction of which the dependent castes can make easy use.

Power is concentrated in the hands of the dominant caste. The main features of this system are well known and have been for many years. The administrators who had to deal with the caste system, as distinct from the writers who merely thought about it, could not afford to miss so important a feature as the dominance of one caste. One caste has direct control over economic resources and it alone has a corporate political existence: the other castes derive their living by a dependent relationship upon the dominant caste, and in themselves they have no corporate political existence. Their political relationships are as individual clients of a master in the dominant caste. Political .ties run vertically in the system and not horizontally: political and economic rank tends to be consistent with ritual rank the dependent castes are not all of equal rank but are organized in several grades, and this is apparent in ritual usage.

These are the main features of caste seen as a political system. But as soon as this picture is put against reality, it becomes obvious that this is an abstraction of a high order. Many facts have to be discarded or accounted for before we can make use of the model. In Bisipara we identified the Warrior caste as dominant. But the Warriors did not own all the land: they had less than 30 per cent of it. On the other hand the Pans who as a dependent caste should have no land at all, had over 20 per cent of the land. The Warriors as a group owned more land than any other group, but their income per head was smaller than that in several other castes. Persons of other caste were not dependent upon the Warriors for making their living. Although the Warriors dominated the village council, since they were by far the largest single group among the clean castes, who alone were eligible to sit on the council, they were far from being able to use an economic sanction, which is one of the bases of the system, to control the other castes. Nor could they make use—at least overt use—of the other basic sanction in the system, force, since this would have been against the law. Lacking both economic and political dominance, in the sense which the ideas about a dominant caste seem to demand, the Warriors were in an ambiguous position in the ritual hierarchy. They claimed to be second only to the Brahmin: the same claim was made by two other castes, the Merchant and the Distiller. None of these castes would accept food or water from one another. The case of the Merchant was not important since there was only one household in Bisipara: but the rivalry with the Distiller caste was continually breaking to the surface of village life in one form or another. Warriors took water from the Herdsman caste (and so did the Brahmin), but they refused it from the Distillers, thus implicity placing them below the Herdsmen in the sale of ritual precedence. The Herdsmen naturally agreed with this, and while they accepted not only water but also cooked food from the Warriors, they refused both from the Distiller. But the Distillers themselves accepted food and water only from the Brahmin, thus claiming from themselves the second place in the hierarchy, which most people allotted to the Warrior caste.

The picture so presented does not fit with the postulate of Warrior dominance. Are we then to do away with the concept of a dominant caste? Before doing this, one ought to examine the system again, not this time as something static, but in its dynamic aspects.

All the variations from the ideal pattern might be comprehensible in terms of a system in motion, just as the presence of sister's sons and outsiders of various kinds can be fitted into the dynamic analysis of the Kond agnatic groups within a village. It might be possible to reconcile the evident disagreement about positions in the hierarchy, by supposing that this is a temporary disequilibrium caused by some outside factor, and that the system is moving all the time towards an equilibrium structure of one dominant and several dependent castes.

The activities of the Distiller caste become partly comprehensible on this hypothesis. A result of 'outside' events they have been enriched, and their former lowly status in the ritual hierarchy (alcohol being polluting) did not match the economic power which they wielded not their position as landowners and men of substance. The system consists of the correspondence of ritual, economic, and political power, and we can then envisage the claims and assertions of the Distillers as evidence that the system is, so to speak, asserting itself, and bringing ritual status into line with political and economic status.

This has allowed us to save that part of the hypothesis in which ritual, political, and economic status are said to correspond. But it has not brought reality any nearer the concept of one dominant caste controlling other dependent castes. Neither the Warriors nor the Distillers are dominant, one over the other: and if this is a movement towards the postulated equilibrium, it seems to have got struck at a point short of the abstract model. There is not one dominant caste, but two castes, who stand towards one another not in relations of ordination, but of equality as rivals. Their mutual ritual 'abhorrence' symbolizes not ordination, but equality.

The events in Bisipara are not part of any repetitive equilibrium, but are a sign of change. This is clear in the case of the Pan untouchables, in Baderi to some extent, and strikingly so in Bisipara. These Pans, in conflict with the clean castes and in particular with the dominant caste, are opting out of the caste system, in so far as it is political, and are entering a wider political arena. In terms of groups, they are exchanging their vertical allegiances within a village for a horizontal political allegiance towards their own caste, and they are becoming a corporate political group.

The concept of a dominant caste *in a village* is becoming one which is useful only as a datum line from which to measure social change. Although struggles and conflicts may still take place within the village between caste-groups (a 'caste-group' consists of members of the same caste who live in one village), nevertheless the political allegiances which are effective at the present day no longer are confined within the village, but embrace a much wider political arena.

The concept of the dominant caste has been used to describe not only the political system of a village, but also of some larger unit, which we may call a region. In large areas of north-western and north-central India the Rajputs are, or were a dominant caste; Nayars were dominant on the Malabar coast; the warriors were dominant throughout the Kondmals; Okkaligas and Lingayats are dominant in different parts of Mysore; and so fourth. In what sense is dominance use in these cases, and is the concept the same as when it is used with reference to village? I shall try to answer these questions with reference to the situation in the Kondmals before the coming of the Administration, and to the situation at the present day.

In one sense, to talk about a regional dominant caste is simply an abbreviated way of saying that the dominance-dependence pattern is found not in one village, but in all, and secondly that the same caste is dominant in all the villages. This is the traditional regional dominant caste. Political relations within this caste are segmentary in one form of another. In a primitive region like the Kondmals the segments consisted of villages and nothing larger: in the more sophisticated Malabar the segments were kingdoms and chiefdoms. But, whatever the complexity of political organization, the political system admitted competition mainly within the dominant caste. The Warriors fought with one another, with the help of their several dependent castes, and they tried to conquer territory, or perhaps to win Kond allies from one another. Political cleavages were within the dominant caste alone.

This does not, of course, mean that in any given stretch of territory there was one and only one dominant caste. In the Kondmals before the coming of the Administration, there were two dominant castes, each dominant within separate systems. In the Kond hills the Warriors were dominant in enclaves within a larger area of Kond dominance.

The situation in Mysore to-day, where the two most numerous castes, the Lingayats and the Okkaligas, complete for power, and where each has localities in which it is dominant, is reminiscent of the situation in the Kondmals before the coming of the Administration. Competition takes place between castes and not within a single caste. But there are also differences. Force is—theoretically at least—irrelevant: and the power that counts is voting power. Although many of the old allegiances persist and the master's clients tend to vote according to his wishes, nevertheless the dominant castes cannot call invariably upon the support of their dependent castes, as could the Warriors in their struggle against the Konds. These dependent castes themselves are likely now to have corporate identity as political units, and to be organized on a horizontal system of allegiances and not a vertical system. They are no longer dependent, although they may be politically allied: they might be termed, metaphorically, 'subordinate allies' rather than dependants. There is a third difference between the 'dominant caste' in the traditional system and the 'dominant caste' in the modern political scene. Although there may be factions and conflicts within a dominant caste like the Okkaligas, or the Lingayats, or the Nayars, such a caste does not segment at the present day into institutionalized hostile groups (chiefdoms and Kingdoms) as it did in the past. It co-operates as a single castes in opposition to other castes. There is, in other words, a radical difference in the structure in which the modern 'dominant caste' operates, from the structure in which the traditional 'dominant caste' operated.

Once again we must beware of the fallacy of thinking that change is once-for-all, abrupt, and radical. To identify a new structure in which a new kind of dominant caste is working does not means that the old structure and the old type of dominant caste has vanished and that we no longer need to bother about it in analysing political relationships within a village. We need it as a datum line against which to measure political change. But it is required for other reasons as well. There are some elements in present-day behaviour which are incomprehensible unless we see them as part of the traditional caste system. We cannot, for instance make sense of the behaviour which symbolizes a difference in rank, unless we also know about traditional, political and economic rank. The fact that the Warriors refuse cooked food from Herdsmen, while the Herdsmen accept food from the Warriors, can only be understood as a means of symbolizing the dependence of the Herdsman upon the Warrior. This dependence existed in the traditional caste system.

Isolation

The question of whether or not villages in India or in other relatively sophisticated peasant societies are sufficiently isolated to be studied as whole in themselves is in many ways similar to this questions about the adequacy of the concept of a dominant caste in a village. Professor Redfield says that a village of peasants in an 'ancient civilization' cannot be isolated in the same way as a tribe which is presumed to be relatively untouched. In abstracting a single social system for the village, the result is too far removed from the reality which it is supposed to represent.

There is no *a priori* answer to this question: it is primarily empirical. It is not even a question about particular *villages.* If the focus of interest is on ritual, for instance, it might well be possible to isolate a single, whole, and coherent social (not of course cultural) system within a village: but in the same village a political or an economic analysis might inevitably lead the enquirer to concentrate on ties which go outside.

Can Baderi be isolated as an object of political enquiry? If we are content to draw a static chart of groups and their normal interrelationships, this can be done. Baderi is a territorial segregated group of agnatic kinsmen who act together for political ends, But this is a meagre description. If we set the structure in motion, and begin to consider process, we must at once recognize that the village is a unit within a larger structure, and that there are individual ties and relationships going beyond the boundary of the village. The mere fact that this is a group of agnatic kinsmen means that brides must come from outside and leads us to describe a network of affinal and uterine relationships, which transcend village boundaries. The process of 'repetitive equilibrium' cannot be understood without taking into account relationship which go beyond both the village and clan. The agnatic structure of Baderi can only be understood as a part of the Balimendi clan, and in its turn the clan structure can only be seen as the product of movements and tensions over the total (Kond) society of the eastern Kondmals. So in the tribal system alone, the unit of study is shifted from the village outwards to the clan, and from the clan outwards to the total society.

Exactly the same is to be said of the other type of political relationship within Baderi—that between the Konds as masters and other castes as dependants. Our ultimate unite for study is the whole group of villages between which the dependent castes may move, and only by taking into account this larger unit can we see how the system could work.

In studying the political relationships between Konds and Oriyas, it is clear that Baderi village is not the significant arena, since the only Oriyas present there are the politically insignificant Oriya Herdsmen, and the only other Oriya who owns a field is the preceptor.

It might them be argued that although we cannot present an adequate picture of political life in Baderi village if we exclude all relationships which go beyond the village boundaries, we can still limit our analysis to Baderi and treat the external relationships as intruding into the system which we are describing. The is to say, we begin to consider them only at the point at which they cross the village boundary: we study their effects in the village but not the systems in which they originate. I have recognized that this has been set in motion by various factors—differential growth of population, the Oriya invasions, and so forth—but I have considered only their effects in the tribal system. Is it always possible to treat outside events in this fashion? Can we always afford to cut them off at the point at which they enter the system which we have chosen to study?

There would be general agreement among anthropologists that outside events which intrude into the social system and originate in non-social systems, can be treated simply as intrusions. If the outside events is an epidemic, or a cattle plague, then we can study the effects of a large number of deaths among people or among cattle on the social system of the village or the tribe or whatever is our chosen unit, without making an excursion into medical etiology. It is not so easy to do this when these non-sociological outside events have themselves some sociological implications. It might, for instance, be necessary to make a study of medical facilities, if we are to understand why they have been patronized by some of the people in our unit of study, and why others have avoided them.

But when the external relationships is what I have been calling a 'bridge-action', then we are committed to making some kind of a study of the system to which these bridge-actions have reference, as well as of the relationships within our chosen unit of study. The rivalry between Liringa and Ponga is purely within the village and within the tribal system: yet to appreciate how each seeks to score over the other we need to know about the Kond-Pan system, and about the Kond-Oriya system: Ponga and Liringa are not simply passive: they are able to manipulate these two systems and the investigator needs at least as much knowledge of these systems as Ponga and Liringa have themselves.

We cannot study social change simply within the boundaries of a village. When bridge-actions lead to change, the system which we are studying may be changing to resemble the system to which the bridge-action appeals[6]. There is no understanding of the behaviour of the Baderi Pans, if we look upon it simply as an act of defiance against the Konds. We will not know the strength or significance of their actions unless we also know about their modern economic affiliations, the Harijan movement, the wider political scene, equality before the law, and so forth. The village of Baderi has been the starting point for an investigation into political systems which far transcend the village. I have found the village to be the best vantage point from which to survey these systems, and from which to analyse the way in which change is taking place. Events in the village provide a text, in the commentary upon which the wider systems are unfolded. The village is not an isolated whole in itself: in a political enquiry it has been merely a convenient field of observation, where several political systems can be seen at work and impinging upon one another.

Tribe, Caste, and Nation

I have shown that tribe, caste, and nation are three different political alignments: three forms of allocating scarce resources, and of uniting to compete for those resources: three different kinds of arenas, in which are engaged three different kinds of groups. I have also shown that these three systems can be placed in a temporal order: that the caste system preceded the national system, and was itself preceded by the tribal system. This is the direction in which political society is changing. But all three system are still in existence and effective political action can be taken by making use of ties in all of them, and by adroit bridge-action from one system to another.

The village has remained an arena within which individuals struggle with one another for power and the possession of land. In a Kond village membership of the community and residence on its territory still appear to be a necessary qualification for taking part in the struggle. There still is, and always has been a political cleavage between individuals in the villages. What has change is the nature of outside alignments which are effective in this struggle: these were, firstly, relationships with other Konds, within or outside the village; secondly relationships with local chiefs and headmen; and thirdly the use that can be made of the administrative and judicial system.

The Kond clans are no longer primarily political units, engaged in the struggle to validate a right to resources, although clan-membership may still have political implications. There is now no competition for land between clans and the clan system has ceased to provide the main political cleavage in the total society. There have been four main cleavages: (i) individual against individual, or faction against faction, within the village; (ii) Kondclan against clan; (iii) clan or group of clans against an Oriya village and its chief; and (iv) Oriya chiefs against one another. The first cleavage continues to-day. The second and fourth are no longer of importance. The third cleavage continues, but it now tends to draw upon wider alignments: it is being transferred, so the speak, to a larger arena. There ceased to be cleavages only within small localities between an Oriya chief and the surrounding Konds, and the society developed a main cleavage between Konds and Oriyas. This cleavage arose partly through the Government's insistence on treating these two categories differently, partly in the manner in which they are engaged in the modern economy, and partly through such historical accidents as the fact that the first Administration was conducted not through the Kui language, but in Oriya. As one would expect, with the improvement of communications—in the widest sense of the word—the struggle for control over resources can now be carried on by larger groups and must take place in a large political arena. Konds and Oriyas, who in the Kond hills formerly were cultural categories, are now becoming political groups. 'Caste' (in the modern sense) is replacing territory as the basis of political grouping.

The analysis of a political system as a logical model is a necessary first step to understanding political activity in the Kond hills: but it is not sufficient to stop at that point. In order to understand actual incidents, or in order to estimate what will be the effect of a particular social reformor a new technique, an analysis of this kind is virtually useless. In a field of activity as complicated as that of the Konds hills we need to emphasize complexity, ad to look not for one political system, but for several. Secondly we need to see individuals not as passive creatures exhibiting for our benefit regularities in behaviour, but as actors who may not only choose between systems but may attempt to twist and amend these systems to their own advantage.

In this book we have largely been content to show that people do behave in this way: that there are several political systems: and that the actors pick and choose between them. Over the last hundred years in the Kondmals some courses of political action have been discarded and different political alignments have been taken up or are in process of being adopted, because they better serve the ends of the actors. To this extent there is regularity in choice: one particular choice begins to exhibit a statistical regularity, and so becomes part of a system: whole another choice ceases to be exemplified, and with it dies a system. We have been able to show why particular choices are advantageous: what, for instance, is the advantage to a Kond of shedding Kond culture and taking on the manners and customs of the Oriyas: why clan memberships nowadays only of minimal political significance. We have also been able to show how the field of choice is itself delimited: why, for instance, the Bisipara Pans can make more effective use of the representative democracy than can the Baderi Pans; why force alone is becoming an ineffective means of gaining political ends, at least in relations between the larger groups. We have showed why individuals have made certain choices in particular situations: why Ponga did not intervene in the Baderi Pan dispute; why neither Ponga nor Nrusingh brought in their commercial relationship why Liringa chose to exacerbate an already difficult situation. At this level I could also make prognoses, and we could suggest what Liringa or the other actors would do in similar disputes.

NOTES

1. G. and M. Wilson, 1945, p. 58. Radcliffe-Brown distinguishes between 'structure' and 'structure form' (1952, pp. 190-3).
2. To an investigator in another science, his decision to act the humble part might have been explicable in terms of his upbringing, or of something else, and in that sense he might not have been exercising a free choice: but, sociologically, we must treat Manda as if he had the choice of several roles in this situation.
3. In consecrating on bridge-actions and on a social field we cannot throw overboard the idea of structure. It would be Impossible to understand the power behind Liringa's threat to invoke the clan to help Manda, if we did not also know of the structure of the clan, and the ties of kinship and ritual, and the way these ties reinforce one another.
4. V. Elwin, 1943, p. 13. 'The souls of the people are soiled and grimy with the dust of passing motor-buses. The village has ceased to be a living community; it is now an aggregate of isolated units,' *et passim.*
5. G.S. Ghurye, 1943, p. 216. 'Tribal sections on joining Hindu society develop an internal organization of the caste pattern, and thus have the regulating and controlling power within themselves.'
6. It is also, of course, possible that bridge-action may result in anarchy.